Developing Overseas Managers
—and Managers Overseas

DEVELOPING
OVERSEAS
MANAGERS
—AND
MANAGERS
OVERSEAS

PAUL E. ILLMAN

A DIVISION OF AMERICAN MANAGEMENT ASSOCIATIONS

Library of Congress Cataloging in Publication Data

Illman, Paul E
  Developing overseas managers—and managers overseas.

  Includes index.
    1. Corporations, American—Personnel management.
  2. Executives.   3. Middle managers.   4. Americans
  in foreign countries—Employment.   I. Title.
  HF5549.5.E45I43   658.4'07   79-54837
  ISBN 0-8144-5587-5

First Printing

CONTENTS

PART II
SELECTING, TRAINING, AND DEVELOPING
THE LOCAL NATIONAL MANAGER

PART III
AND NOW, SOME WORDS TO THE
LOCAL NATIONAL MANAGER

INTRODUCTION

The Target Audience

Before we get to the heart of things, it seems proper to identify the audience to which this book is directed. Who might benefit or gain a few ideas that would be helpful in the whole matter of developing overseas managers?

First, there is the home-office executive who is responsible for selecting and preparing the U.S. manager who is to go overseas. Second, there is the U.S. manager himself. Third, the book may help the local national manager who is the subject of the American company's development efforts. Finally, but to a lesser degree, it may help the foreign national who visits or is transferred to a post in the United States.

The Home-Office Executive

When an American is sent abroad to manage a function and then fails, usually the failure is not really his fault. In one respect, of course, it is, but in another the blame should be placed elsewhere. Either he was the wrong person from the beginning—the choice was the wrong choice—or, and this is very possible, his preparation was hopelessly inadequate.

Whichever the case, the responsibility has to fall back on the shoulders of the home-office executives who chose the manager and then gave him whatever indoctrination in the overseas assignment he might have received. When the wrong manager is selected, or his preparation is sketchy or nonexistent, don't criticize him if things don't work out as planned. He had too much stacked against him from the start.

The executive who chooses and prepares the U.S. manager needs to know everything the transferee needs to know and will experience. If he doesn't, it's a case of the blind appointing the blind—with the potential for a costly failure.

Sending a person and his family abroad, especially to a developing country, is hardly the same as moving him from New York to Boston. The fact that he was successful in New York augurs well for success in Boston but not necessarily in Bombay or Buenos Aires. Things are so radically different abroad that the selecting officer has to be an authority on the type of person who is most likely to succeed as well as on the culture and customs of the country in which the U.S. manager will live.

While this book makes no attempt to analyze customs, habits, and mores on a country-by-country basis, it does discuss some of the more important and common traits found in the developing societies. In the process, it emphasizes the behaviors and emotional strengths the successful candidate should possess, in terms of both day-to-day living in the foreign country and ability to develop local national managers.

For the selecting and briefing executive, then, the hope is that at least some of the chapters will help him be a little better prepared to choose wisely the overseas candidate and ready him for his international assignment.

The Manager Himself

One intent of the book is to provide a vehicle by which someone potentially interested in an overseas post can evaluate himself and decide whether he really wants or is emotionally equipped for such an assignment. Once he is better armed to analyze his own attitudes and temperament, as well as those of his family, he may decide that moving lock, stock, and barrel to some developing country simply isn't worth the sacrifice. Or, after the self-analysis he may conclude just the opposite. He then can present himself as a viable candidate who at least has a reasonable idea of what he and his family are likely to encounter.

For the manager who is finally accepted to go abroad, Part I of the book will acquaint him with some aspects of the culture, especially what is happening beneath the surface in the developing societies, the clash between traditionalism and industrialization, and some aspects of managing, motivating, and communicating in such societies. Part II then leads him into the specifics of selecting the local manager, orienting him to the company and the job, and carrying out an effective training and development program.

In brief, for the U.S. manager, the book is designed to help him adjust to the local way of life in a developing country. It then proceeds to suggest proven means and methods that will assist him in the process of developing his local staff, with special emphasis on the local manager.

The Local National Manager

In most cases, the local manager reporting to a U.S. expatriate is in the dark. He doesn't know what the expatriate has been told, what his role abroad is, what admonitions or instructions he has been given, or what the U.S. manager is trying to accomplish through the various training and development programs he has established. It would seem only fair, and probably contributive to a better interpersonal relationship, if the local understood his American boss and had a clearer picture of what the American was trying to do. Parts I and II will help clarify the American's role, what's expected of him, and his more important managing and development responsibilities.

Local nationals may also be unclear on what the U.S. manager expects of them or how they should conduct themselves in the performance of their tasks. Some locals learn this rapidly, some slowly, some never at all. In the hope of expediting the learning process, Part III outlines the probable expectations the American manager has of the local national, along with some thoughts on how the local can conduct himself to become the complete employee, one ready to assume a more responsible position in the organization.

One other concern may also be important to the local manager. Part II proposes what the U.S. manager should do in preparing for, selecting, orienting, training, and developing his local subordinate. The same principles and steps apply to the local when he has to select and develop his own staff. The suggestions in Part II, adapted as necessary, may thus be useful to him when he faces similar responsibilities in the management of his unit.

The Local National Visiting or Transferring to a U.S. Post

To a somewhat lesser degree, the book has relevance for the local manager who is either visiting the U.S. home office or being transferred to a position here. The more he understands our business orientation and some elements of our culture, the easier he will find it to live among us. The book is in no way a study of American culture, but references to it can't be avoided, especially when comparisons are made between life in a developing country and life in ours.

There's another side to this as well. The emphasis placed on the American's need for sensitivity to others in a foreign culture might also remind the local of the importance of equal sensitivity when he visits us. We, too, bleed when cut and don't appreciate attacks on or violations of our traditions, habits, and customs by outsiders.

Sensitivity, like preparation, is a two-way street. Gestures or actions that are acceptable in his culture may be offensive here. Arrogant behaviors toward people of nationalities he considers his inferiors at home aren't likely to be tolerated. Flamboyant displays of wealth will probably generate only disdain. While the book doesn't get into this from the American point of view, if the local can see the same principles applying to him in reverse when *he* is the foreigner abroad, that may be one byproduct that will make his travels to other lands more productive and rewarding.

With the above as audience definition, let's move to the first matter under consideration. . . .

PART I

Selecting and Preparing the Manager for an Overseas Assignment

1

First—
Is the Right Person
Going Overseas?

Four Candidates—Who Should Be Selected?

You're responsible for selecting a manager for an overseas assignment. The country to which he[1] will go is in transition, moving from underdeveloped to developed. The person you select will be charged with setting up a department or section, running the operation, and, you hope, developing a local national to take his place. The tour of duty is to be three years, with the contract renewable for two years after that. You have four candidates who have indicated interest in the assignment. Which would you choose?

LARRY NUGENT

Larry Nugent wants to be selected for the overseas assignment his company has just announced. As a bachelor with no family obligations, he feels it would be an ideal opportunity for a 31-year-old manager on the way up.

---

[1] Throughout the book, it is assumed that a man is being sent overseas and that the local nationals he is supervising are also men. The reason for this male orientation is simply that women are rarely assigned management positions in developing countries. It's not that they lack the qualifications or the potential to do the job but rather the cultural traditions would make it extremely difficult for them to supervise local male subordinates with any degree of success. Women, while highly respected and protected in the underdeveloped nations, are relegated to the home, child-bearing and -rearing, and care of the household.

   Once in a great while, the wife of an expatriate may find a job in a local business or government office and might rise to a supervisory position. If this occurs, however, it is because of a particular skill she possesses, for example, as computer programmer or as an English language teacher.

   In other words, managing in the developing world is a man's responsibility. For that reason, and that alone, the book focuses on the male as the U.S. manager abroad and as the local national subordinate who is being supervised and developed.

The job, he realizes, would take him to a country that is just developing, but that doesn't bother him. In fact, he's intrigued by the idea. Having majored in history and archaeology in college, he has always been interested in ancient lands and their people.

In reviewing Nugent's qualifications, you know that he is strongly oriented to the people side of the job. He makes friends easily and has always tried to create a family atmosphere in any department he has managed. He doesn't believe in strict discipline or in setting up a long list of personnel regulations. These things, he apparently feels, only develop barriers between the people and him. Instead, he prefers a relaxed working environment in which human needs and congenial relations are the primary concerns.

His supervisors haven't always agreed with this style of managing, but you have to admit that it has certain advantages. The employees undoubtedly like Nugent, and a social esprit de corps exists that is not characteristic of some of the other departments. While there is a fair percentage of turnover and absenteeism, morale seems generally high—if the relatively few grievances and situations demanding disciplinary action are any criteria. Production, however, lags behind the established quality and quantity standards.

Technically, Nugent is as qualified as any candidate for the job, and he is certainly strong on the human side. Still, you have some doubts. Is he really the man to take on this assignment? If so, why? If not, why not?

On a scale of 1 to 10 (with 1 representing almost certain failure, 10 almost certain success), how would you rate Nugent's chances if you selected him for the job?

ARTHUR BRAXTON

As you review Arthur Braxton's qualifications for the same job, these facts come to light:

He is 29, is married, and has two children aged 10 and 7. He is a college graduate with a bachelor's degree in economics and a master's degree in business administration. Highly skilled technically, he's always been a slave to production. Getting the work out on time and in accordance with all standards is one of his primary objectives.

Although he has many friends off the job, he's essentially a loner in the office. Usually the first one in and the last one to leave, he drives himself hard while demanding the same from his people. There is no time for frivolity or socializing in Braxton's day. It's the god of production that rules.

To ensure top quality and quantity, he sets departmental objectives and work standards, makes the key decisions, and solves operating problems that arise. Blessed with a high energy level, he's everywhere at once and knows exactly what's going on throughout his department. If, in his frequent inspections, somebody makes a suggestion or offers an idea, he might listen, but that's about all. What people say or think doesn't particularly interest him. They're there to work and are being paid well to do that and that alone. At least, that's the impression you get from observing him.

But—the work gets done, much to Braxton's pride. His reputation for running a tight, productive shop is well-established.

Again, on a scale of 1 to 10, how would you rate Braxton?

DAN MATTHEWS

Dan Matthews, age 34, is a middle-of-the-roader. Securely settled in suburbia with his wife and three children, ages 14, 11, and 8, he is occasionally involved in community affairs, belongs to a good (but not the best) country club, and enjoys his Friday-night poker and Saturday round of golf with the boys.

At work, he seeks an acceptable balance between the demands of production and the needs of his people. What comes out of his department is neither outstanding nor inferior. "Acceptable" probably describes it best. The morale of his people is all right, the discipline is reasonable, and they seem generally satisfied.

In problem-solving or decision-making, Matthews likes to get the thinking of everyone. He usually does some sort of vote-taking before arriving at a solution. If a deadlock then develops, he's not averse to deciding the issue by flipping a coin or seeking advice from a disinterested third party. When it comes to setting departmental objectives, he sometimes determines the objectives himself but feels more comfortable when he can get his subordinates to participate. Either way, the objectives are usually attainable without too many demands being placed on anyone. Rules and policies, he feels, are to be obeyed—which means that he goes by the book. What the book says is what counts. In following this allegiance to the written word, he apparently feels a comfortable sense of security.

Things are all right in Matthews' shop—not bad, not good. It's an acceptable average that he seems to like. He's proud of his department but apparently doesn't want to do anything that would draw undue attention to him or it. A nonextremist, he holds the philosophy: do the job and don't make waves.

With these traits, is Matthews a good risk in an overseas assignment? Rate his chances for success on the 1-to-10 scale.

ERIC BENNETT

The fourth candidate, Eric Bennett, is married, is 35, and has three daughters ranging in age from 13 to 17. He has a liberal arts degree from a small Southern university.

In considering Bennett, you see him as a high achiever who tries to mesh the needs of his production with those of his people. His style is to encourage maximum participation of his people in the objective-setting, problem-solving, and decision-making processes. He seeks to get the best thinking possible before deciding an issue or determining a course of action. This practice takes time, of course, but it has produced better ideas while opening up communication channels among all concerned.

When the situation demands, however, Bennett can move quickly from the so-called democratic style to the very firm role of deciding matters by virtue of his authority. Normally, he makes this switch only after all ideas or recommendations have been examined and group agreement on the best course of action can't be reached. In an emergency, too, he can be very autocratic. For the most part, however, he isn't comfortable with this style and reverts to it only infrequently.

Bennett's focus is mostly on the future, although he uses the past to provide guidelines and alert him to traps that should be avoided. In the same vein, employee mistakes are discussed and used as opportunities for growth, not for recrimination or scolding. Some of his people seem to resent this "tomorrow" orientation because of the pressure they feel it places on them. Others, however, like it. It gives them a sense of challenge and accomplishment.

The climate Bennett creates is fast-paced, with concentration on quality and quantity. Because of it, most of his subordinates are committed to their tasks, dependable in performance, imaginative in their suggestions, and constructive in their criticisms. When something goes wrong, Bennett can get tough, but he is rarely forced into that position.

Do you think the characteristics Bennett has displayed at home would work overseas? Would the national employees respond to the climate he has been able to establish at home? Again, rate his chances for success in a developing country on the 1-to10 scale.

Now that you have evaluated the four candidates, hold your decisions and then come back to them after you've finished Part II. On the basis of what follows, were you right? Or have you changed your mind about the type of person the overseas operation needs? Remember that the successful candidate is going to a developing country—not Japan, England, or a similar industrialized part of the world. The job is a line position with direct authority over local national management personnel and employees.

Briefly, What's the Difference?

Working and living in a foreign country—especially a developing country—is a far cry from a casual visit or the whirlwind tour of the vacationist. One-week junkets may be fun; the inconveniences, language barriers, and cultural differences may be tolerable or even exciting. Escape from the unpleasant, however, is as close as a taxi ride to the airport.

Not so with the U.S. manager abroad. He faces unique demands. If he is emotionally prepared and educationally equipped for a world vastly different from the one he has known all his life, the likelihood of success is greatly enhanced. If he is unprepared or ill-equipped, he may find the assignment abroad frustrating, discouraging, and costly—to him, his family, and his company.

Through various quirks of questionable logic, many companies fail to appreciate the importance of managerial preparation. As was noted in the Introduction, success in New York does not assure success in Bombay or Buenos Aires—or Turkey or Saudi Arabia. Moving from an industrialized society into one that is developing or in a state of transition poses challenges that can be overpowering. Unless conditioned for the new way of life, the most competent manager at home may find his overseas assignment an experience to be forgotten as rapidly as possible.

To Begin at the Beginning—Operator or Developer?

You, in the home office, have decided to send someone overseas. Whether it is to head up a new plant, solve some critical operating problems, or replace a manager whose time has come to return home is momentarily of secondary importance. The point is that someone is going. Before even thinking about the individual or screening the candidates, however, you need to make a key decision: How do you want the manager to function in the new assignment? What *role* do you want him to play?

To clarify the word "role": The individual going abroad first has to know what he's expected to accomplish in the assignment. The purpose, once defined, normally determines how he is to function and whether his role is to be an *operator, developer,* or a combination of the two—an *operator/developer.* Each role is different, and each produces its own on-the-job managerial style:

   ○ *Operator.* In this role, the manager is to see that the work gets done and that production objectives are met. His primary responsibility is to run his portion of the business. How he does it is of less importance than the results he produces—results in terms of product or service quality, quantity, timeliness, and costs.

In performing as an operator, the manager will, in all likelihood, have local national subordinates reporting to him, perhaps in various management capacities. Typically, however, he immerses himself in the work, maintains tight control, delegates sparingly, communicates only the essential, and assumes the major responsibility for the success of the operation.

The operator is a "doing" manager in every sense of the word, with no conern for developing his subordinates or preparing any one of them to replace him. To get the job done is his only purpose.

   ○ *Developer.* The developer has an entirely different role. He is charged with the training, coaching, and long-range growth of the local staff. The company may plan to have a fair portion of the foreign operation managed by nationals, and his job is to broaden their skills for increased responsibilities as well as to hone their present-day skills.

The operator is in the thick of the battle. The developer is more on the sidelines as a coach, a counselor, an adviser. The first is responsible for product quality, the second for human excellence.

   ○ *Operator/Developer.* The role of this manager is to meet production objectives while simultaneously developing the local national management employee for advancement within the organization. As the locals learn and grow, he consciously relinquishes more and more operating responsibilities to them while gradually assuming a sideline position as a consultant and coach. When at least one subordinate becomes capable of taking his place, his job is finished and he goes home. He has literally worked himself out of a job—which was why he was sent abroad in the first place.

There can be many reasons for sending a U.S. manager overseas: personal growth, broader exposure, fire-fighting or problem-solving, opening a new plant or new market, testing for potential advancement, and so on. Yes, even getting dead wood out of the domestic operation—"It's Ankara or you're through."

Whatever the purpose, the manager must clearly understand what is expected of him. Once that has been defined, his performance should be measured accordingly. All of which sounds quite basic and simplistic. Unfortunately, however, too many managers end up in foreign posts without clear direction or mutually agreed-upon objectives. Typically, they then focus on the work, become highly involved and directive, and disregard other responsibilities such as subordinate development. If that is their expected role, fine, but if the home office wants them to be developers as well as operators, they're in a failure mode. Only they don't know it.

What should the manager's role be? Well, that depends on the company and the job to be done. In most cases the practical role is that of operator/developer—especially if the company plans a long-term tenure in the international arena. The reasons for this are many and will be discussed at the proper time. Suffice it to say now that this role generally promotes profitability, a positive corporate image, and managerial economy.

Next—the Candidate

Let us assume the manager abroad is to be an operator/developer. Now comes the task of selecting the best person for the job. A lot more is involved—or should be involved—than finding a willing candidate, cutting the transfer papers, and holding a bon voyage party. That's the old way and the costly way, as many organizations have belatedly discovered. While the possibility of failure can never be eliminated, the risks can be minimized if a little care is exercised.

Consider for a moment some of the likely ramifications of a wrong decision. One ramification is certainly to the company itself in terms of its mission abroad—whether the mission is sales, marketing, production, providing support, or supplying a service. Reputations spread rapidly, and if the company is cursed with several "wrong" people, it will inevitably pay the price.

Then there is the matter of operating costs. Sending a manager abroad involves a considerable dollar investment, especially when housing, educational allowances, fringe benefits, overseas pay increments, transportation, the shipment of household goods, and the like are added on to the manager's base salary. For a $30,000-a-year executive, all these costs could easily add up to $50,000 or $60,000—just to get the executive to where he is going and see him through the first year.

If he then proves to be the wrong choice for whatever reason, he has to be brought home and relocated, and the whole process of finding a suitable replacement must begin again. The costs echo and re-echo—for the company, for the man himself and his family, and for the mission abroad. This is a pattern too often repeated, especially by companies new to doing business overseas. Despite all the recent literature to the contrary, the tendency remains strong to believe that a manager who has succeeded in New York will automatically succeed in New Delhi. Indeed he may, but it's far from automatic.

Another repercussion of a wrong decision is the effect on the national employees, particularly those in supervisory positions. Supposedly, along with other purposes, they are there to learn Western technology and Western managerial skills. Since they have had little previous exposure to the industrialized world, their thinking and behavior are shaped by the example set before them.

If the American boss is dictatorial, uncommunicative, or abrasive, subversive rebellion is one probable result. Another is that the nationals may adopt the same behavior traits when they are placed in positions of authority. Their own reactions to negative leadership are forgotten as they emulate the style of the American. They may feel that the ways of the U.S. manager, repulsive as they seem, must have some usefulness since this person is the product of the greatest industrial power on earth. And so the nationals walk in his footsteps, or at least make the attempt. With limited opportunities for comparison, the local manages as he has been taught. The wrong lesson may be learned but, once learned, is perpetuated as he grows in position and responsibility.

Finally, selecting an unqualified candidate can have serious repercussions on the man himself and his family. Countless examples are recorded of aborted tours of duty, unhappy wives, frustrated children, even broken families because of inadequate preselection screening or preparation for the assignment. Oh, the U.S. manager may struggle through his tour, but at what cost to the company, to the national subordinates, to himself, to the solidarity of his family? The less determined individuals, facing conflict on and off the job, give it all up and come home. Preventable? Yes, if some of the stop-and-go signals outlined next are observed.

Typical Causes of Failure in Overseas Assignments

Occasionally, but very rarely, does a U.S. manager abroad fail because of technical incompetence. He usually knows his job and is highly skilled in his chosen professional field, be it marketing, finance, production, or whatever. Failure stems far more frequently from behavioral traits and an inability to adjust to the foreign way of life. In plain terms, it's a human relations and social failure rather than one born of technical inadequacies. Typical causes include:

PERSONALITY

Personality has many definitions and facets. In essence, it's the image an individual projects to the rest of the world. Is it an image of warmth, openness, and helpfulness? Does it engender trust and confidence in others? Does it draw people to the individual because others sense his concern for and interest in them? Is the individual outgoing, friendly, and helpful in his interpersonal relations?

Conversely, does the person project an image of cold efficiency, of mistrust, of personal insecurity? Does he seem to be a one-way communicator whose egocentrism blinds him to the needs and wants of others? Is he a driver whose only concern is production and who has minimal regard for those responsible for the production?

The home office doesn't need a battery of psychological tests to discover behavior traits like these. How the potential candidate has managed right here at home will offer some pretty accurate clues about his personality. If the intended overseas assignment is to be long-term and the desired role is that of an operator/developer, don't send the hard-driving autocrat. He probably won't make it. He doesn't have what it takes to meet the full requirements of the job.

One trait that particularly irritates local nationals is a demeanor of superiority. It makes little difference where the U.S. manager might be—Europe, Asia, the Orient, or the Middle East. Any denigrating comparisons of life there with life in the United States are certain to create antipathy and conflict. This is especially true in the developing countries. Presumably the U.S. manager is there, at least in part, to help those who are less advanced technologically, who are moving from underdevelopment to industrialization. The national is well aware of his country's technological backwardness. He doesn't need an egotistical foreigner to remind him of it. Nor does he need a foreigner who degrades his way of life, his time-honored culture, and his deeply ingrained social customs.

Once again, the presence or absence of a superior attitude can be fairly well determined by studying the candidate's behavior in the jobs he has already held. For example:

- Is he always absolutely certain that he is right, regardless of what others think?
- Does he plow ahead, disregarding the advice or counsel of others?
- Is he boastful about his achievements, his family, his social position?
- Does he scorn others or retort sarcastically when suggested actions or decisions differ from his?
- Is he domineering and autocratic in the management of subordinates?
- Does he abruptly reject new ideas submitted by subordinates?
- Is he a know-it-all in attitude and behavior?

If any of these questions raise a red flag, there is a good reason to pause in the selection process—maybe even to stop entirely. A holier-than-thou attitude at home could grow into the holiest-of-all attitudes in an overseas capacity. Should that occur, the ticket for the manager's early return will quickly be written.

INTOLERANCE

The world abroad, especially in the developing countries, is a far cry from what the U.S. manager has known all his life. This is no earthshaking revelation, but the differences can be rather earthshaking to one who thinks he can get along with the Arab just because he gets along with the American.

The American abroad needs an open-minded attitude if he is to accept and tolerate foreign habits, attitudes, and behavior. We have our culture; the countries of the rest of the world have theirs. Ours works for us, and theirs works for them. There is no right or wrong—there are only differences.

Too frequently seen in key jobs abroad are archetypes of the ugly American. These are the managers who scoff, laugh, and sneer at local customs—the managers, wrapped in the flag of national chauvinism, who make it known that "the only right way is the American way." They can't tolerate the normal government infringements in their businesses. They vocally resent the religious restrictions on their personal freedoms. They object to the food and are openly irritated by the long business luncheons where everything but business is discussed. They are frustrated by the difficulty of driving ahead, obtaining prompt commitments, and getting things done on time.

At the root is an inability to accept, and thus tolerate, other customs, cultures, and ways of life. As a guest in the host country, the American must act like a guest if he is to be treated like one. Open discourtesy and voiced intolerance beg a response in kind. When this sort of conflict between an American and the locals surfaces, the American's chance of success is about 1 in 100. Local nationals are most artful in their ability to sabotage an intolerant expatriate.

INABILITY TO ADJUST

This is not the same as intolerance. The U.S. manager may accept and indeed respect the local way of life but find himself incapable of adjusting to it. Perhaps for him the climate is unbearable, the frequent electrical failures too frequent, the telephone service too unreliable, the shopping too challenging, the payola repulsive, the requirement to bargain annoying, the language barrier insurmountable.

Again, he may accept and understand these elements of life but find they just aren't worth fighting. Rather than adapting, he longs for the ordered efficiency of life back home.

To evaluate this ability to adjust, certain psychological tests will help, but so can a review of the candidate's work history. How has he reacted when changes in methods or operating procedures have been imposed on him? Can he alter his position or change his mind when new facts about a certain situation are revealed? If he had been transferred from one location to another in the States, how quickly and easily did he settle down in the new location and adjust to the new job? To what extent does he show an open mind on controversial matters? How effectively does he seek the best solution to a problem even though he may have already voiced his own opinion?

These are just a few clues that indicate the ability to adjust, adapt, and accept. Suffice it to say that rigidity and inflexibility are common contributors to failure overseas.

LACK OF APPRECIATION OF CULTURAL DIFFERENCES

More will be said about this in Chapter 2, because failure to appreciate or accept the differences in culture and social customs is another of the causes of failure abroad. Often, the fault lies in lack of preparation for the foreign assignment rather than in personal traits or attitudes. Despite the availability of excellent cross-cultural orientation programs, too many companies still feel that such exposure would be nice but not necessary for their person. "Too costly," "Too time-consuming," "He'll catch on," "We need him there right *now*."

Maybe you do need him there right now; maybe he *will* catch on. But is it worth the risk? It's easy to say yes if you don't care about the man, his family, the costs, and the company's overseas reputation. If you do care, even a one-week concentrated course on the host country's culture, social mores, religion, government, family relations, and language will be well worth the small investment.

Giving the manager some exposure to what he will encounter is essential—and that applies to the accompanying family members as well. Otherwise, the culture shock may be greater than what even the most tolerant can accept. The intensity of preparation varies, of course, with the country to which the manager is being assigned. A post in London will hardly present the life-style differences that are found in Singapore, Kuwait, or Saudi Arabia. There *are* differences everywhere, however—in business practices, etiquette, customs, the meaning of time, government regulations, language, and so on. If the U.S. manager is not aware of these differences, whether major or minor, he is certain to make mistakes that could prove very costly to him and to the company he represents. The risk is not worth the small investment of time and money.

These, then, are the most common causes of failure abroad. Potential candidates should be carefully screened, with particular attention to personality (especially lack of a superiority complex), tolerance, and ability to adjust. If the screening results here are positive, the next step is to make sure the successful candidate receives the necessary cross-cultural orientation from people who have been where he is going and know what they are talking about.

A manager who has the basic character strengths and is supported by proper preparation will be well-equipped to take on the new assignment. Success is not guaranteed, but, other things being equal, the risks of failure are minimized. Which is probably all anyone could ask.

The Bases for Success

Yes, the personal traits and adequate preparation are essential ingredients. But additional qualities—qualities closer to the job itself—are needed if the probability of success abroad is to be increased. The potential candidate should be examined from the viewpoint of three specific skills: technical, managerial, and human.

TECHNICAL SKILLS

Perhaps the most obvious, these are usually the first to be considered in screening a candidate. Essentially: "Is he qualified for the available position?" If not, further investigation is futile. You don't send a computer expert to oversee an international marketing program.

Technical skills, as the term is used here, refer to the required knowledge and proven ability of the candidate in his particular field of expertise—production, marketing, purchasing, materials management, industrial relations, or whatever. These are the learnable management technologies that require prior training and experience. They are the skills the host country is importing—or the parent company is exporting. Proficiency in his own field is thus expected and assumed of the U.S. manager.

Knowledge that is based solely on theory and business school preachments, however, is not enough. Experience and a proven track record are necessary if ideas, principles, and theory are to be translated into practical on-the-job application. Last year's MBA graduate with little real-world experience is not the best risk in an overseas assignment.

MANAGERIAL SKILLS

As important as the technical skills are, they are not *management*. Whatever his professional qualifications, the U.S. manager is not expected to boil out a truck carburetor, make eight customer calls a day, or weld a leaking pipeline. He may have the expertise to do any of these, and more, but that's not why he is there. His job is to *manage* either those who supervise the workers or the workers themselves.

This responsibility brings in a whole new set of skills that are above and beyond technical proficiency per se. Managerial skills include the ability to:

- o Establish results-oriented goals and objectives.
- o Plan—to achieve some desired result.
- o Organize—the work, the people, the workplace.
- o Lead—the people to execute the plan.
- o Control—to maintain the predetermined standards of quality, quantity, timeliness, and costs.

Within these basic functions, management also means the ability to define jobs clearly and explicitly; to set challenging yet attainable performance standards with each subordinate; to delegate as many responsibilities as the capabilities of the subordinate will permit; and to train thoroughly, coach wisely, and develop carefully those reporting to the manager.

Effective management creates a climate of openness and trust—a climate where freedom of expression is encouraged and the right of the subordinate to make an occasional mistake is understood. Effective management is knowing when to become personally involved in the operation and when to leave the people alone (the Principle of Exception). It is keeping people *currently* informed on how they are doing and conducting performance-related appraisal interviews based on fact, not feelings or opinions. In the healthy organization climate, the communication channels are open—down, up, across, and diagonally. The boss shares the information he can share; he welcomes ideas from subordinates; rumors are minimal; the people know what's going on.

Deficiencies in skills such as these are what produce the "doing" manager. He is the sort of person we've all seen—the superactive manager who is busy all day, breathing down the necks of his people, changing plans, revising priorities, issuing orders, answering questions, solving problems the people *could* solve, making routine decisions—and driving everyone around him crazy. That is not managing by any definition.

What about the overseas candidate? How has he performed in the past? Is he a *doer* or a *manager?* You don't need a psychological test to answer that. A little observation and a few chats with his subordinates will tell you what you want to know.

Select the manager, not the doer. The doer may have all the technical expertise, but, except in the most technologically backward and illiterate parts of the world, his closely held authority and constant interference in day-to-day work will be highly resented. The worker abroad, like the American employee, will respond to effective management practices.

HUMAN SKILLS

Along with managerial skills, some basic human or interpersonal skills are essential in an overseas assignment. For example, *empathy*—the ability to see things from the other person's point of view—is important anywhere in dealing with people. It is even more critical, however, when working with and supervising others whose culture and values are so different from the manager's.

The ways of the local people may seem strange, incongruous, or illogical to the American. But they are the products of centuries of history, and they make perfect sense to the local nationals. Rather than criticizing or mocking, the American manager should try to remove some of his biases or prejudices and see things from the local's point of view.

Empathy for the national as an employee is equally important. It is a stressful experience to work in an industrialized complex with perhaps limited technical knowledge and language ability. In the Western world and in Japan, the stress may not be that acute, but it definitely is in the developing societies. Patience and understanding are demanded of the U.S. manager in such situations.

Openness, honesty, and *trustworthiness* are traits the local employee looks for in his American supervisor. Make no mistake about it: he initially views the U.S. manager with suspicion. It is a wait-and-see attitude. If he then concludes that the manager can't be trusted, in either word or deed, the manager is quickly marked as a "tourist"— one who is there for the money and whose primary concern is "What's in it for me?" Once a manager is tagged with that label, the workforce has marvelously subtle methods of undermining his effectiveness and abbreviating his stay among them. The right word to the right ear is often all that's necessary. In Saudi Arabia, for example, with the plethora of princes and members of the royal family, it's not difficult to get a message to a government official. Without hearings or debate, the official often has the power to see that an expatriate is quietly but promptly dispatched home.

If this route isn't taken, countless small but erosive techniques are employed within the company itself. These eat away at the manager's ability to function. With his power diluted, he goes home voluntarily or is recalled by the home office.

On the plus side, however, the local will become almost slavish in his devotion and support when he finds that he is working for a person he can trust. It may take some time because of early suspicions, but when an open interpersonal relationship is created, marked by obvious respect and demonstrated honesty, the manager will have won for himself a dedicated follower.

Other human skills, such as warmth, a genuine concern for others, the willingness to help the local employee grow and develop, patience, and thoughtfulness, are the personal attributes that identify the successful executive abroad. These attributes, when coupled with technical competence and managerial expertise, strengthen the American role in the developing as well as the developed world. At the same time, they are fundamental to the forging of a productive local workforce—a workforce that can make or break the organization that has planted itself on the country's soil.

"But," you say, "what's so different about any of this? The same thing is true right here at home." Sure it is. People are people. The difference is that at home there are a common language, a common culture, and a diverse industrial complex that allows the disgruntled employee to quit one job and find another next door or around the corner. There is a commonality that simplifies communications and understanding. Even so, how much labor strife have we generated in the States because of our failure to manage wisely or respect human values? The same applies in England today, where the economy is being shattered by militant unions and bitter workers. Nor is the picture much brighter in France, Italy, or other industrialized nations.

It is no different here at home—except that we have continually violated some of the very basics that we're asking the manager abroad to practice. In the developing countries, with their differing cultures and social values, trust and respect come even more slowly. Furthermore, although local employees generally lack a union of any measurable strength to speak for them, they find ways of their own to control or remove those whom they have learned to mistrust.

The end result may be the same as in the United States—labor unrest, lowered production, the eventual replacement of the incompetent manager. Abroad, however, the cost to the company, especially the cost of manager replacement, is considerably greater and thus more serious. The price of managerial failure there is high by any yardstick.

Therefore, companies in the international arena should exert every possible effort to minimize the potential of failure. It all begins by selecting the right person in the first place and then preparing him to meet the challenges he will face.

Why Is the Candidate Willing to Be a Candidate?

The possibility of an overseas assignment still has its fascination, its aura of romanticism. Finding managers who at least want to be considered for an assignment is usually no problem. Finding the *right* manager is something else.

Several aspects of this "rightness" have already been reviewed. Another question is pertinent, however: Why is Joe Smith willing to be a candidate? What motives does he have for throwing his hat in the ring?

Some points to be explored: Is Joe applying because he sees this as a short-term, self-advancing step? With a couple of years behind him, does he want to return to a bigger job, a better title, a healthy pay boost? Is he going with a "What's in it for me?" attitude?

If these are his reasons, the home office would do well to file Joe's application in the appropriate resting place. Joe will probably fail. He is too self-centered to make the necessary sacrifices or adjustments. His eye is on the final exit visa and the day when he can get back to "civilization" and the good life at home.

On the other hand, suppose Joe sees this as a self-advancing step (which it should be) but one in which he can make a commitment in terms of the organization and its well-being. Suppose he sees the assignment as a growth opportunity for himself and an educational experience for his family. Suppose he sees it as an opportunity to make a meaningful contribution to his company and to the development of the host country. What then?

Quite obviously, this Joe is a good risk—all other things being equal. He will probably do his best to adjust, learn the language, and manage his unit with intelligent sensitivity. Naturally Joe is in it for himself—who isn't? We're all selfish in that respect. He sees more to the role, however, than the narrowness of his own personal advancement.

The successful Joes, especially those who venture into developing societies, have to have a bit of the missionary in them. They have to see themselves as apostles of the developed, industrialized world. They are abroad for the benefit of their company while contributing in their own way to the growth of a developing country.

Personal motivations largely determine behavior patterns and performance in any environment. In remote locations, however, those motivations can generate behaviors that will make or break the manager. It would be well to determine what motivation prevails before telling Joe: "Congratulations! You're going to Dubai."

Don't Forget the Wife

Joe's all set. He has the technical ability and seems to be emotionally as well as psychologically equipped for Dubai or wherever. But, if he's married, what about his wife? Is she equally equipped to make the change to an entirely different way of life? Can she adjust and adapt? Does she have interests other than housekeeping that would occupy her time and her mind? There's a limit to how much dusting, vacuuming, and cooking one can do, especially in a small apartment or when she's hired a houseboy for those very purposes.

If Joe and his wife are housed in a company compound with other Americans, she may make enough friends so that she doesn't fall victim to frustrating boredom—a boredom that's very possible if the culture of the country limits her freedom. However, compound living in a restricted environment also has its dangers.

In one case with which the author is familiar, a group of American wives, having little to do and isolated from the city proper, began getting together in the early afternoon for coffee or tea. These daily social respites gradually became less satisfying, so beer or wine replaced coffee and tea, and it wasn't long before smuggled scotch or homemade hard stuff took over from the beer and wine. More than one woman turned into a chronic alcoholic by the time the tour of duty was over.

Then there is the story of Maynard, which David M. Noer cites in his book *Multinational People Management.*[2] Maynard and his wife were sent to eastern Europe to do work with one country's government. Everything was fine. Maynard loved the job and apparently had made an excellent start. After two months, however, everything blew up and Maynard was recalled, to the considerable embarrassment of his company.

The problem, as Noer says, wasn't Maynard: it was his wife. Back home, she had been a right-wing activist. Frustrated in her efforts to buy fresh meat and vegetables, frustrated by the inadequate housing and the completely bureaucratic way of life, she began to attack the whole way the society was run. She was right; the system was wrong. Her public denouncements forced the company to bring Maynard home when he was just two months into an 18-month assignment. Some sort of investigation into his wife's interests and activities, plus a briefing on what she could expect in an iron-curtain country, would either have prepared her for the experience or convinced her that this wasn't the post for her. Had that been done, Maynard probably would have refused the opportunity or not been chosen for it at all.

Don't overlook wives. They can make or break their husbands, particularly in a developing country.

---

[2] Washington, D.C.: Bureau of National Affairs, 1975, pp. 52–53.

A Familiarization Trip

True, there's a cost attached, but it's eminently unfair to send a husband and wife abroad unless they've had a chance to see the country and how people really live there. Travel folders are for tourist consumption and rarely paint an accurate picture. Even if books from the library or the latest State Department publications are up to date (which they usually aren't because of the rapid changes in the developing societies), the written word can never replace going, seeing, feeling, and breathing life as it is.

Give the couple a week or two to investigate housing, shopping, schools (if children are involved), churches, transportation in the city or area, what the people (especially women) wear, living costs, and so on. If they're going to be in the country for two or three years, they deserve the chance to see what they're getting into. Then they can make an intelligent go or no-go decision. Otherwise, they're jumping blindly for the "glamour," the "education," the "chance to travel," or a dozen other rationalizations that may or may not be valid.

A familiarization trip is the only way to minimize the potential of failure. It won't eliminate the potential, since failure has many fathers, but at least those who are being asked to go will have a better idea of what to expect. The money spent now could save thousands down the road, to say nothing of the transferees' welfare and the company's reputation.

Conclusion

As much of this chapter indicates, many managers have been sent abroad who should never have passed the first screening interview. Settling in a distant country 10,000 miles or so from home is hardly the same as moving from New York to Los Angeles or from Minneapolis to Miami. Here there are no language barriers, the supermarkets are comparable, the laws are basically the same, and modern medical facilities are always available. The inconveniences are minor, the culture shock minimal.

Going abroad is another matter. Culture shock isn't just a textbook term: it's a very real emotional condition that can seriously affect a person's outlook on life and his performance on the job. Unless he is prepared for it, both by his own temperament and by being taught everything possible before he departs, a hopeless feeling of entrapment is a real possibility. Visiting a strange land as a tourist is one thing.

To live in that land, if only for a year or two, is an entirely different story.

Choosing the right man—and the right wife—is the first step. Next comes the preparation. If both stages are done well, and the manager knows clearly what role he is to play, his chances of fulfilling his mission are excellent. The wrong choice can be disastrous. The right person will be a credit to his company, to himself, and yes—without becoming melodramatic—to his country and the system he represents.

2

Second—
Is He Ready to Bridge
the Culture Gap?

The typical U.S. manager was born into and has grown up in a culture that has always been oriented toward commerce, trade, and business. Since our nation's founding, these have been part of our life, our tradition. In this we are unique, for nowhere else in the world has what we broadly call "business" been such an integral element of a country's history and heritage. Nowhere else has business held such a position of dominance in the life patterns of a country. And nowhere else is the tradesperson regarded with the same degree of esteem or so respected for his accomplishments. The legend of shoeshine boy to president is strictly an American one.

Business—a Peculiarly American Tradition

Since our earliest days, we have had the best business and highest production because the best brains have gone into business. In Puritan times, it was the merchant who made things work and the businessman who took the risks to build the mills and shops. For the immigrants, many of whom arrived as indentured servants or were fleeing oppression and poverty, it was the businessman who provided jobs, paid wages, and loaned money to help others set themselves up in businesses of their own. Risk-taking was encouraged, and it was the merchant and businessman who took up the challenge. They spearheaded the development of an empty land.

Capital was invested in forges, fences, and factories—not castles or monasteries. There was minimal religious influence to limit business, no military class to control it. In those early days, the scholar or the artist was of little importance.

As the wilderness of 3,000 miles was tamed over a period of 300 years, the businessman was catapulted into dominance. In the seat of leadership, he set the pattern and tone of the culture—a pattern and tone that prevail even today. It is in this tradition that we are indeed unique, because we are still a business-dominated society. Despite some recent attacks on its ethics and morality, business remains strong and fundamental to our way of life. Those who enter it view it as an honorable pursuit.

Although perspectives are changing, this attitude toward business has not been shared by the rest of the world. In the Far East, for example, the people who dealt in trade were traditionally among the least respected members of society. First was the scholar who taught others how to live. Then came the farmer, followed by the carpenter or artisan. At the bottom was the businessman, trader, or shopowner.

In England, business is more highly regarded now than in times past but still not to the same degree as here. Until recently, a man went to Oxford or Cambridge and then sought a position in foreign or civil service. If he chose a business field, it was typically banking or investments, not trade. On the Continent, law and diplomatic service were the favored professions for the educated.

The American manager, reared on and trained in our business principles and practices, should be conditioned for what he will probably face abroad. In a good part of the world, he won't find the same enthusiasm for productivity, achieving objectives, high performance standards, punctuality, and the like that he brings to the job. His ideas of what is important probably won't mesh with those of the Indian, and certainly not with those of the Iranian since the 1979 revolution and removal of the Shah.

Indeed, it makes little difference where he goes. In South America, the Orient, Asia, the Middle East, and even Europe, the local businessman conforms to *his* traditions across the conference table, not ours. In the same mold, so does the employee.

In most developing countries, the local employee is still the product of a society where, if the father was a carpenter, the son is a carpenter. His parents made the decisions for him and they chose his wife for him. Born into a particular social stratum, he had learned that this is his lot in life. Thoughts of rising out of it are foreign to the culture and his training.

Times are changing, but the influence of centuries of changelessness is still powerful in the developing societies. Contributing quite dramatically to the change is the advent of machinery and technology, coupled, in some cases, with a national wealth heretofore inconceivable. The oil-rich Emirates, Saudi Arabia, Kuwait, and Iran are common examples of societies thrust abruptly into the twentieth century.

With these rapid changes, the traditional society experiences discontinuity. It begins to break up. Old guidelines and tenets that once provided direction become diluted. Questions begin to be asked about them. As industrialization moves in, confusion arises about what is right, moral, or sacred. A gnawing discontent with the past is mixed with a fear of the future.

Arabs smoke their water pipes in sidewalk cafes while staring at black-and-white television screens. A laborer straddles a tawdry donkey that is slowly pulling a water cart, while a jet aircraft whines overhead on its final landing approach. Is it any wonder the developing countries are confused? The old is disappearing and the new is not yet understood.

This is not meant to imply that national managers in these developing societies are ignorant or naive. Far from it. Many are highly educated and are brilliant in the management of their business affairs. They may be flamboyant, but they are also shrewd in their investments and use of capital. At the lower levels of the organizational hierarchy, the same intelligence and potential exist. But there is uncertainty about what is right and what is wrong. There is a conflict between newfound wealth and ancient traditions. There is a conflict between imported American management techniques and the nationals' own historic patterns of life.

Into this mélange enters the U.S. businessman. He has never experienced their culture, and the local citizens know little, if anything, of his. At best, an uneasy accommodation can be expected—unless the American is aware of the transition that is taking place and is determined to accept it and do what he can to smooth the path into the future.

Other Gaps to Be Bridged

A full-scale review of national or regional cultural differences around the world is beyond the scope of this book. In the developing countries, however, there are some areas of commonality that produce gaps the American must be prepared to bridge. Below are a few of the more common ones.

ATTITUDES TOWARD TIME

Time, and the lack of concern for it, will probably frustrate the newly assigned U.S. manager as much as anything. If he has an appointment to be in someone's office at 10:00, he may cool his heels in the waiting room for one or two hours before being summoned by his host. Similarly, meetings rarely start on time; promised delivery dates aren't met; employee tardiness is routine; and it seems to take forever to get anything done.

Patience and understanding are two of the manager's better allies in adapting to this different attitude toward time. Pleadings or arguments will be of little avail. Telling a garage mechanic that "I have to have my car by 3:00 tomorrow afternoon" is to ensure that you won't get it. *Mañana* and *bukrah* both mean "tomorrow," but tomorrow doesn't mean *tomorrow;* it just means some time in the future. The Arab mechanic may politely acknowledge your request with the reply, "Tomorrow, *inshallah,*" or "Tomorrow, if God wills." If the car is not ready when promised, it means that God has ordained otherwise and that something of greater importance has arisen.

The American, if prepared, will accept and adapt to the time "gap." He'll learn to set a new date for a meeting that never took place; he'll requisition materials and supplies with an extended lead time; he'll learn to add months onto the estimated completion date of a new building. Above all, he'll learn that arguments and visible annoyance produce nothing. They are self-defeating, arousing only enmity and further procrastination.

RELIGIOUS INFLUENCE

Religious influence in most of the developing countries is still powerful and predominant. This is especially so in the Moslem world. The true Moslem abides literally by the word of the Koran and the preachings of the Prophet Mohammed. As just one example, the Moslem employee obeys the commandment to pray five times a day and will tolerate no interference with this obligation. Work may be interrupted by the call to prayer, but the U.S. manager can do nothing about it—nor should he even attempt to. Tampering with the national's religious requirements is emphatically taboo.

During Ramadan, the Moslem's month of penance and fasting, little productive work can be expected. He fasts from sunup to sundown, abstaining completely from food, liquid, and tobacco, and then feasts quite sumptuously throughout the night. Most companies shorten the working hours for the month, and at first the toll of fasting-feasting and little sleep isn't too noticeable. After ten days or so, however, the growing fatigue and growing irritability militate against getting any meaningful work accomplished. The month, coupled with the three-day Eid Al-Fitr holiday that follows immediately, can be a very frustrating period for the production-oriented American.

Again, however, there is nothing that he can or should try to do about it. In one case, a U.S. manager demanded that his immediate subordinates maintain the normal working hours of 8:00—4:30 during Ramadan instead of the abbreviated day. His order was quite properly disobeyed, and he lost face for trying to enforce the unenforceable. You don't tamper with religious obligations or cultural habits without paying a price.

ATTITUDES TOWARD WORK

Work attitudes are another source of potential frustration. The local is accustomed to a leisurely pace in which socializing on the job, frequent tea or coffee breaks, casual interruptions of meetings, and missed deadlines are all part of the routine. The American manager, schooled in efficiency and production, may find these behaviors disturbing and disruptive to his own objectives, but there is little he can do to make any drastic changes. The "old" is not easily put aside, nor is the "new" readily adopted.

As Aaron Lippman says in his book *The Colombian Entrepreneur in Bogota* [1] (paraphrasing Max Weber's observation in *The Protestant Ethic and the Spirit of Capitalism*):

> Protestantism and Puritanism provided an incentive for dedication to work while restriction of consumption (i.e., frugality) was considered a virtue. Catholicism, on the other hand, had not provided an ethical legitimation of an achievement-orientation aimed at worldly success. Directly opposed to the Protestant concept of business as a "calling" was the Augustinian view that business was in itself an evil, for it turned men from seeking true rest, which was God.

Whether in Latin America, the Middle East, or the Far East, the American devotion to work is not shared. Even Europeans fail to understand our long hours, seemingly total dedication to the job, and full briefcases. To most non-Americans, life is made up of many other pursuits of greater significance. Business or trade has never been a valued component of their culture.

Accompanying this fact are regional values that affect the local person's thinking and behavior on the job. For example, in an Indian home, discussions designed to further business interests are considered a discourtesy to the guest. This is a social occasion, and to bring up such matters would violate the host's principles of hospitality.

[1] Miami: University of Miami Press, 1969, pp. 35–36.

In Latin America, several meetings, dinners, or luncheons with a prospective customer might be required before the subject of business is even raised. If the American (*North* American, that is) is to be successful, a relationship of friendship and trust must first be created. In effect, the Latin buys the *person* and then does business with him. The American's concerns are facts, figures, and product; the human being with whom he is dealing is secondary.

For the Saudi, manual labor is studiously avoided. He never enters trades such as carpentry, painting, plumbing, or garbage collection—especially if he is from the upper class. He considers working with his hands beneath him. In Saudi Arabia these jobs are performed by the Yemenese and the Sudanese.

The typical European manager works hard at his job but is usually satisfied when he is finally able to provide a good home for his family and educate his children. Then he prefers to enjoy the more important things in life, such as good books, good wine, an automobile, and periodic tours around the Continent. He is not driven to expand his organization, if he owns one, or to seek a higher position for the sake of prestige. An American might say that he lacks ambition. Actually, he simply has a different set of priorities in life.

The Japanese, despite all of their industrial influence, still mirror many of their ancient traditions in the workplace. Lifetime employment is the rule, with all sorts of protective paternalism extended by the company. Seniority is more important than efficiency—an offspring of the Oriental's time-honored respect for age. The preservation of self-esteem, or face, is an ever present concern. Social failure or discharge from employment means a loss of face in the eyes of the individual's family, relatives, and friends. In serious instances he will choose death rather than continue to live in disgrace.

Japanese decision-making is typically bottom-up and by consensus. Suggestions and solutions to problems are submitted through channels to the proper decision-making authority where, after thoughtful consideration, the recommendation is accepted or rejected. If it is accepted, the word goes back down to those responsible for implementation. The process is much slower than in the United States, but acceptance and implementation of change are both greater and faster.

Conversely, American management makes decisions more rapidly, communicates them down the line, and then encounters as many negative reactions as positive ones. This is particularly true when new operating policies or practices are being introduced. The Japanese system involves the people; they become a part of the very decisions or actions they are being asked to follow. Reception under these conditions is obviously much more positive than under our management-by-dictate practices.

Similarly, in the Japanese system, responsibility is basically shared. If a decision proves to be wrong, no one loses face. Many people were involved in arriving at the final decision, so the finger of blame can be pointed at no specific manager. This is one reason why delegation, as we conceive it, is not a widely accepted management practice in Japan. Delegation empowers an individual to act autonomously, if he chooses, rather than by group agreement of consensus. Should he act on his own authority, any mistake or error in judgment is immediately exposed. The guilty party is easily identified, and loss of face is likely.

While many changes are needed in our own managerial practices, the system works well for us. To the Japanese, however, it runs counter to their traditional and paternalistic culture. They have great respect for our technical expertise, but our way of managing the human element is not theirs.

So attitudes toward work vary from region to region. The one strain of commonality is that all attitudes differ from ours. Wherever the American goes abroad, he can be certain that the work ethic he takes with him will conflict, to one degree or another, with that of his host country. Too many overseas managers have failed to appreciate that simple fact—until, perhaps, it is too late.

NEPOTISM

Nepotism is a standard practice in most of the world, but especially in the developing countries. The family looks out for itself—a practice that stems from the strong family ties that are so much a part of ancient cultures. Assuming that they have the authority to do so, fathers bring sons and relatives into the same company, and brothers bring brothers. Looking out for one another is considered a basic family responsibility.

In a somewhat similar vein, some developing countries employ a national nepotism—meaning that local nationals are hired over perhaps more qualified foreigners. In Kuwait, for example, the government stresses the hiring of Kuwaitis and, once they are on the payroll, protects them by law against termination for all but the most serious of offenses. Termination for mere ineptitude or undependability is next to impossible. The same is generally true in Saudi Arabia and other countries where the employment of nationals is considered essential to economic growth.

For the American, "nepotism" has a negative connotation. Elsewhere, however, it is an accepted practice with no hint of negativeness attached.

ATTITUDES TOWARD THE FAMILY

The family, as just suggested, is the local national's highest (or almost highest) priority. As summarized by many Saudis, their devotion is to "God, family, and country"—in that order. The job, and the local's responsibility to it, is well down the list in order of importance. It has significance primarily because it ensures the income necessary to feed and protect the family. A sick child gets the father's attention first. He may leave work to take the child to a doctor or the hospital, come in late for the same reason, or not show up at all. The death of an uncle, aunt, or cousin warrants time off to attend the funeral.

In Latin America and in the Middle and Far East, the family is the center of the local employee's life. It is the unit that provides food, shelter, and protection for all its members—immediate and distant kin alike. It is not uncommon to find one brother financially supporting another brother or sister, a cousin sending a monthly check to a second cousin, or a father depriving himself of all but the essentials of life to send a son to a university in the United Kingdom.

On an expanded level, this devotion to family is easily translated into a devotion to country. The typical local is highly nationalistic and outwardly patriotic. While aware of his country's deficiencies, he is nevertheless extremely sensitive to derogatory remarks about it. An attack by an outsider on his country and culture will be met with the same vehemence as an attack on his family and its reputation. The expatriate who indulges in demeaning observations had better be prepared for retaliation. The local won't take that sort of thing lying down, no matter how right or wrong the expatriate might be in what he has said.

By comparison, the American probably isn't all that different. His concern for his *immediate* family is no less, and the same might be said of his patriotism. He is prone, however, to try to submerge family problems or illnesses and plod ahead with the job. The American child with a simple cold is treated at home; the local national will take time off from work and drive the child to a physician. We worry about the well-being of our wives, sons, and daughters; the local is concerned with the whole family network. We're proud of our country and its global reputation (although national masochism seems to be the current vogue). Defending our country from external verbal abuse comes as naturally to us as it does to local nationals.

We are, however, a conglomerate of races and nationalities that have been absorbed into the mainstream of life. Most of the developing countries, on the other hand, are "purer" in the sense that they are more homogeneous ethnically and racially. To a measurable degree because of this, the local's nationalism is more vocally expressed. For example, a developing country often places great importance on the establishment of its own flag-carrying airline. There may be only a couple of airplanes, but as they land at foreign ports, they signal to the world that "We are." Nationalism is an extension of the family-centered life-style of the local. Both, then, are important for the U.S. manager to understand if he is to relate effectively to his local employees.

ATTITUDES TOWARD AUTHORITY

Authority, and attitudes toward it, stem from family relationships. Most local employees have come from a family where the father was the dominant figure. He made the decisions, issued the orders, and controlled the household. At school, the employee learned to listen, take notes, recite from memory, and not question the reasoning of the teacher. Obedience and respect for authority figures were ingrained in him. As he moved into the work scene, he carried with him this same respect for those who now supervised him.

Respect for authority, however, has two meanings. One is the respect accorded to the position and title, while the other is earned by the individual through the way he uses the power granted him by the title. The two don't always go hand in hand. Power that is abused or misused is power lost.

Practically everywhere, the expatriate manager is expected to oversee and direct the operation. It is he who plans, organizes, coordinates, communicates, and controls. At the same time, he is viewed as a protector and a provider. He is the father figure in the world of work. This implies an element of paternalism, of personal interest in his subordinates, of ensuring a sense of security. But it also implies some measure of aloofness and avoidance of too much of a buddy-buddy relationship. The manager must maintain a delicate balance, not being too much *a part of* the subordinate group and yet not too far *apart from* it. The typical local, in a caste-like way, sees his manager as being above him. Excessive friendliness is troubling to him. Finding the proper balance is not easy for any manager, but it is essential if he is to earn the respect his position warrants.

One of the main complaints against American managers is not their friendliness but their remoteness, their lack of visibility. A frequent comment of supervisors in a Kuwait firm was that no one ever saw the top management people (all expatriates) except on rare social occasions. They just didn't bother to walk around, chat briefly with the people, ask a few questions, and be seen. They were remote—to an extreme.

The best policy is the open-door policy, in reverse. Whether the manager is local or expatriate, he should get out from behind his desk, walk through the open door, and be *seen*. The employees may respect the authority granted to the office, but they won't respect the incumbent if he remains isolated in his executive suite.

All of this—the father-figure, paternalism, visibility—creates another problem, however. Americans believe in organization structure, the chain of command, an orderly flow of communications. Not so elsewhere. It's not unusual to find a worker in the manager's office or a first-line supervisor bypassing all intermediate levels and taking an issue directly to the managing director or whomever the top person might be. In Saudi Arabia, the "lowliest" bedouin knows that he can have an audience with the king—a freedom that has been extended into the business world.

A greater respect for channels is beginning to develop as Western ideas of organization discipline spread. The U.S. manager, however, should be neither surprised nor irritated if he finds his people occasionally going around him to some higher authority. In the process of industrial development, the practice will gradually come to a halt.

PAYOLA

Payola—the old game of palm-greasing—is as normal a way of doing business abroad as it is repudiated here at home. A payoff to win a contract or get an agreement signed is routine. *Baksheesh,* the Arab word for it, goes on in major business dealings just as it does with shopkeepers and merchants. You want something? Okay, you'll get it—for an aside consideration.

As Americans, we may not like the custom, but it's a fact of life in many parts of the world. Before criticizing the practice too harshly, we should remember that our moral values are not shared everywhere else. Bigamy is illegal here, but Moslem law permits as many as four wives, as long as all are treated equally. Who's to say we're right and they're immoral, or vice versa? The same rationale applies to *baksheesh,* payola, or whatever you want to call it. Just because we are in Rome doesn't mean that we have to do as the Romans do, but we should be very careful not to criticize what they do or how they do it. When value differences emerge, we would be wise at least to try to accommodate and understand the other side. We might as well, because it's very unlikely that we'll effect any changes in long-held customs and habits.

These, then, are some of the common cultural gaps the manager abroad has to bridge—time, religious influence, work attitudes, nepotism, attitudes toward family and authority, payola. The list is hardly complete, but it is representative of the more pronounced differences between the U.S. manager's inheritance and what he will find in the developing parts of the world.

Properly prepared for the differences, he will find the culture shock less threatening to him and to his family. Then, if he remembers that he is representing the only country in which business and trade have been a vital part of its entire history, he will perhaps be a bit more tolerant of those who are moving from a traditional society into industrialization.

The United States and the Host Country: Some Things the Manager Needs to Know

Common though the ugly American abroad may be, the ignorant American is even more prevalent. Without question, the vast majority of U.S. managers abroad know their business and are highly competent technically. The ignorance comes to light when they are asked questions about their country and when they ask questions about the country in which they are based.

With the spread of television and American movies, most locals have a Hollywood-made impression of the United States. Their curiosity has been aroused, and they will ask many questions, most of which the U.S. manager should be able to answer. But, you might say, what does that have to do with the job to be done—running the plant, marketing the product, setting up the management information system?

The answer: nothing. But the manager should keep in mind that he is representing both his company and his country while abroad. He is an ambassador-without-portfolio, like it or not. He should be familiar with the pros and cons of democracy and capitalism. His purpose should not be to impose our system on others but to explain it so that others will better understand us and can then draw their own conclusions about which system is best.

Some questions about life in America—such as those on housing, education, food, prices, wage and salary scales, and entertainment—

can be answered from the manager's personal experience. The areas noted below, however, often do not enter into our daily thinking or conversation. Yet they are subjects of interest to most local nationals, and therefore should be reviewed by the manager before he heads abroad.

ABOUT THE UNITED STATES

The Structure of the Government

This may seem elementary, but the lessons learned in a high school civics class have perhaps dimmed with time. Since our structure is unique, a brushup would be in order. This is hardly the place for such a review, but a few suggestions, in outline form, would include:

The Constitution

The U.S. Constitution was adopted in September 1787 and became effective on March 4, 1789. It established:

1. Organization powers; restraints; methods of election of the executive, legislative, and judicial branches.
2. Powers of the states and their relation to the federal government.
3. Representatives of the states in Congress.
4. Provision for the national debt; the supremacy of the Constitution; federal laws and treaties; methods of amending and ratifying the Constitution.
5. The Bill of Rights—to protect the individual and clarify his rights.

Basically the Constitution establishes:

1. Government by the people and for the people.
2. A system of checks and balances and limitations on the power of the Presidency.

The Structure of Congress

Congress consists of the legislative and executive branches of government. It is structured so that:

1. The two branches control each other.
2. Each problem is thoroughly discussed and exposed to the people.

State Organization

1. Each state is a small version of the national government, having a similar organization with both legislative and judicial branches. The governor is the top executive.

2. State laws differ because of Article X of the 12th Amendment to the Constitution, which states: "The powers not delegated to the United States by the Constitution nor prohibited by it to the States are reserved to the States respectively or to the people."
3. States differ in their:
   a. Methods and amounts of taxation.
   b. Regulations pertaining to driving, licenses, and traffic.
   c. Educational systems.
   d. Legislation—for example, right-to-work laws and blue laws.

The Two-Party System

Methods of nominating and electing:

1. National representatives.
2. State representatives.
3. Local representatives.

Two aspects of our government structure are particularly confusing to foreigners. The first is the apparent inability of the President to make a commitment to another government and then act accordingly. President's Carter's 1978 proposal to sell military equipment to Israel, Egypt, and Saudi Arabia is a case in point. The Arabian man-in-the-street could not understand the delay, the Congressional arguments, and the eventual watering down of the President's offer. He found it confusing that the most powerful office in the land could not commit and produce. Once the foreigner understands our system of checks and balances and the sharing of power by the executive and legislative branches, it makes sense to him.

Another area of confusion is the role of the states and how they function. A not-infrequent question from a local who has never visited our country: "What papers would I need to go from one state to another?" And from those who *have* visited here: "Why are the laws and regulations different in states that may be next to each other?" Some of the better educated or more widely traveled nationals know the answers. The typical employee does not, but he knows enough about us to be curious.

The Pluralism of Our Society

The United States is not an either-or society. Born in conflict and searching for freedom, the country has, over the years, attracted wide mixtures of people seeking the right to believe, worship, and work as they wish. This accounts, in part, for the difficulty one has in describing the "typical" American. The mixture of inheritances has produced the pluralistic society in which we live.

We have, for example, no national symphony orchestra but perhaps 500 to 600 locally sponsored symphonies. There are two major political parties, but within each is a wide range of views spanning from the far left to the far right. When neither of these parties meets a particular need, people band together to form their own political organization—for example, the Conservative, Prohibitionist, Socialist, or Communist party.

Religious affiliations are just as varied. Along with the traditional Catholic, Protestant, Jewish, and Greek faiths are the sun worshippers, snake worshippers, followers of Zen, and so on. And, unlike countries that have just one or two prime universities, we have nearly 2,700 two- and four-year colleges.

Decentralization versus a central concentration of power so common in developing countries is what makes us unique. States' rights and local pride are important to Americans who prefer to solve their own problems rather than look to the federal government. The sharing of power and responsibility at the grass-roots level naturally creates a divergent society in which differing interests, values, and life-styles are comfortably accommodated. While our system is not without its problems, it has worked well for over 200 years.

Crime

Unfortunately, people abroad hear the worst about us—which puts crime near the top of the list of things foreigners associate with the United States. In the tightly controlled societies, crime does exist but it is not a major problem as it is here. A point the U.S. manager should keep in mind, however, is that many acts we classify as "criminal" are perfectly legal elsewhere—gambling, prostitution, the use of certain narcotics, and payola. Americans have put moral strictures into law, which accounts for a good part of the nonviolent lawbreaking that goes on. And since we have a free press, those acts we deem wrong or criminal are exposed for the world to see.

Whether or not one agrees with the leniency of the courts today—the illegality of capital punishment, the system of parole, and so on—it is clear that in parts of the world where punishment is swift and severe, the crime rate is negligible. Saudi Arabia's practice of public beheadings for murder and chopping off a hand for repeated theft are rather effective deterrents. In Kuwait, where the drivers seem bent on proving their machismo when they get behind the wheel, some fairly drastic actions were taken recently by the Directorate General of Traffic to tighten up the regulations. For example, according to the Traffic Law Penalties that were issued in September 1978, an offender can be imprisoned up to three months and fined up to 100 *dinars* (about $350) if he drives an unlicensed vehicle or one whose insurance has expired, drives recklessly, races without official permission, or drives a vehicle without the knowledge or approval of its owner. He can be imprisoned up to one month and/or fined up to 50 *dinars* ($175) if he drives a vehicle opposite to the traffic direction, exceeds the speed limit, or uses the vehicle for a purpose other than that prescribed by its license. These are stiff penalties for traffic violations, but they were needed—and the effect on the driving population has been quite remarkable.

Our crime rate, whatever the cause, is high by most standards. Whether that's because we classify more deeds as criminal or because of the relative leniency of our judicial system is up to sociologists and psychologists to determine. The fact remains that it has created a negative image of us abroad. It's hard to anticipate the number of times a U.S. expatriate will be asked: "Is the crime really as bad as we've heard?"

When the question does arise, there is admittedly no easy way to answer it. Some suggestions, however, would include these:

○ In the concern to protect both human and civil rights, the United States has more laws and regulations than most countries. The individual, then, has more opportunities to behave in ways, either knowingly or unknowingly, that are considered illegal. An example: a resident of Ohio, making a cross-country automobile trip, buys liquor in Missouri and transports it across the state line into Kansas. He is observed purchasing the liquor near the state line and is arrested as soon as he enters Kansas. The fact that he did not know that Kansas had a law prohibiting importing liquor from another state is of no consequence. He is convicted of a crime and fined accordingly.

○ Even in the most wealthy nations, there are pockets or centers of poverty, of the have-nots, the disadvantaged. Seeing affluence all around them, and sparked by the drive to escape some of their deprivation, the have-nots are strongly tempted to take illegally from the haves. When the deprived (or anyone, for that matter) once begin criminal activities, an important psychological barrier is broken. Having stolen once, it's easier to do it the second time, still easier the third, and so on. This is one reason why people just released from prison frequently revert to the very behavior that put them there in the first place.

○ Newspapers, radio, and TV are free to print or announce whatever they consider newsworthy. Crime, of whatever nature, is thus openly publicized, trials are covered in detail, the details of the criminal act fully exposed. The frequency with which crime appears in the media does not reflect the frequency of crime as such. It makes news and is so reported.

○ Movies and television shows also distort reality, or at least give foreigners a distored image of the United States. But films that depict gang wars, clever jewel thefts, bank robberies, even murder (for example, "In Cold Blood"), attract audiences. In their way, they are exciting and gripping—but they still distort reality.

○ The judicial system presumes a person innocent until proven guilty. Unless guilt is proved beyond a shadow of a doubt, an offender may be freed by a jury of his peers. A clever defense lawyer can be so persuasive that even one who has admitted his guilt before he was read his rights may be released. This does not mean that he will return to criminal acts, but the ease with which he escaped punishment is hardly a deterrent.

○ The leniency of the courts in meting out punishment has undoubtedly contributed to lawlessness. The punishment does not always fit the crime. Much of the leniency, however, can be traced to the concern for human rights and the reluctance to punish appropriately if there are any extenuating circumstances that would justify a light or suspended sentence.

Again, totally convincing answers are hard to give when the local national inquires about our crime rate. Some of the above, alone or in combination, however, may suggest a response that will have an element of validity. The American can't deny that we have a crime problem, but he can perhaps persuade the local that it is not the all-pervasive problem he may have been led to believe.

Profits and Capitalism

Here is a source of frequent discussion—or arguments, especially if the local employer has been influenced in any way by Communist propaganda. Capitalism, U.S. style, isn't understood because few countries are capitalistic. Socialistic is a much better description.

To say that capitalism has been distorted abroad is an understatement. In fact, right here at home the ignorance about corporate profits and return on investment is surprising. Ask a few Americans what they think a fair percentage of return would be after all expenses and taxes are deducted, and you're likely to get replies such as, "Oh,

I suppose about 15 percent," or "Well, I guess 20 to 25 percent would be reasonable." This is a little off base. Ten percent is considered a fair return, but how many companies even net that? The national average today is about 5 to 7 percent, with many companies lucky to realize 3 or 4 percent. That's cutting things rather close, and it wouldn't take much to turn black to red.

Despite all the negative things said about it, capitalism is not evil. Certainly when profits are hoarded and not plowed back into research, plant expansion, and new equipment, there is every reason to condemn those responsible for at least immorality if not criminality. Profit used wisely, however, ensures growth, jobs, and worker security. Without a profit—even a 1 percent profit—everyone loses.

Rather than being embarrassed when called a capitalist, the American at home and abroad has the right to acknowledge the fact with pride. The system he represents has brought more benefits and opportunities to more people than any other, past or present. Anyone who tends to doubt this should study other political and economic systems and then decide which one he would prefer to live under.

For the local national, the principles and workings of capitalism are of no little interest. He is curious; he likes to ask questions. The U.S. manager, then, should be prepared to field the questions and to represent the American system with accuracy and truthfulness.

The Fundamentals of Foreign Policy

Some research into foreign policy, particularly the policy relative to the manager's host country, is a requisite before going overseas. Ample information is available through the State Department, the manager's congressional representative, or, if need be, the U.S. embassy in the host country. However obtained, at least a bird's-eye grasp of our foreign policy is not only helpful to the manager but expected by the local national. The manager can be sure that questions will be asked.

On this matter, a word of caution is in order. Where alliance to the United States is fragile or even nonexistent—as in eastern Europe, the Arab world, and parts of Latin America—political discussions can be dangerous. A strong defense of Israel, for example, is a match to a can of gasoline to a Palestinian or a Syrian. Negative comments about OPEC, the Berlin Wall, or Russian tactics in Angola or Sudan raise grave possibilities of conflict with the local person—depending, of course, on the host country and the person's particular political orientation.

The best advice: Don't begin or get drawn into political discussions in any but the obviously pro-American countries. It's in order to answer questions, of course, but answer them factually and without personal editorializing. Feelings run high, particularly in the developing countries, and many an American has paid the price for thoughtless outspokenness on tender political issues. Caution and tact will be the manager's best allies.

ABOUT THE HOST COUNTRY

Obviously, what the U.S. manager should know about his host country can only be suggested because of the differences among nations around the world. Test yourself before heading for that overseas job. For the country to which you are going, make sure you can answer these questions:

1. What is the form of government?
2. How is the government structured?
3. Who is the king, amir, monarch, or president?
4. What does the flag look like?
5. What role, if any, does the government play in business?
6. What taxes, if any, do expatriates pay? The people themselves?
7. How widespread is social welfare? What is covered in the welfare program?
8. What is the prevalent religion? Have you read any of the sacred writings?
9. What influence does the religion have on day-to-day life?
10. What are some of the more important social and cultural standards?
11. What are the attitudes toward divorce, remarriage, and extramarital affairs?
12. What are some words, gestures, or types of body language that are resented or considered profane?
13. What is the language?
14. What are the local attitudes toward alcohol and drugs?
15. What sort of literature will pass customs and be admitted to the country?
16. What are some of the laws and regulations that must be obeyed or that could easily be violated through simple ignorance?
17. To what extent is the country underdeveloped, developing, or developed?

18. What are the major industries and products? The chief exports and imports?
19. What are the principal natural resources, and what importance do they play in the nation's economy?
20. What are the size and population of the country?
21. What is its history?
22. Is it pro-Western, pro-Communist, or neutral?
23. What are the important holidays? How are they observed?
24. What are the favorite recreational activities of the people?
25. What medical facilities are available—qualified doctors, hospitals, clinics, dental care, and so on?
26. What medicinal drugs are available or not available? To what extent are prescriptions necessary to obtain medicinal drugs?
27. Who is allowed to drive? Men and women? Men only? Minors?
28. How are drivers' licenses obtained?
29. What visas are necessary to enter or leave the country?
30. What foods are prohibited? What foods can you import for personal consumption?
31. What is the normal dress of the local men and women?
32. How should expatriate wives dress in public? Slacks? Shorts? Long dresses? Bare arms? Covered arms? Does their manner of dress make any difference?
33. To what degree is makeup permitted or discouraged?
34. What is the role of women in the country? Are they allowed to work? Mingle freely with men at social affairs? Serve as hostesses at mixed gatherings in their own homes?
35. To what extent are servants available for domestic work?
36. How much do housing, food, utilities, gasoline, telephone service, and automobiles cost in the country?
37. What schools are available for expatriate children and teenagers?
38. What English-language newspapers and magazines are easily available?
39. What is the local currency? What are the bills and coins? The dollar exchange rate?
40. When shopping, to what extent are you *expected* to bargain over the asking price?
41. How do people greet each other? Shake hands? Embrace? Kiss?
42. What are the local-language expressions for "Good morning," "Good night," "Hello," "How much?" "No," "Yes," "Thank

you," "Please," "Yesterday," "Today," and "Tomorrow"? Will you be able to communicate with taxi drivers and waiters in restaurants?

43. What activities are available to expatriates, such as jobs for wives, social organizations, and community involvement? What entertainment is available—movies, night clubs, private clubs, and so on?

44. What protocol is expected when you are invited to a local national's home? A gift, before or after the event? A thank-you note? Do you arrive early? Late? On time? How do you know when it is time to depart politely?

45. Finally, when these questions have been answered, is this where you want to go for the next X months or years?

A little research in the library will answer most of these questions. Another source is the country's desk officer in the State Department or one of its consulates, which are located in various U.S. cities. Other avenues for information are Americans who have returned from a tour of duty in the country (not tourists), nationals who are studying at universities here, and specialists in the area, such as college professors.

The most effective preparation, however, is to enroll in one of the programs specifically designed to orient managers to the overseas scene. To cite only a few, there is American University's Business Council for International Understanding (BCIU) in Washington, D.C.; the American Graduate School of International Management, in Glendale, Arizona; the American Management Associations' three-to five-day seminars; and New York University's Graduate School of Business Administration.

Participation in these and similar programs around the country is mushrooming as more and more managers are trying to ready themselves for overseas assignments. The only trouble is that too many continue to go abroad unprepared, ill-equipped to face the new life that awaits them. The effect of ignorance on them and on their companies is hardly worth the little bit of time or money that may have been saved. The Boy Scout motto "Be prepared" is excellent counsel to the American about to work and live overseas.

Conclusion

When an American fails abroad, it is almost always the fault of human relations. The mistakes so often made are flaunting of Americanism; ignorance of or disrespect for local customs, habits, and life patterns; intolerance of cultural differences; self-imposed social isolation; impatience with nationals; or scorn for the people.

International companies cannot depend solely on the technical abilities of their managers. They need managers who are also well prepared for the assignment and possess high levels of managerial and human skills. Of course our expertise is what is being imported, but we are being closely watched and evaluated on:

- How effectively we contribute to the physical well-being of the host country.
- The integrity with which we perform our functions and meet our responsibilities.
- Our effectiveness in training and developing the local managers, who can then contribute actively to the industrialization drive.

The world is changing rapidly, with the developing nations caught up in the vortex of political, social, and economic explosions. The quickening transition from traditional to developed societies is putting a strain on the people as well as generating confusion about what is right—old values or new demands. Into this environment, the U.S. manager must move with caution, respect, and understanding. He is a representative of the "new" and is thus not fully trusted—because what he represents isn't really understood.

But when the U.S. manager is emotionally and intellectually prepared for his new post, the chances are good that he will manage the affairs of the company with the intelligence necessary for success. If he has been wisely chosen and properly oriented, the likelihood of a productive tour of duty is very great.

For an in-depth study of this entire subject, see the paper by Edward C. Stewart, "American Cultural Patterns: A Cross-Cultural Perspective." [1]

[1] Pittsburgh: University of Pittsburgh Press, 1971.

3

The Impact of
Transition on the
Developing Societies

As has been mentioned before, the parts of the world that are in a developing stage face fundamental and shattering changes. The move into industrialization is causing revisions of old values while introducing new and not-yet-understood technologies. There is much questioning of what was, coupled with an apprehension about what will be.

If the American manager is headed for a post in western Europe, Great Britain, Australia, or Japan, these changes aren't of much consequence. Those areas aren't developing; they have arrived. It's a different matter, however, in most of Latin America, Africa, the Middle East, and Southeast Asia. These areas are in transition, and the effects of transition have a bearing on how the U.S. expatriate manages and develops the nationals reporting to him.

What exactly does the term "developing nation" mean? Typically, it means a country that is gradually moving from a feudal, primarily agrarian way of life through the various stages of growth until a fullblown state of industrialization prevails. The societies that have reached this last level of sophistication have normally done so over a period of many years. The development has been a slow, evolutionary process during which changes in societal values and mores have been painlessly absorbed. There is no shock, no shattering conflict when natural growth and development take place.

In a sense, a nation is like a human being; both need time to adapt and adjust to the demands of development. A baby becomes a child, then a teenager, a young adult, and finally a mature adult. If properly trained and guided through these stages, he is presumably prepared to assume the full responsibilities of adulthood. However, if a 12- or

48

15-year-old is suddenly forced to take on the responsibilities of maturity, fear and uncertainty are inevitable. Similarly, if a nation undergoes too rapid a transition, internal conflict is inevitable.

Stages of Economic Growth

Walter W. Rostow developed a concept of growth that counters the Marx-Engels theory that a state moves from feudalism to capitalism to socialism to communism. In his book *Stages of Economic Growth: A Non-Communist Manifesto,*[1] Rostow proposes that five stages of development exist: (1) the Traditional Society, (2) Preconditions for Take-off, (3) Takeoff, (4) the Drive to Maturity, and (5) the Age of Mass Consumption. A broad summary of the characteristics of each stage appears in Table 1.

What may be interesting to note is that many of the developing countries still maintain some of the traditional-society characteristics. Limits on vertical mobility continue to exist, coupled with a certain locked-in fatalism. The family remains the focal point around which life revolves; clan or tribe loyalties are still strong even though some dilution is evident.

The countries that have been thrust into transition (Stages 2 and 3) because of their critical natural resources, such as the oil-producing nations, find the move from one stage to the next particularly difficult. As a Saudi professor remarked only a few years ago, "Saudi Arabia is galloping rapidly into the eleventh century." That was in the 1960s. Today, Saudi Arabia and its fellow OPEC members are being thrown into the twentieth century. No natural evolution this, in which changes can be absorbed gradually. Instead, it is an abrupt leap from an ancient, relatively static society into the world of today. This is a traumatic change for any people and needs to be recognized as such by one entering their society.

Another way to look at the status of nations is to compare them in terms of per capita wealth. *U.S. News and World Report,* in its July 31, 1978, issue, divided the world's nations into three categories:

Poor: those with a gross national product of $550 or less per person.
Less poor: those with a GNP of $551–$2,000 per person.
Well-to-do: those with a GNP of more than $2,000 per person.

[1] Cambridge: Cambridge University Press, 2nd ed., 1971.

TABLE 1. Rostow's stages of economic growth—characteristics and times at which each stage was reached.

STAGE 1 Traditional Society	STAGE 2 Preconditions for Takeoff	STAGE 3 Takeoff	STAGE 4 Drive to Maturity	STAGE 5 Age of Mass Consumption
Basically agrarian	Rumblings of science	Old blocks and resistance to growth overcome	After takeoff, long period of sustained growth	Shift toward durable goods and services
Little scope for vertical mobility	Modest expansion of world markets	Growth increases	10–20% of national income invested, permitting output to outstrip population increase	Increases in income that permit purchase of luxuries over basic food, shelter, and clothing
Family and clan/tribe associations important in social organization	External intrusions shock traditional society and bring ideas of better things to come	Increased investment in social programs—up to 10% of national income	Growth in international trade	More office and skilled workers
Fatalistic outlook—son is what father was	Some evidences of capital reinvestment	New industries expand rapidly	Economy can produce anything it wants	Increased allocation of resources to welfare and security
Political power in hands of few who own or control land	Commerce widens	Profits reinvested	Import of capital unnecessary	Emergence of welfare state
	Development of centralized political state and growing nationalism	New class of entrepreneurs expands	Development of suburbia	Economy geared to consumer
Undeveloped nations (as in parts of Africa, Latin America, and Asia) still in this stage		New techniques in agriculture and industry	Drive to achieve privacy—home, car, and so on	Content with somewhat lower growth rate
	U.S.: 1770–1815 Western Europe: late 17th and early 18th centuries Kuwait and Saudi Arabia: 1940s–late 1960s	Expansion and greater influence in world	Improved transportation	Development of urban problems
		England: 1783–1805 France: 1810–1860 U.S.: 1845–1860 Germany: 1850–1865 USSR: 1890–1914 China and India: 1950–1960 OPEC countries and parts of Latin America: 1970s	Living standards up, wages up, leisure activities up	High transportation costs
			U.S.: 1860–1910 England: 1805–1850 France: 1860–1910 Germany: 1865–1910 USSR: 1914–1955	U.S.: 1913–1914 Germany: 1950s France: 1950s England: 1915–1917 Japan: 1950s USSR: still in Stage 4

On this scale, the geographic distribution was as shown in Table 2. The information presented there can be summarized as follows:

Area	Poor	Less Poor	Well-to-do
Western Hemisphere	6	17	5
Europe	1	5	23
Africa	40	6	2
Asia	16	9	10
Pacific	4	1	2
Total	67	38	42

In essence, 7 1 percent of the world (105 countries) is either poor or less poor. The remaining 29 percent (42 countries) is considered well-to-do.

Wealth in itself, however, is not an accurate gauge of *development*. For example, Kuwait is considered the wealthiest per capita country on earth; the Emirates and Saudi Arabia are close behind. Nonetheless, all are still in Stage 3, with many of the Stage 2 characteristics remaining and only a few of those of Stage 4 present. National wealth does offer a measure of development—and in many cases an accurate measure, as in Africa or North America. But it doesn't tell the whole story, especially when the exploitation of natural resources catapults a country into undreamed opulence.

Societies in Stages 2 and 3, whatever their riches, are ready for new techniques in industry and agriculture. For the most part, however, their level of sophistication requires training and assistance. At the same time, the door is open to clashes between ancient values and the modern managerial principles the U.S. manager is trying to impart. A few illustrations:

o *Objective-setting and planning.* Through the centuries, the devout Moslem has believed that tomorrow has been planned according to God's will. If objectives and plans fall within what God has willed, then they will materialize. If they don't, it's foolish to spend too much time in this effort.

These attitudes are changing, of course. Among the political leaders, planning has become an essential managerial skill—and they are very adept at it. At less sophisticated levels, however, some of the deeply imbedded religious convictions still persist. Installing management by objectives or setting up an elaborate budget planning system may be an exercise in futility at this point in time.

o *Delegation.* This is something intermediate-level managers beg for, but once they are granted certain levels of authority, they tend

TABLE 2. Geographic distribution of per capita wealth.

Area	Poor	Less Poor	Well-to-do
WESTERN HEMISPHERE	Bolivia El Salvador Grenada Guyana Haiti Honduras	Argentina Barbados Brazil Chile Colombia Costa Rica Cuba Dominican Republic Ecuador Guatemala Jamaica Mexico Nicaragua Panama Paraguay Peru Uruguay	Bahamas Canada Trinidad and Tobago United States Venezuela
EUROPE	Albania	Cyprus Portugal Romania Turkey Yugoslavia	Austria Belgium Bulgaria Czechoslovakia Denmark East Germany Finland France Great Britain Greece Hungary Iceland Ireland Italy Luxembourg Netherlands Norway Poland Spain Sweden Switzerland USSR West Germany
AFRICA	Angola Benin Botswana Burundi Cameroon Central African Empire Chad Comoro Congo Egypt	Algeria Ghana Ivory Coast Mauritius South Africa Tunisia	Gabon Libya

TABLE 2. (continued)

Area	Poor	Less Poor	Well-to-do
AFRICA (continued)	Equatorial Guinea Ethopia Gambia Guinea Guinea-Bissau Kenya Lesotho Liberia Madagascar Malawi Mali Mauritania Morocco Mozambique Niger Nigeria Rwanda Sao Tome and Principe Senegal Sierra Leone Somalia Swaziland Sudan Tanzania Togo Uganda Upper Volta Zaire Zambia Zimbabwe Rhodesia		
ASIA	Afghanistan Bangladesh Bhutan Burma Cambodia China India Laos Nepal North Korea Pakistan Sri Lanka Thailand Vietnam Yemen-Aden Yement-Sana	Iran Iraq Jordan Lebanon Malaysia Mongolia South Korea Syria Taiwan	Bahrain Hong Kong Israel Japan Kuwait Oman Qatar Saudi Arabia Singapore United Arab Emirates
PACIFIC	Indonesia Papua New Guinea Philippines Samoa	Fiji	Australia New Zealand

to avoid grabbing the ball. Authority means having the responsibility to act or decide; acting or deciding, however, presents the opportunity for error; and errors reflect on the individual, causing him to lose face with his superior, peers, and subordinates. To the Latin, Asian, or Oriental, losing face is to be avoided at all costs. This is why, as was noted before, the Japanese favor their system of bottom-up group decision-making over the approach employed in the Western world.

A second factor in authority-avoidance is the fear of a superior wielding his power in a punishing way should the subordinate err in judgment or action. The arm of punishment is a long one in many of the developing societies, and the mere threat of it is enough to emasculate any system of delegation the U.S. manager might wish to initiate.

This is not to say that the local employee won't accept delegated authority. He will, but once the assignment has been made, he often avoids taking action on difficult matters or solving knotty problems until he has talked things over with his boss. Once he knows, or thinks he knows, what the boss would do, he then implements what is really the boss's decision. It's a case of delegating upward to escape full responsibility for whatever he does.

Here is where the boss has to be a patient coach. He should help the subordinate think through the issue at hand and help him arrive at the best solution. He also needs to make it known by word and deed that the subordinate has no reason to fear either punishment or loss of face if the results of a decision or action are not always what was hoped for.

Every decision involves the future, and no one has yet been given the gift to foresee the future with 100 percent accuracy. So, convey the attitude: "We're in this together, Mr. Subordinate. Let's talk things over first, if you think it's necessary, but otherwise do what you believe is right. I'll back you, and you don't have to be afraid of the consequences if what you do goes wrong." And then support those words by the way you react when something doesn't turn out the way you think it should!

While the Thais, the Middle Easterners, the Latin Americans, and the Japanese are highly individualistic, the cultures in which they have grown up don't encourage them to thrust out and act autonomously. The fear of being wrong, or of not having the right to be wrong, is still a powerful deterrent.

○ *Socializing.* The inherited tradition of socializing, siestas, or frequent coffee or tea breaks conflicts with the American's concept of efficiency and performance dependability. The gung-ho American who sweeps into his job with all-business, no-nonsense proclamations will find himself punching at clouds. This is a climate that conflicts with the local's traditional way of life.

  o *Families and "arrangements."* The American, on arrival, may be surprised at the number of local managers who have side businesses that can affect the application of good business practices. He may be equally surprised by the family networks that exist outside the company itself and their influence on the way people function on the job.

As Alison R. Lanier said in her AMA briefing *Your Manager Abroad: How Welcome? How Prepared?*, "Every purchasing agent in Spain has an uncle in Barcelona, a cousin in Malaga, a nephew in Granada with whom he has 'arrangements.' . . . Salesmen have similar networks, well worked out and well intrenched."[2] There is always the local person who says, "It may cost a little more, but I know where I can get it for you this afternoon." The "where" is probably a brother's store or an uncle's shop. The American would be wise not to try to buck the system. If the company has "always" done business with a particular supplier or vendor, there's probably a good reason— even though it's likely that the article could be obtained less expensively elsewhere.

These family networks militate against sound business practices, but they exist. The U.S. manager should make haste slowly and not try to change an embedded way of life.

Despite obstacles such as these, the expatriate manager has an important role in the developing society. He is the external catalyst who is helping to hurry the society through the stages of growth. He is an expediter in a forced transition, and the fact that it is forced makes his job difficult.

In a more ordered process, the people subconsciously or naturally change from old ways of thinking and behaving and adopt the new. In so many parts of the world, however, people are conscious of and troubled by cultural changes that are occurring as the technology of industrialization overtakes the society. An imposed advance to Rostow's Stage 4, or even Stage 5, presents one set of problems for the people and another set for the imported manager. If he is aware of what is going on, however, he has a better-than-even chance of accommodating to the prevailing conditions.

[2] New York: American Management Associations, 1975, p. 21.

What the U.S. Manager Has Going for Him

Despite some likely problems, the U.S. manager has many pluses going for him in a developing society. One of the most important is the desire of the local national to learn. Keep in mind the strong sense of nationalism that typifies him. Highly patriotic, he sees his country developing and wants to be a part of that development. He sees his country's increasing influence in the world and wants to contribute to that influence.

At the same time, he's well aware of what he doesn't know, of what he must learn if he is to make any sort of meaningful contribution. He is thus a willing student if the teacher is patient and empathic. Most nationals respond to *individuality* in their leaders. They look for charismatic leaders to whom they can relate with personal enthusiasm.

Americans and Europeans can accept uninspiring bosses if they have the technical competence to offset a neutral personality. Followers of "the individual" cannot. That's one reason why manager visibility, as mentioned earlier, is so important. The more the U.S. manager works with each subordinate on a personal level, providing the necessary training and coaching, the better will be the response. Most nationals will master the new technologies quickly when they are under the tutelage of one who clearly has a genuine interest in them as human beings.

People in the developing societies are envious of the technological advances made by Western civilizations. They know enough about us to know what they want. At Stage 2 or 3 in the process of economic growth, the drive to move on is much more than a superficial desire. Even where extreme national wealth exists, the people are well aware that they are still dependent on foreign expertise to run their industries and guide them in their agriculture. The yearning for national self-fulfillment is strong—they want it, they'll work for it, and they look to the U.S. manager to help them achieve it.

For an interesting discussion of nationalizing management, particularly at the higher organizational levels, see pages 193–203 of *The Multinationals,* by Christopher Tugendhat.[3]

3 New York: Random House, 1972.

4

Modern Management Techniques: Do They Work in Developing Societies?

Chapter 2 touched on the two facets of management: management technology and management philosophies, theory, and style. The first relates to the manager's knowledge of and skills in his particular business function, such as sales, marketing, production, purchasing, or finance. These can be viewed as the "hard sciences"; they are reasonably precise, or very precise, and can be taught or learned.

The second facet of management concerns the manager's philosophy of *how* to lead and direct others so that the principles of sales, marketing, and so forth come to life and produce the desired results. The manager's philosophy is inevitably expressed by his visible behavior on the job and the style he projects in the actual process of leading and directing his subordinates. One facet is purely technical knowledge while the other is better described as management *methodology*. So when we use the word "management," both aspects of it should be kept in mind.

Now—does modern management work in the developing societies? With some exceptions, the answer is yes. The technologies can generally be installed and made part of the operating system fairly easily so long as the facilities and hardware are available. At the same time, production methods may have to be simplified or revised downward to accommodate the less sophisticated skills of the workers. Government requirements can affect financial and accounting procedures as well as personnel policies. Certainly sales, advertising, and marketing approaches have to be adjusted to the local ways of doing business. In summary, despite political and cultural variations, it is safe to say that the Western management technologies can be adapted to the developing society.

The same is basically true of management methodologies and style—if (and it's a big if) the U.S. manager is truly a follower of

57

modern management practices. Should he still believe that the big-stick autocracy of the 1920s and 1930s is the way to get the job done, he's going to have a problem. The beliefs he holds about the meshing of his human and production resources will determine his observable style; his style will then determine how the people respond to his leadership and the extent to which they will follow him.

Within the broad area of management methodology is a variety of skills the effective manager employs to accomplish his technological purpose. Included are the functions of forecasting, objective-setting, planning, organizing, leading, directing, coordinating, delegating, setting performance standards, training and development, conducting performance appraisals, utilizing management information systems, controlling, and the like.

Do these work in developing societies? Will they be accepted and then practiced by local subordinate managers in the supervision of their own people? Again, with a few exceptions, yes. Chapter 3 indicated some potential obstacles when it comes to objective-setting and planning in Moslem cultures. The same is true of delegation there and in Japan. But the obstacles aren't insurmountable, nor are they necessarily even major. The techniques of establishing long-range goals, setting results-oriented objectives, and developing specific plans to achieve objectives are entirely transferable to local people. They want to know how to shape the future, on the assumption that the future they are planning is within God's will.

Equally transferable are the principles of organizing a department. These include the arrangement of the workplace, the flow of materials and products, the formation of work units, and proper work assign-ments. Involved as well are the organization structure of the depart-ment or company itself, the span of control, the purpose and func-tioning of channels, and staff and line responsibilities.

In the same vein, the local national wants to know how and what to control, the purpose of control, and how to interpret feedback and crank it into the planning process. He is impressed by the usefulness of meaningful job-performance standards and their value in conduct-ing objective performance appraisals. He wants to learn how to com-municate effectively and break down the barriers that clog the com-munication pipelines. He wants to master the techniques of training so that he can develop his own subordinates to full potential.

Merely examples, these are some of the skills the U.S. manager can teach the local subordinate. They are highly transferable, and they do work in a developing society.

To repeat, however: there can be obstacles to either management technology or methodology. There are two basic types of obstacles—environmental and organizational.

Environmental Obstacles

Because of the nature of the society, the people may have a relatively low educational level that would make it difficult for them to grasp the intricacies of some technologies. Or there could be certain legal or political regulations that affect the manager's freedom of action, such as being required to hire an employee against his will or not being able to terminate a nonproducer.

Social barriers are very possible wherein members of one tribe won't work with or for those who are members of what they consider to be an inferior tribe. Responsibility to the family versus responsibility to the job raises another potential obstacle.

If the economy of the country is booming, with an equivalent pay scale, work might be considered an unpleasant interruption of more hedonistic pastimes. Count on absenteeism, tardiness, and turnover in such an economy. At the other extreme, a poor economy may have an uneducated workforce that compounds production difficulties.

Organizational Obstacles

These include overstaffing through forced employment of local workers or understaffing because of a scarcity of qualified people. Controls can range from the excessive, where detailed records and regular accounting to a government office are required, to an organization with little followup or data about performance. A technical necessity such as a preventive maintenance program is often talked about but rarely gets off the ground.

Efforts to motivate the workforce frequently falter, so the company misguidedly relies on money to placate the people. Often, management doesn't recognize the difference between genuine motivation and manipulation. The result: everybody gets an annual "merit" increase, regardless of his performance, in the hope of buying productivity and corporate loyalty. Motivation is a common obstacle, but it is more the failure of management, local or expatriate, than the result of any trait indigenous to the society.

The availability of materials, parts, and supplies is frequently a real problem. A machine breaks down and a part has to be ordered from

London or Amsterdam; tools that are common in the United States just aren't available. Supplies requisitioned from the States may sit in customs for weeks before being released to the consignee. You want a pad of flip-chart paper to go on an easel for a presentation? Perhaps it can be obtained locally, but when it arrives it may be gummed down the side of the pad instead of across the top, and the holes the vendor has drilled may not match those on the easel. This despite detailed instructions at the time the order was placed.

Minimizing the Obstacles

Environmentally and organizationally, the U.S. manager's frustrations can be considerable—but that's all part of working in a developing society. If the society were as technically advanced as ours, the manager might not be there at all. The local people would be running the show.

Minimizing the obstacles and barriers can be boiled down to three admonitions:

1. Most important, the *right* U.S. manager must be selected. That, by now, is hopefully apparent.
2. Well-tested practices that work at home have to be adapted to the local environment. They can't be forced on people who are not conditioned to our way of life.
3. The manager must accept the barriers as a fact and then, with patience, try to break them down through the application of sound management principles. Some barriers the manager can overcome; others he can reduce; still others he will never change because they are government- or religiously inspired. These he must learn to live with, which he can if he possesses the necessary tolerance and flexibility.

Good management is good management—everywhere. The difference lies in how the principles are applied. Latin America is still a society of *patrones* and peons. Power is important. The owner of a firm is the master, the caudillo. From him comes all. Sharing of that power through assumption of power responsibilities at the lower levels is a relatively new and not widely accepted practice.

In all the developing countries, the concepts of power and rule by fear must change before delegation, lower-level decision-making, and lower-level problem-solving will be fully effective. Western nations and Japan have relatively consistent understandings of the language and techniques of management (*relatively* consistent, that is). Such is not likely to be the case in most of the Third World and in societies making the transition to development.

The transfer of management technology is not difficult. Any people with sufficient learning ability can be taught to sell, keep books, control inventories, set up a data processing system, or manufacture a product. These are so-called sciences in that they are based on facts and technical principles. They require knowledge first, and then the skills to put the knowledge to work. Both knowledge and skills can be taught; both can be learned. In that sense, U.S. technology is highly transferable.

Management methodology is another matter, however. It, too, can be taught and learned, but the process is slower. In many cases, human attitudes and interpersonal relationships have to change, or be changed, before a certain philosophy will become acceptable. To use delegation again as an example: the techniques of delegating can be installed with little difficulty. What takes time is creating an emotional climate in which delegated authority is not only sought but welcomed. It takes time to convince people who have learned to fear authority that there is nothing to fear. It takes time to persuade those who are afraid to act because they are afraid of making mistakes that it is no sin to be wrong. The words to convince or persuade can be said, but they mean little when inborn emotional attitudes have to be changed before traditional obstacles are lowered. The same is true when the manager tries to instill the concepts of efficiency, punctuality, effectiveness, and product or service excellence. What each is can be explained. To get local people to achieve each is another matter, especially when lifetime habits have oriented them in other directions.

The U.S. manager can't teach management methodologies, philosophies, and styles by forcing them on the local people. Too many intangibles, such as beliefs, values, and cultural inheritances, are involved. His only approach is to explain what he means, put his preachments into action, and, by example, establish a pattern of leadership that others will emulate.

This is the role of the operator/developer who gets a job done while simultaneously developing local national subordinates. He will make modern technologies and methodologies work by adjusting them to the dictates of the culture and patiently educating his subordinates in the new ways of production and business. Will the locals respond to such a manager? Almost without exception. Try it and see.

5

Understanding
the People Side of
the Overseas Job

It may be carrying coals to Newcastle to talk to a manager about something as basic as human behavior, especially if he has met the criteria essential for an overseas assignment. Yet, a fair amount of experience in training both U.S. and foreign national managers has shown that a sizable majority have little understanding of why people respond or behave as they do on the job.

Without understanding, the manager is leaving himself open to errors of omission or commission that could create a multitude of personnel problems—all quite unnecessarily. Not being aware of what makes people tick is just as dangerous as ignorance of the production resource. Technical *and* human skills are essential for management effectiveness.

Basic Drives

It makes no difference where one works in the world: people have fundamentally the same drives, needs,[1] and behavior traits. What makes them *appear* different are the levels of national and individual development and the avenues that are culturally accepted for expressing their basic drives and needs. Within those parameters, each person behaves in a way that will allow him to satisfy his drives—drives that were common to people long dead, to those living today, and (unless human nature changes) to yet-unborn generations. Simply stated, these drives fall into four categories: hunger, thirst, self-perpetuation, and self-preservation.

---

[1] Basic needs of people that relate to motivation will be discussed in detail in the following chapter.

In most work situations, only one of these—the self-preservation drive—exerts any meaningful influence. People of course have to eat when they get hungry; they have to drink when thirsty; and the urge to perpetuate the species is universal to all living things. Behavior resulting from the need to satisfy any of these three, however, is rarely seen in the office or on the shop floor.

To be sure, someone who is suffering from malnutrition will have severe problems; on a milder level, an employee may become irritable if he's missed his breakfast or lunch; a field hand will find work impossible in 120-degree heat when an adequate supply of water isn't available; and where men and women work together, evidences of the species-perpetuation drive occasionally appear. For purposes here, however, these and related behaviors are relatively infrequent on the job. It is the fourth one, self-preservation, that creates most of the behavior—favorable or unfavorable.

The self-preservation drive can be further broken down into two elements:

○ The instinct to protect oneself from harm, danger, and death. (This is the preservation of the organism, of life itself.)

○ The instinct to preserve and protect one's *ideas, ideals,* and *self-esteem.*

While certain kinds of work may pose potential bodily harm, they are more the exception than the rule today. Only occasionally are working conditions so bad that behavior caused by this element of the drive is evident. It is really the second element that has the most meaning for the manager. From this comes much of the behavior, both constructive and destructive, with which the manager has to cope.

First, some explanations of the terms "ideas," "ideals," and "self-esteem."

IDEAS

An idea is an opinion formed on the basis of a person's knowledge or belief about something. In other words, it's a thought, a mental concept, or a rationalization.

Say you're convinced that something you've known and believed over the years is absolute fact. You repeat it to others with complete confidence. What you are saying is unquestionable and indisputable. Your faith in the fact is so strong that if someone else doubts you or implies that you have your facts wrong, you might become stubbornly argumentative in defense of the idea.

But then another person comes along who has more accurate information on the same subject. He convinces you that what you had believed to be fact was not so. Little by little, you relinquish your position and give up the idea. Hard reality can't be denied. To hold to your position would be illogical.

Ideas are important, and we will fight to preserve them—until it is proved to us that we were wrong. At that point, we usually discard the old and may quite easily adopt new and very different ideas. While this part of the self-preservation drive is always present, it is primarily mental and intellectual. It is thus not as strong as the drives relating to ideals and self-esteem.

IDEALS

Ideals are something else. In the context used here, an ideal is a feeling, belief, faith, or value. While an idea is intellectual, an ideal is emotional. The feelings an individual has about his family, his religion, his country, his job, and other people are "ideals," whether positive or negative in nature. They are nonrational (not irrational) emotions that are almost impossible to describe or explain to others.

Try to convince a Christian that he should become a Moslem or a Moslem a Christian by the sheer weight of intellectual reasoning and see what luck you have—particularly if the other person is devout in his faith. You are dealing with emotions and beliefs that may be deeply entrenched and passionately defended. Or get into a political argument with an Iranian Shiite and attempt to convince him that the Shah's efforts to modernize the country were right. A healthy defense of the strict Moslem ways is likely to result. Old beliefs and long-held emotions aren't changed by verbal brilliance—which is one reason religious or political arguments are such a waste of time.

Ideals, then, are highly personal feelings about something. They are strongly defended when threatened and are not easily, if ever, discarded. The drive to preserve a deep-seated ideal is too intense.

If it weren't for this, how many of the world's problems could be resolved overnight? The USSR versus the Western world; the Lebanese conflict with the rightists, the leftists, the Christians, and the Moslems; our relations with Cuba and Chile; the hard-line stand of the Iraqis and Syrians against Anwar Sadat; the whole Middle East scene—these differences aren't rational and intellectual but emotional, born of the drive to protect fundamental ideals. Logical debate between nations around a conference table is likely to be no more productive (except for minor concessions) than a strong Democrat trying to convince an equally strong Republican that he should change parties.

This is one reason why the manager sent abroad must possess tolerance and empathy. It is why he simply can't afford to look down his nose at a less developed society or make fun of its beliefs and culture. He's playing with some very intense emotions when he does, with outright aggression on the part of the local nationals a probable result.

SELF-ESTEEM

Of even greater importance to the manager, however, is the matter of self-esteem. By definition, self-esteem is both:

1. How we look at ourselves—our self-respect and self-concept.
2. How we want the rest of the world to look on us—the image we hope to project to others.

In business and industry, more behavior probably results from the drive to perserve self-esteem than from almost any other cause. A few illustrations:

o A boss publicly reprimands an employee in the presence of other workers. The employee's self-esteem is immediately hit. If the reprimand was warranted, his own self-image may be damaged, his confidence shaken, his view of his own abilities tarnished. If the reprimand was not warranted and he knew that it wasn't, nothing destructive has taken place so far as feelings about himself are concerned. One-half of his self-esteem is still intact.

But the second half comes into the picture. How about those who heard the reprimand? Did they agree with the boss? Are they more or less laughing to themselves at the employee and enjoying what they heard? Has he been degraded in their eyes? At the moment, he has no way of knowing how he now appears to "the rest of the world." The second element of his self-esteem is in question and will remain so until he can get some reading on the way others feel about him.

The employee's reaction to the reprimand depends on his own character and personality. He may argue back with angry vehemence; he may quietly but firmly defend himself; he may say nothing; or he may just pack up his things and walk off the job, either temporarily or permanently. One thing is absolutely certain, however: this employee, in some way, at some time, will get back at the boss. He will retaliate. It could be sabotage, spreading stories or rumors, absenteeism, intentionally careless work, filing a grievance, termination, or whatever. But retaliate he will. The boss damaged his self-esteem, and this his pride will not accept without revenge of some nature.

○ An employee has worked for some time on an idea that he believes will improve a phase of the operation. When he submits it to his boss, he's told to quit wasting time on things like that and get back to work.

Nobody heard the dialogue, so the second part of his self-esteem wasn't affected. But what about the first? The boss degraded him and made him look foolish. His pride was hurt. His future behavior? Retaliation in some form is certain. At the very least, it's improbable that he'll ever submit another idea to *that* boss.

○ A local national approaches his Western supervisor and says: "I just don't understand what I'm supposed to do in this process. Would you explain it one more time?" The supervisor: "My God, I thought I'd made it clear! Why didn't you tell me you didn't understand? You people are all alike—you won't listen and can't learn."

It takes little imagination to picture how this employee feels or what he will say to his co-workers back on the job. Again, retaliation is a certainty.

A manager may gleefully make it known that "I sure told him off" or "I got that guy straightened out." Perhaps he did tell him off or straighten him out, but that's about all he did. The odds are a thousand to one that the other person won't change, and they are ten times greater that he'll get back at the manager in his own way, in his own time.

While the negative, or the "hurting," has been stressed so far, there is a positive side to this matter of self-esteem as well. Help an individual have greater respect for himself, build him in the eyes of his peers (but not at their expense), build the group in the eyes of management—and then watch the response. It is as rewarding to strengthen self-esteem as it is harmful to damage it.

The drive to preserve self-esteem is a powerful force in human behavior. Some call it "pride," others call it "face," but whatever the word, it's the same thing. If there is any difference in the visible reaction, it's a difference born of culture. The American is taught to have a thick skin. "Don't be so sensitive," we are told when we react to criticism with displeasure. We may try to hide our feelings, but we're usually not very good at it. Attend a sensitivity-training session sometime and see just how stalwart we are when others "level" with us and tell us what we're doing that bothers them. The Asian, Latin, or Oriental tends to be more overt in his sensitivity to loss of face, but this again is a product of culture, not of any basic human difference.

One other aspect of self-esteem should be noted. If the way we think of ourselves is the same as the way the rest of the world views us, things are in balance. Presumably we are well-adjusted. But there can be variations, as the following four conditions illustrate:

1. A person is proud of himself. He feels that he is realistic and objective about things. He believes he is doing the best he can at home and on the job. He can look at himself in the mirror with a clear conscience. Since he holds this self-concept, one-half of his self-esteem is healthy. At the same time, if those who know him (or know of him) have confidence in him, respect him, and trust him, the other half of his self-esteem is secure. His positive opinion of himself is shared by "the rest of the world." A healthy balance exists.

2. A person sees himself as clever, witty, indispensable. Others view him as an egotistical bore with little of value to recommend him. Things are out of balance here.

3. An individual has little respect for himself. For whatever reasons, he feels that he is a failure who has not achieved his personal goals. He has been true neither to himself nor to his family. The rest of the world, however, considers him to be a success by any standard. He has achieved, has given of himself, and is essential to his family and community.

This is another case of imbalance—and not unfrequently a cause of suicide when one's self-image is at the depths. The world says, "How could he have done such a thing when he was so successful and had so much to live for?"

4. A person is no good and he's very aware that he's no good. The rest of the world agrees, holding him in equal disdain. There's a balance here, albeit one that is unhealthy and negative.

Preserving self-esteem, in terms of either internal or external evaluations, results in all sorts of behavior patterns both on and off the job. This is a fact of human nature that no manager can afford to overlook if he hopes to work successfully with other people—especially in the developing societies where saving face is so fundamental to the culture. The only clues that can be suggested to him are: (1) be alert to the constant presence of the drive, and (2) exercise every precaution when dealing with local nationals to avoid hurting their self-esteem. Reprimand in private, correct gently, teach patiently, and coach wisely. Otherwise retaliation will follow, with the manager inevitably paying the price.

The manager's task is to achieve objectives through the help of his people. There's no better way than by showing confidence in and respect for those on whom he depends for his own success.

The Self-Centeredness of Behavior

The human animal is essentially self-centered. That doesn't mean he isn't generous, altruistic, or helpful to others. He is, and the evidences of man's humanity to man are countless (as are evidences of his inhumanity). On the other hand, concepts such as establishing self-esteem, saving face, preserving personal dignity, and doing what one feels is best for oneself are highly self-centered. Traits such as these fall under what is called the Benefit Concept.

The Benefit Concept says that people behave as they do at a particular moment because they *feel*, at that moment, that it is to their advantage to behave that way. Ten seconds later they may discover that such was not the case, but that is later—after the fact or act. As Combs and Snygg [2] put it: "But everything we do seems reasonable and necessary at the time we are doing it. . . . At the instant of behaving, each person's actions seem to him to be the best and most effective acts he can perform under the circumstances. If, at that instant, he knew how to behave more effectively, he would do so."

The Benefit Concept suggests that we are all selfish, that we behave in self-centered ways that are personally rewarding. This is true in a sense, but we need to look at the other side of the coin as well.

The words "benefit," "advantage," and "selfish" mean more than greed or "What's in it for me?" They also imply feelings of inner satisfaction—an intangible reward for having done something meaningful for others, a sense of goodness or internal warmth. Say you stop along the highway to assist a stranded motorist whom you've never seen before. He pays you nothing, you ask for nothing. As you drive away, however, you feel just a little better for what you have done.

Did you plan out your stop and calculate the benefit it would bring you? Of course not. It was an instinct or a feeling that caused it, and you benefited from it through an internal satisfaction. Conversely, if you failed to stop, you felt that that would be more beneficial to you. There was probably no sense of satisfaction, but it seemed to be the more advantageous decision at the time you made it.

---

[2] Arthur W. Combs and Donald Snygg, *Individual Behavior* (New York: Harper & Row, 1959), p. 17.

The Benefit Concept is clearly operating in people who never help others or who avoid involvement in any affairs outside their own homes. They are doing what they do because they feel it is beneficial to *them*. The concept, however, also can be seen operating in "unselfish" acts.

People save the lives of others, perhaps at risk of their own; they give money to charities, often anonymously; they give alms to the poor; they donate time to company or community causes; they do small and thoughtful things for others. These are acts of generosity committed without thought of material reward. They are merely the positive side of the Benefit Concept, with the only reward being internal feelings of satisfaction. Yet, since a reward is involved, we can still view such actions as self-centered.

Now let us transfer these ideas to the shop, the field, the office. There are always employees who are constant complainers. There are those who do a lot less work than they could, and what they do isn't done very well. And there are employees who intentionally violate rules and policies—who arrive late, are frequently absent, and are constantly stirring up trouble.

These are perfectly rational people; they behave as they do because it gives them some internal satisfaction. Destructive or obstructive acts are their way of getting back at the supervisor. The fact that their behavior may be harmful is inconsequential. It's still rewarding in the sense that it provides some emotional benefit, and is likely to continue until they (1) no longer find it personally rewarding, or (2) know that punishment of some nature will ensue unless the disruptive behavior ceases.

Understanding the Benefit Concept can help the manager to appreciate the sources of some of the constructive and destructive behaviors he sees on the job, as well as to understand his own conduct and the effect it might have on his work group. The better the grasp he has of the basics of human behavior, self-evident though these basics seem, the more effectively he can lead his people for productive results.

The Law of Effect

Related to the Benefit Concept and the self-centeredness of behavior is the Law of Effect, proposed by the psychologist Edward Thorndike. The law basically states that behavior that is rewarded tends to be repeated, while that which is punished tends to be discarded.

People don't intentionally move into situations they know will be punishing. Then why is there crime? Crime exists because there's always the chance of getting away with it (reward) and the potential of not getting caught (punishment). By the same token, people behave in ways that increase the probability of reward. By nature, they're on a track of reward-seeking and punishment-avoidance.

Within the Law of Effect lies the clue to shaping behavior through the *reinforcement principle.* "Reinforcement" means that favorable acts, decisions, and performances, if rewarded, tend to be repeated. When there is no reinforcement, the act loses significance and is eventually dropped. Acts that are punished also tend to be discarded.

Reinforcing desired behavior doesn't mean that every positive action is rewarded with a letter in the employee's file or a merit increase. When something has been done well, just a word from the supervisor may be all that's necessary: "That was a good job you did yesterday." "I liked the way you handled that problem." "You're coming along fine." "That's the way to do it." Little by little, this sort of positive reinforcement encourages the subordinate to repeat the behavior that has brought recognition from his supervisor.

In a similar vein, punishment is not necessarily a reprimand, demotion, or letter in the file. It, too, may be no more than a comment at the right time: "Let's not do it that way. Try this approach." "How about watching the time a little more closely? This is the third day this week you've been late." "This report isn't complete. Let's see what you need to do to get it right." "Why did you feel that you had to go around me and talk to my boss first?"

These make it clear that the manager isn't satisfied with a certain level of performance or a specific behavior pattern. He hasn't "punished," in the literal sense of the word, but he has indicated that changes are necessary. As people gain nothing by persisting in the "wrong" ways, they try to avoid punishment by altering their behavior. If the manager now *rewards* the changes as they occur, he will gradually be shaping productive behavior patterns.

Unfortunately, both here and abroad, punishment is far more prevalent than reward. People need assurance that what they're doing is right. Too many managers, adhering to the archaic practices of 50 years ago, follow the policy that: "Unless you hear from me to the contrary, everything's going okay." In other words, no news is good news.

All this does is tell people what *not* to do. It doesn't encourage them to channel their efforts in the right direction and to build on their strengths. Positive reinforcement is the green light that says: "Go. Keep on doing what you're doing." It is encouragement. Negative reinforcement, or punishment, is a red light that discourages a certain behavior but may not always point out the right way to go.

Negative reinforcement is necessary, but it shouldn't be the principal tool the manager uses to get the job done. The more the positive is applied, the better will be the performance and the less will be the need to resort to the negative.

The worst climate of all is one in which there is neither punishment nor reward. No one says anything. The people are never commended for what they do well, and there is no punishment for what they do poorly. The good workers slip into mediocrity, and the rest just hang on. As a result, product quality settles into a rut of inferiority that, through the absence of managerial action, becomes permitted if not actually encouraged.

"But," you might ask, "why is all of this any more important overseas than in Dallas or Duluth?" Basically, it isn't. People are people. Keep in mind, however, what is happening to a developing people in a developing country. They are shifting, or are being wrenched away, from the easy, traditional habits to a highly organized, industrial way of life. They are anxious to learn for their personal as well as national advancement. They are sensitive about the fact that they have to rely on external expertise for development. They are individualistic and proud. And the need to save face may produce a marked sensitivity to both reward and punishment, to praise and criticism.

Soft criticism and tempered praise work wonders when people are trying to master strange technologies and methodologies in their leap into the twentieth century. Assuming he has the necessary education, the local employee is highly trainable—when treated with respect and understanding. In this, he differs not a whit from the American. It is the other conditions cited above that demand a patient U.S. manager who understands human behavior and the forces that are affecting the people he is supervising. In that context, the Law of Effect can be a powerful instrument in the development of the local employee.

The Power of the Group in Determining Performance Standards

Whether the manager likes it or not, the employees, as a group, exercise considerable influence in determining the speed at which group members work and the eventual quality of the product. Peer pressure and the informal leaders within the group are powerful forces that the manager can either fight or utilize.

As one example: A highly qualified new employee comes to work. At the outset, his attitude and performance are everything the manager could ask. For the first few months, his superiority over others in the group is pronounced. Gradually, however, a change sets in and it isn't long before he's no better or worse than anyone else in the unit. The manager, in frustration, asks, "What happened?"

"What happened" is simple. The group had its own production and behavior standards, and its influence on the newcomer was sufficient to tell him: "Either conform to the way *we* do things—or else." The "or else" is social isolation from the group or any number of other punishments the group selects.

The new employee, if typical, wanted to be accepted by his co-workers when he first began. He wanted to be a part of them. At the same time, he may have been looking for a job that would provide advancement opportunities and a chance to make use of his talents. Beginning with enthusiasm and genuine interest, he soon learned that something would have to give. Either he would continue at his present pace and become an outcast among his peers or he would have to descend to the group norm and become "one of the boys."

Acceptance by the group is a potent motivator. The decision can be hard, but the average new employee usually surrenders. Sometimes this means doing less than he could, but it may also mean keeping his work from falling *below* the group norm. The employee who is dogging it, making too many mistakes, or shifting his workload to other group members will be isolated just as quickly as the overproducer. The standards must be generally met. Otherwise, group punishment is inevitable.

The key is *social acceptance*. This is the cement that holds a group together. Most people crave it and will do whatever is necessary to achieve it. Of course, there are exceptions. Some people's ambitions or personal standards drive them on to perform at their best, regardless of what their peers think about them. These are the outproducers, the doers, the achievers. Rarely, however, are they the leaders in the work group. Their very behavior has isolated them from the group, with the result that they are targets for the slings and arrows of their peers rather than their models.

Say a job opens up that involves direct supervision of the group. Who's going to get the promotion? Higher management, studying the potential candidates, reviews the performance of the hard-working overproducer and says, "That's the man!" So this former outcast gets the job. Once in it he often rubs his hands with glee and says, in effect, to his new subordinates, "Now I've got you." Because of the way they treated him when he was theoretically one of them, he becomes tough, demanding, and autocratic—the typical straw boss of yesteryears. A good producer; a poor supervisor. Unusual? Not really.

The blame for this should really be placed on the management that selected the overproducer. Not that he shouldn't be promoted, but management's failing was that it didn't look closely at the relations between the worker and the rest of the group. The mere fact of isolation is usually enough to raise a warning flag. When it is accompanied by above-standard performance, the dangers of removing that person from the group and placing him in a position of authority over it are perhaps not worth the risk. By contrast, if the individual is truly a leader, has gained the respect and acceptance of his peers, and is still an above-standard producer, the choice for advancement is obvious and probably carries zero risk.

What can the manager do about these group-established standards—especially if they are lower than what he thinks is right? On the one hand, nothing; on the other, everything.

He can do nothing if he demands, threatens, coerces, or punishes. He has already created a climate that has produced an element of rebellion. The less-than-acceptable performance level is evidence of that. Anti-company attitudes probably exist that won't be changed by heavy-handed management practices. The group will continue its foot-dragging, its flurry of busyness when the manager is in the area, its corner-cutting, its pattern of mediocrity.

So many American managers have gone into overseas posts and tried these tactics. With their work-ethic rearing and much "we'll-get-'em-on-the-ball" gusto, they have pleaded, punished, conned, and coerced—all to little avail. The mediocrity continues; the job is just a job, with the paycheck the only compensation.

But, there is a brighter side. The manager can be most successful in raising group standards if he uses the right approach. He can set a pace that brings out the best in each employee, new or old. To do this, he first needs to keep in mind such matters as self-esteem, the Benefit Concept, the Law of Effect, and the power of positive reinforcement. These apply to a group as well as to an individual and offer the manager a wide range of opportunities to create the effective workforce he wants. Here are some of the things he can do:

- Consult regularly with his people, especially the informal leaders, on matters such as working conditions, tools, equipment, safety measures, rules, policies, and procedures.

○ Involve some, many, or all employees in the setting of unit objectives and establishment of plans to achieve the objectives.
○ Keep the communication lines open so that his people know what is going on and he knows what is of concern to them.
○ Delegate certain decision-making responsibilities to those best qualified to make the decisions.
○ Encourage his people to solve the problems they are capable of solving, without having to run to him for solutions.
○ Reinforce desired behavior—publicly, privately, individually, and groupwide.
○ Ensure that his people are properly trained and are kept current on new procedures, methods, and techniques.
○ Jointly set performance standards with the group and particularly with the informal leaders.

This is hardly a complete list, but it does suggest that the manager can utilize the power of the group to achieve better performance. Instead of becoming its victim, he should be its beneficiary. A whip and the iron fist won't do it; sound management practices will.

People aren't by nature anti-company or anti-management. They're made that way by the environment in which they work. Remember that the typical worker in a developing country respects authority. He responds to it, however, only when that authority respects him. Should he find it to be otherwise, he can drag his feet with the best of them.

Frustration—Causes and Symptoms

Most people, no matter where they are or what they are doing, try to adjust to the conditions in which they find themselves. They want to adapt so they can exist with relative peace and satisfaction. If the conditions are reasonably compatible with their own ideas and standards, adjustment isn't too difficult. If there is little compatibility and adjustment is difficult, the result is usually frustration—with problems almost certain to follow.

Webster's defines frustration as "a deep chronic sense or state of insecurity and dissatisfaction arising from unresolved problems." We might add to this that the deep dissatisfaction usually arises from conditions over which the individual has little control.

The words "deep" and "chronic" are important because they bring frustration into focus. Every person faces situations that are not what he'd like them to be. If these are brief or not very important to him, no "deep" or "chronic" dissatisfaction arises, no evidences of frustration appear. It's another matter, however, when he faces unresolvable problems or completely incompatible conditions—whether on the job, in the family, or in a foreign culture. The dissatisfaction becomes deeper and more chronic, with frustration emerging as a very real emotion.

This is where the manager comes in. Employees may become frustrated by job conditions or problems they can't solve. They then begin to behave in certain ways which should clearly signal to the manager that something is wrong—something that needs attention *now*.

To be more specific, following are six types of reactions or behavior patterns that are usually symptomatic of frustration. An individual may display more than one of these simultaneously, but for simplicity's sake each is summarized as a separate, distinct reaction to a frustrating situation.

AGGRESSION

This is a fighting behavior—an attack on the person, the situation, or the thing that is blocking the individual's efforts to achieve some goal. The attack may be direct or indirect, physical or verbal, as these examples illustrate:

Employee A feels that he's in competition with Employee B for promotion to a certain job. He sees B not just as a competitor but as a block that he can't overcome. B is spending a lot of time in their manager's office and seems to be the leading candidate for promotion. Employee A feels there is little he can do about the situation, so his frustration grows.

Being the type of person he is, he becomes aggressive and attacks directly. He starts arguments with B; he finds fault with what B does; he begins to spread stories about B's lack of efficiency or integrity; he criticizes him in front of others; he doesn't hesitate to make innuendos about his ancestry or whether his parents were married when he was born.

A's aggression here is nonviolent. He hasn't physically attacked B but has chosen to do so verbally. The effects, however, may be more serious and long-lasting than a physical attack, which is generally short-lived.

In another case, Employee C is severely reprimanded by his boss for something he failed to do. Given no chance to explain, C becomes angry and frustrated. Not daring to fight back directly, he broods all day and then takes his frustration out on someone else—often his wife, then his children, and maybe finally the family cat.

Quite frequently, an individual doesn't know exactly what it is that is blocking his path and therefore doesn't know whom or what to blame for his frustration. He can't attack directly, so he finds a substitute on which he can turn his aggression. In a work situation, the substitute is usually management in general, with the aggression manifested through open criticisms of management, complaints, grievances, malicious rumors, absenteeism, sabotage, and the like.

Aggression may also be directed at machines, material, or equipment. Intentional damage by frustrated workers is hardly a rarity in plants and factories. Slowing down the operation or doing something that will cost the company money is the employee's way of getting back at those he feels are the cause of his frustration. The behavior may be childish, but it at least serves as a temporary escape valve to relieve some of his antagonisms.

When behaviors such as these persist for any period of time, management would do well to look closely at itself and the climate within the organization. Aggression may be a natural response to frustration, but it should not exist in a well-managed company.

RATIONALIZATION

Rationalization is the act of giving a reason for a decision, action, or particular situation. In simple words, it's making excuses. By so doing, the individual justifies his behavior and protects his self-esteem.

Excuse-making shows up in many ways on the job. One of the most frequent is for the employee to blame something or some person for his own failure. If he's having trouble doing his work correctly, he condemns the equipment, the materials, the lack of information given him, the unrealistic schedule, poor training, etc., etc. Normally he has little difficulty convincing himself that external conditions, not his own lack of ability, are the causes of his failure. "The boss never gives clear instructions." "The people in inspection don't know what they're talking about." "Nobody tells us what's going on." "Why don't they plan things better?" "The boss won't listen."

Another evidence of rationalization is "sour grapes," or the effort to make something one can't get seem less important or desirable than it is. It's the old fable of the fox trying to reach the grapes that were out of reach. "Oh well," he said in frustration, "they're probably sour anyway."

Employee D has been trying to get a better job for months. A vacancy finally occurs, but he doesn't get the job. He then goes around saying, "I didn't really want that job in the first place. The little extra money isn't worth all the headaches." Eventually he may convince himself of this, too, as he substitutes supposed conclusions for his real feelings.

The opposite of sour grapes is "sweet lemon." Here, the attempt is to make the best of a bad situation. Employee E is forced to take a job he neither likes nor wants. Rather than complain aloud and admit that he had no control over what happened to him, he begins to cite some of the advantages: "It pays well." "It's nearer to home." "It's a lot easier." "The hours are good."

Actually, he would have much preferred another job, even if the hours and pay weren't as good and it took longer to get to work. Given no alternative, however, he tries to rationalize away his real feelings about being required to accept something he didn't want in the first place.

Sour-grape and sweet-lemon reactions are common, and they do have the advantage of helping us justify a situation that is not the way we'd like it to be. In that sense, neither is entirely unhealthy.

Rationalization is usually not a destructive or otherwise harmful outlet for frustration. At the extreme, however, the behavior resulting from it can be quite unproductive. The person who is continually making excuses for himself isn't going to try to improve. After all, he has things or people other than himself to blame for his problems. It's a case of "If only *they* would straighten up, everything would be fine."

WITHDRAWAL

This is an effort to escape from a frustrating situation. There is no attempt to try to solve the problem or cope with it; the individual simply runs away from it.

Employee F had many ideas for improving methods in his department. Every time he made a suggestion, however, his manager brushed him aside with comments such as, "Well, they'd never buy that upstairs," "It's a good idea, but . . . ," or "You're not paid to think—get back to work and do what you're supposed to do." To a creative person who wanted to make a contribution, this was a frustrating, defeating situation. Gradually, he began to come in late and take a day off now and then; finally he resigned to work for another company. He reacted to a problem he couldn't solve by withdrawing from it entirely.

People also withdraw by daydreaming. A certain amount of this is natural, but when it becomes a substitute for the real world—when an employee fails to be realistic and down to earth—it is a harmful pastime. Instead of actually getting things done, he daydreams his day away. Things are too frustrating on the job, so he escapes mentally.

Another common escape mechanism is to get "sick." This is seen all too frequently in the developing countries. Under pressure, the employee develops a wide variety of pains, aches, and physical ailments no physician can diagnose. When symptoms of illness occur (most of which are psychosomatic), he feels completely justified in physically withdrawing from a situation he is unwilling to face.

REGRESSION

This is going back to a less mature level. It's a breakdown of constructive problem-solving abilities, and can be so extreme that it involves a return to childlike behavior.

Take the case of a worker who's having trouble with a machine. He tries to repair it but it still won't run properly. In frustration, he starts kicking it, pounding on it, maybe actually destroying it. He's acting just like a little boy who gets angry at a toy and ends up jumping on it.

Regression is expressed in many ways: sulking when we can't get what we want or have our way about something; exaggerating or lying about who we are and what we have done, all in the hope of impressing others; shouting or swearing when job pressures become too heavy; refusing to do anything unless the boss is around and tells us exactly what to do and how to do it. An individual who regresses may be fully mature and highly educated, but at the moment, he is behaving like an emotionally unstable adolescent.

FIXATION

Fixation is a behavior that is repeated over and over, despite the fact that it has already proved unsuccessful. Say an employee is having trouble performing a certain task because he's using the wrong technique. His supervisor shows him the right way, but he still clings to the old method—even though he knows that in so doing he'll probably be criticized.

Fixated people are stubborn and often unreasonable, but they don't see themselves that way. They insist that they are merely persistent or cautious. They refuse to accept change and don't want to consider new ideas or other ways of doing things. Inflexible in thought and action, they have little ability to solve problems or overcome the situation that is causing their frustration.

Unfortunately, the more they are punished for their "stubbornness" and criticized for their inflexibility, the greater becomes the frustration and the stronger the fixation. It's a vicious circle, with neither the manager nor the individual successfully breaking the pattern.

RESIGNATION

This is to surrender, to adopt the belief that nothing can be done about one's frustrating situation. Every supervisor has had experience with listless employees who have no real interest in their jobs—who show no enthusiasm or desire to work, whose general attitude is "I don't give a damn." It's a surrendering behavior, similar to withdrawal except that the resigned person stays in the frustrating environment. He doesn't try to escape from it; he just gives up.

Resignation is common among those who have experienced frequent failure. Despite efforts to solve their problems in the past, they haven't succeeded and now are no longer even willing to try. This individual is usually pessimistic. Lacking confidence in himself and his abilities, he makes no attempt to improve, gain experience, or learn anything new. Not uncommonly, he has lost faith in people and is thus a poor leader (if he should ever become one) and a reluctant follower.

Resignation is probably the most common symptom of frustration in the work situation. Management can discipline the aggressive employee and the one who costs the company money by withdrawing, but it's difficult to punish the worker who says, "I'll do my job and no more." Resignation then becomes a comfortable and relatively safe means of expressing frustration.

AN OVERVIEW OF THE FRUSTRATION-INDUCED BEHAVIORS

The behaviors described above are the ones people most commonly exhibit when frustration exists. One person may display a single symptom while someone else could resort to two or three over a period of time. It's not unusual, for example, to see aggression followed by fixation or resignation and ending up with permanent withdrawal. As a brief recapitulation, the behaviors are:

Aggression: hostility; a fighting behavior.
Rationalization: making excuses.
Withdrawal: escaping.

Regression: a return to childlike behavior.
Fixation: stubbornness; inflexibility.
Resignation: surrender.

In an overseas assignment, particularly in developing countries, direct physical aggression against authority is rare. This is contrary to the culture and training. Indirect verbal attacks, however, are common when foreign managers create or perpetuate a frustrating organization climate. (We're speaking here of frustrations relating to the job, not government or political matters. There, direct physical attacks against ruling powers are not at all unusual.)

More common is withdrawal evidenced by absenteeism and tardiness. A fair amount of daydreaming can also be expected. Actual termination from a job is sometimes the course taken but it is more often avoided *unless* comparable work is available elsewhere. The labor market determines whether the employee quits in frustration or puts up with what he's got just to be sure he has a paycheck.

With complete withdrawal unlikely, resignation is the next most frequently observed symptom: "Since I can't escape, I'll surrender." This person feels he has no other alternative. Once he is resigned to his fate, regression or fixation may appear, disappear, and emerge again. Withdrawal through absenteeism or tardiness can be expected, along with some rationalizing and excuse-making. Resignation is a state of defeatism that opens the doors to some or all of the other manifestations of frustration.

These behaviors occur, however, only when there is a *deep, chronic dissatisfaction arising from unresolved problems.* Emotionally healthy people in situations that they find congenial don't act in these ways. You don't see the symptoms in a well-managed company or a well-ordered home. They do appear, however, when a U.S. manager, without proper preparation, suddenly finds himself in some strange culture that he neither understands nor finds compatible with his way of life. Insecure and dissatisfied, he can do little except struggle along and count the days until he's on the flight home for good.

Of course, he has the option of complete withdrawal, but that could jeopardize his job at home as well as his future. In their frustration, however, too many managers do just this. Escape becomes more important than the job future.

If the frustrated manager chooses to complete the assignment, a common consequence is that he creates a frustrating climate in his own unit. He may arouse much ill will if he becomes aggressive— ruling with an iron hand, issuing orders, criticizing, and verbally attacking those around him. Should he surrender, the place will run by itself with no one really caring what happens. Sprinkled in may be excuse-making: "If only they'd give us the right tools, we'd get the job done"; "If I had some decent people around here, I'd be able to achieve the objective"; "What's the matter with those people? They can't remember anything!" Now toss in a little fixation or regression and you have all the ingredients for failure abroad.

The more frustrated the manager, the greater is the chance that he will create an equally frustrating working climate for his people. And on and on it goes, with frustration compounding frustration in a never-ending cycle of deepening, chronic dissatisfactions. Unfortunately, this is a story too often told when the unprepared American arrives on the foreign scene.

Conclusion

This chapter has offered a brief overview of some of the elements of human behavior as they relate to the work situation. There has been no attempt, obviously, to talk about the id, ego, and superego; the extrovert, ambivert, and introvert; and so on. Only those aspects that seem important to the manager in supervising a group of people on the job have been discussed.

In any society, the challenge of coordinating people to maintain a continuing high level of performance is a stretching challenge. It is far more stretching than usual in a developing society, with all of its attendant differences from our own society and our lifetime of experiences. To meet the challenge, a basic understanding of human behavior is essential. Without it and the ability to read the signs before him, the American manager *might* be able to lead his people effectively, but the odds are not in his favor.

Technical skills, managerial skills, human skills—these are the three legs of the management stool. The instability of the stool is obvious when any leg is missing or shorter than the others. The one leg that is almost certain to be strong is the technical. The other two? Well, there is where the stool becomes unsteady. Effective management abroad demands strength in all three areas if objectives are to be achieved.

A final comment relating to the people side of the job: managing the human element would be relatively easy if one were directed only by logic, rational thought processes, and cold intellect. That, however, is not the case. Feelings and emotions determine our behavior just as much as logic and rationality. This observation is aptly summarized in a quote from an unknown source:

> And so we are forced to give up the idea that human beings are primarily creatures of reason, acting on the basis of thinking and thinking on the basis of fact. Rather, we have to see them as partly rational and partly emotional, and to understand them, individually or in groups, we must understand their moods, sentiments, desires, wishes, beliefs, attitudes, and values; and the effect of all of these often greatly exceeds the influence of reason as such.

6

Motivating the
Overseas Workforce

The manager arrives at his post abroad, qualified and prepared. Whether he inherited it from a predecessor or fashioned it himself, let's assume that his department is well organized. Objectives are clear to everyone, the staffing is complete, the people trained to do the job. The necessary materials, equipment, and funds are on hand. At this point, he should be able to sit back and watch things happen according to plan.

Regretfully, it doesn't always work that way. The real challenge to the manager's abilities is just beginning. Now enters the responsibility to integrate the production and human resources so that departmental goals and objectives are achieved and predetermined performance standards are met. Just because the people know *what* is to be done doesn't mean they will do it. Creating the *desire* to achieve is the challenge the manager faces. This is the role of motivation.

But first—is there any major difference between motivating people at home and motivating them in a developing country? Basically, no. People are much the same everywhere and generally respond to the same stimuli. Peripherally there are some differences, which will be discussed in this chapter. Second—do the current concepts of motivation work in a society just moving into industrialization? Yes they do, though there are a few exceptions. The problem is that the current concepts have been tried too infrequently, with the result that local supervisors learn the outdated practices that were in vogue 30 or 40 years ago. More on that later, as well.

What Is Motivation?

A manager has, say, 25 subordinates working for him. The question is: Can he motivate them? In response, most managers say, "Sure. Of course I can. That's my job." Are they right? *Can* the manager really motivate? The answer is *no,* and failure to comprehend this point has caused many failures in motivating efforts.

If I say that I can motivate you, I am really saying that I can get you to do what I want you to do. You respond the way I want you to respond. Who, then, is motivated? I am, not you. You are conforming for other reasons—fear, security, tenure, or whatever—not because you are internally motivated to accomplish what I have asked. My efforts to move you in this case are not motivation, they are manipulation. And there's a big difference between the two. The master puppeteer dangles his wooden images on a series of wires as they respond to his movements and dance his jig. *He* is the one who is motivated; they are manipulated to help him achieve his objective.

This is the fallacy that has been held by innumerable managers. They have misread the true meaning of motivation, employing instead the lures and tricks of manipulation. The typical methods used over the years to get people to move boil down to four—the four C's:

COERCION

The Romans built 75,000 miles of roads with slaves and whips; the Egyptians erected the pyramids with the same forceful means. Throughout history and into the Industrial Revolution, owners, entrepreneurs, and managers have relied on their power over others to achieve their purposes. Coercion, fear, threats—these were the tools of management in U.S. industry until approximately the middle of this century. Was the product a more motivated workforce? Hardly. The growth of trade unions, anti-company belligerency, and labor-management conflict are the obvious outgrowths of coercive supervisory practices.

Despite all we know—or should know—about motivation, coercion continues to exist today. Fear and threats are still used far more often than necessary. Dictation is preferred to collaboration; mistrust prevails, with mutual trust between leaders and the led a rarity. This should be the enlightened age of industrial relations. The old techniques, however, are apparently still too embedded to permit the intrusion of modern thinking. Enlightenment hasn't been able to penetrate the darkness of antique practices.

Does this imply that coercion should never be used? Of course not. There usually comes a time when force (nonviolent) is the last recourse. A directive, a pay cut, suspension, termination, or disciplinary action of some nature may be required. Then force, if you will, is in order. But this should be the *last* resort; the threat of it should not be the initial effort to motivate.

COMPENSATION

"Work harder and you'll get more"—the old lure dangled in front of the employee to encourage greater production. Coercion is the stick, compensation the carrot. This goes back to the scientific-management period of Frederick W. Taylor, with its emphasis on monetary incentives to improve productivity. Financial incentives do have an effect on production, but they don't develop truly motivated people. The only exceptions are increments such as bonuses and merit programs, but those have a meaning quite different from routine wage and salary adjustments.

Assume that a company gives an across-the-board pay increase to everyone. Management then sits back and waits for the explosion of motivation and improved performance. It waits—and it waits—and it waits. The thoughtfulness of management apparently goes unappreciated, its generosity unthanked. Cost-of-living differentials are essential, and perhaps seniority should be recognized and automatic increases granted because someone has spent another year on the job. Fine. A healthy compensation program provides for these. However, management should not expect them, either separately or together, to strengthen employee motivation. They prevent *dissatisfaction;* they do not generate motivation.

Now consider a company that has a "merit increase program." Misguidedly, management annually grants everyone an increase, regardless of his or her performance. The amounts may differ, with the minimum performer getting 2 percent and the high producer 10, but the idea is that the raises are all for merit. So the 2 percenter goes home and announces that he got a merit increase. "If it's merit," he says, "I must be doing a good job. If I'm doing a good job, why should I do anything differently next year?"

How about the 10 percenter who got the maximum increase? He looks at the average and below-average performers, who also received "merit" increases. His reasoning is that for all his efforts he was awarded only 5 percent more than Janet, who is an also-ran, and only 8 percent more than Mike, who is barely hanging on. He's not enthusiastic when he analyzes things that way. In fact, this sort of system can be a demotivator while at the same time opening the doors to unnecessary internal conflict as people compare increases and the word spreads about who got how much.

Merit raises can be a potent motivating instrument, but their value is grossly diluted when they are granted to all employees without regard for what they have done or how well they have done it. The value is equally diminished when across-the-board "merit increases" are granted to compensate for cost-of-living rises or to maintain the proper internal salary structure. Give raises to meet inflation, to reward seniority, to be competitive in the marketplace, but identify them for what they are. They certainly aren't "merit," in the truest sense of the word.

A merit program is essential but must be used judiciously. Only those whose performance is well above the established job standards should be rewarded. This makes the system an esteem-builder and a symbol of recognition "for what *I* have done." It thus serves as an effective prod to do even better in the future. Used in this way, money *is* a motivator.

Why all the emphasis on this? Simply because many companies abroad, both U.S.- and locally owned, misuse the merit concept. They either have no program at all to reward excellence, or they apply it across the board. When an existing program is misused, it costs the company unnecessary money and perpetuates performance mediocrity.

If the U.S. manager has any influence in his company in this regard, he is urged to establish a good merit review and compensation system. The selective distribution of merit funds will produce the results he wants if it is properly administered. Otherwise, it's a waste of money.

CON

A con game, as everyone knows, is a way of manipulating or tricking people into doing something. In the work environment, con games include the superficial human relations techniques that used to be taught to managers. For example: call people by their first names; know all about their families, hobbies, and interests; ask them about their weekends and vacations; be sure to send them cards on their birthdays. If you do these things, Mr. Manager, your people will respond to your interest in them with enthusiasm and motivation. As General McCauliffe said: "Nuts."

Other human relationists have preached: "Give your people a feeling of belonging, a sense of participation in operating matters." That's poor advice, too. People need more than a "feeling" or "sense" of belonging; they need to *know* they belong and *know* that their ideas or solutions to problems are both essential and wanted. This the manager doesn't do with tricks or parroted clichés. He does it by the way he runs his organization on a day-to-day basis. A human relations approach, if soundly practiced, is invaluable. Employed to con people into a motivated state of mind, it doesn't work and never has.

In some parts of the world, paternalism is used as another con. In Japan it really isn't a con because it is accepted and is an integral element in the traditional management-employee relationship. The same is largely true in South America and, to a degree, in the Middle East. Much depends, however, on the extent of the paternalism. People expect certain benefits or privileges granted by the company, but when these become excessive—when they are not what the employees would have asked for, had they been consulted—corporate generosity backfires.

One case cited by Brannen Hodgson in his book *Overseas Management*[1] describes the efforts of the Anglo-Iranian Oil Company to care for its employees. Along with housing, the company provided shops, stores, movies, recreational facilities, and restaurants. Complete health and dental care were available to all. The people really wanted for nothing.

How were all these "gifts" accepted? More with nonchalance and criticism than gratitude. The employees, though better treated than any other employees in the area, did not display any particular loyalty or dedication to the company because of its paternalism. They knew the company could afford these things anyway. As Hodgson says:

> Paternalistic employee relations policies fail in the long run because they perpetuate, or create, attitudes of dependence. Employees do not learn to satisfy their desires by their own efforts. Instead, they depend on their employers to solve all their problems. Once the philosophy of dependence has been implanted . . . and centered on the employer, any feelings of dissatisfaction will lead to complaints against some policy or omission of the company. No other cause for unhappiness or unsatisfied desires is likely to occur to them.[2]

People feel locked in when too much is gratuitously provided by the all-knowing company. Anti-company and anti-foreign sentiments are common outgrowths. If the employees want a swimming pool and ask for a swimming pool, then provide one. But charge a small fee for its use so they will feel that it's at least partly theirs, that they have an investment in it. And don't give them a pool just because someone in management "thinks" they want it.

[1] New York: McGraw-Hill, 1965. Account taken by Hodgson from Stephan H. Longrigg, *Oil in the Middle East* (London: Oxford University Press, 1954).
[2] *Overseas Management*, p. 155.

CLICHÉ

The fourth "C" smacks of the human relations gadgetry. "Give 'em the big picture." "Here's a real challenge." "People—our most important resource." "Atta boy!" "We're number one." "I know you can do it." "Win one for the Gipper." "Mother, flag, and party."

The pep talk, the emotion-laden imprecation, the catch phrase—these are supposed to stir the adrenalin in Joe or José or Ahmed as he does battle for dear old Alpha Zeta Company, Inc. In the right place at the right time, the cliché may have some value. By itself, it is no motivator. Still, it is one of the techniques managers use even today to get their people moving.

So, these are the four C's. Do any sound familiar?

Then What Is the Answer?

If the manager can't motivate his people, and if coercion, compensation, cons, and clichés don't motivate, what then *can* he do? To say it is easy; to do it is something else. But the effective manager can *create an organization climate that causes his people to become self-motivated.*

This is not playing with words or drawing fine lines. There is a major difference between trying to move people the way you want them to move and developing within them a self-motivation to do what should be done. True motivation is internal. It's a feeling, deep and important, within a person that causes him to pursue a given behavior or course of action. It's not the result of external manipulations but rather of the quality of leadership exercised by the manager. That leadership establishes the climate, and the climate determines the degree of self-motivation.

Now, in a healthy work environment, the human relations techniques mentioned earlier have a place—only they are no longer techniques as such. When the boss asks about your weekend, you know he's interested; when he inquires about your family, you know he means it; when he sends you a birthday card, you know it's not a gimmick. These are no longer tricks or manipulative con games to get you to work. He's fashioned a climate that inspires the best in people, and you know that his interest in your welfare is genuine. What was phony before is honest now—even though the words may be identical.

I define motivation as "the creation of an organization climate that causes people to *want* to contribute actively and constructively to the attainment of established goals and objectives." This is the manager's responsibility, and what the manager can do to create that climate is the theme of this chapter.

This Concept of Motivation in the Developing World

"Come on, it's different here," objected one U.S. manager in a developing country. "All that stuff you teach in the States is fine, but it won't work with *these* people. I've been here long enough and I ought to know." The only thing this manager didn't know was what he didn't know—if that makes sense. He was a lot more wrong than right, as the performance of his local employees clearly demonstrated.

The real meaning of motivation isn't clearly understood abroad. Many of the basics of human relations aren't either, or else they're constantly being violated by expatriates and locals alike. It's a matter of the boss ordering and the subordinate jumping; the boss acts, the subordinate reacts. There is little of the subordinate jumping out on his own, taking things into his own hands, and being willing to accept risk.

There are exceptions, of course, but the climate overseas is more reactive than proactive, which to some degree is understandable. The concept of having to *command* when one is the schoolteacher, policeman, father, or boss is deeply entrenched. So is the belief that when one is in a subordinate position—as a student, citizen, child, or employee—one is expected to follow orders, to obey. The command-obey syndrome is a cultural trait that has not yet been tempered to any measurable degree. The skills of acting with independence and rebelling in a constructive way when disagreeing with the boss are anything but highly developed.

The source of this syndrome is easy to explain, but the syndrome itself is being reinforced and perpetuated by overseas managers' lack of understanding of what motivation is and what methodologies will create a climate in which it can flourish. The nationality of the manager—American, British, German, Dutch, Mexican, or local—makes little difference. The vast majority still think *they* do the motivating, that it's up to them to move their people to action. So out come the four C's, individually or in combination. Then, when no burst of motivation appears, the manager resorts to more and more coercion to get the job done. What these managers don't realize is that their people are already motivated. They're motivated to work for or against management. They don't need the four C's. What they need is the chance to have some personal control over what they do and how they do it. Within the established guidelines, they need freedom, but a freedom that isn't followed by harsh recriminations should they fail in an assignment or not measure up exactly to the boss's standards.

Experience in the developing countries proves rather clearly that the local manager or employee will demonstrate strong evidences of self-motivation if:

1. He is properly trained in the work and knows what to do.
2. The desired end results of whatever he's asked to do have been defined.
3. Guidelines or limits in terms of policy, expenditures, and time have been established.
4. He is left alone to do the job.
5. He knows he can go to his boss at any time for guidance or support when he reaches an impasse.
6. He knows he won't be berated if things don't work out exactly as the boss wanted.
7. He is immediately reinforced for the things he does well.

A case in point: A young, bright Pakistani was employed in Saudi Arabia as an office clerk in a company where the author was working. His performance under an American manager was adequate but hardly outstanding. When a management training program was introduced in the company, he was eventually put in charge of collecting and packing all the course materials so they could be shipped to either Beirut or Istanbul, the cities where the course was to be conducted. Altogether the shipment usually consisted of 14 or 15 separate pieces, including metal trunks, projectors, flip-chart easels, a flannel board, and so on. It was the Pakistani's responsibility to have everything transported to the airport, boarded on the aircraft, and cleared through customs at the destination.

The assignment was an exacting one, requiring care, close attention to detail, and a lot of physical hauling and tugging as well. It also demanded a personal finesse to enlist the help of taxi drivers, porters, hotel personnel, and even customs officials without having to hand over excessive gratuities.

At the beginning and throughout the life of the assignment, management tried to establish the seven conditions listed above. The employee was trained and told what had to be done, and the end results were defined—everything had to be at the meeting place by the prescribed time and nothing, absolutely nothing, could be missing. From that point on, if he had questions or a problem he couldn't resolve himself, he came to management and got the help he needed. Otherwise, he was left to do the job on his own.

As to his performance—it couldn't have been better. He took on the assignment with a thoroughness and enthusiasm that no one had guessed he had. Not once, while we were associated with him, did he fail us. Every single course item was unfailingly there. If a customs clearance problem arose, as it often did in Istanbul, he always seemed to find a way to solve it. If the collator of the manuals omitted a page, he found a way to get it reproduced. Even when a silent-pulse tape player failed to function during a dry-run practice session, he, with no knowledge of mechanics or electronics, worked for hours one night to try to repair the instrument. Finally he succeeded, and to say that he had a sense of accomplishment is a considerable understatement.

Given the desired results, the guidelines, and freedom to do things the way that was best for him within the guidelines, this young Pakistani, who was merely average as an office clerk, became the very example of excellence. If there was any dissatisfaction with something he did, it was discussed on the spot. By the same token, his achievements were immediately reinforced. He had a challenge; he knew where he stood in the eyes of management; and he responded with every evidence of self-motivation possible. A year later, he was promoted to a supervisory position in the company's management training department—a rather unique post for a Pakistani in Saudi Arabia.

The point of all this is that the employee wasn't motivated by any external force. Management didn't command, as such, or manipulate. It merely tried to create the proper climate for self-motivation.

Was management brilliant? Not at all. It did understand, however, and tried to apply the principles of motivation that are almost always successful. In this case, the employee made management look good when the courses got underway. Management trusted him, and he supported management—an ideal team organization.

What follows in this discussion of motivation, then, does have pertinence in the developing societies. The ideas presented here are designed only to suggest some things that the U.S. manager can do to create a greater level of pro-company self-motivation. Not every idea will apply in every situation in every location; there are bound to be exceptions. Generally speaking, however, the research conclusions and principles reviewed aren't limited to employees in the United States or the industrialized West.

Some Research—and the Implications Abroad

Much work has been done over the past 40 to 50 years in an effort to unravel the mystery of what people want from a job and what motivates them to perform productively. Social scientists, behavioral scientists, and psychologists have been busy, and their findings should have meaning to any manager, with perhaps special significance to one in a developing country. Out of the myriad of writings on the subject by highly qualified professionals, four are being isolated for review here. To the student of management, each will be familiar territory. To others, there may be new ideas here that could assist in the structuring of a healthy organization climate.

THE HAWTHORNE EXPERIMENTS

One of the most important studies in the early research on motivation was the work of a group of Harvard scientists at Western Electric's plant in Hawthorne, Illinois. The leader of the group was Professor Elton Mayo. The experiments took place between 1927 and 1932, and were originally designed to determine the effects of lighting and working conditions on employee productivity, fatigue, and job monotony.

The scientists first selected experimental groups, measured their current productivity and efficiency, and then began a series of changes in lighting, temperature, humidity, and other conditions. At the same time, the researchers informed the group members that certain rest breaks had been authorized by management. They suggested that the members themselves get together and establish a schedule that would allow each person to have his break but not so the flow of work was interrupted. In other words, not everyone could be off at the same time. Keep in mind that in those days coffee breaks were a rarity in the plant or factory. Furthermore, management was still operating under the influence of scientific-management concepts and efficiency engineers; group or team organizations didn't exist. The work was arranged to minimize social contact and maximize output.

As the experiments proceeded and the various changes in working conditions were made, levels of productivity and efficiency were recorded. With each change, both improved. The effects of better lighting, temperature control, and physical conditions on worker performance seemed undeniable.

At some point, the decision was made to take away some of the improved conditions to see what effect that would have on productivity. To the surprise of the researchers, productivity remained at the level it had attained and never did return to the original level recorded when the experiments began. A lengthy series of interviews was then initiated to explore the reasons for this phenomenon. Some of the reasons, or conclusions, reached were:

○ The group members indicated that being selected for the experiments made them feel they were set apart from the other employees—were more or less the plant elite—and that their status was higher as a consequence. This gave rise to the theory that employees perform more effectively when they are given special attention, a response called the "Hawthorne effect."

○ The people were more productive when working in groups rather than in isolation.

○ Wage incentives alone did not determine product output, even when people worked on a piece-rate basis.

○ The freedom to determine their own rest-break schedule had given the people the knowledge that they had some control over their own working environment.

When the Harvard group conducted similar interviews elsewhere in the plant among those who had not participated in the experiments, they found little but apathy and frustration. The people felt that management was stripping them of any positive attitudes they may have had, that management had destroyed any desire to cooperate, and that the lack of concern for the human element versus production demands was self-defeating.

This second series of interviews was important because it demonstrated how an informal group could sabotage management's efforts to increase productivity. The groups set their own standards, and once these were set, management found itself almost powerless to stop what Mayo called "massive foot-dragging." At the same time, the employees took pride in the techniques they had developed to *look* busy when they really weren't.

As a result of the entire experiment, the researchers came to some conclusions that are significant in any study of motivation:

1. People like to work. It is natural for them to want to do something worthwhile, constructive, and productive.
2. When a person does not like to work, the reason will usually be found not in him but in some social or psychological condition associated with the job.
3. Physical surroundings and working conditions have little direct, major effect on morale.

4. Employees fear the loss of a job, even when other jobs are easily available, because of the implications of being fired.
5. Work is primarily a group activity, with social relationships and interdependencies normal and natural.
6. Work is the primary social force in the average worker's life. (Meaning that he spends more time with the people at work than with anyone else except his immediate family. Work therefore provides him with most of his friends, although he may have closer or better friends off the job.)
7. Attitudes toward the job are influenced by situations within the work group.
8. The informal group has strong social influence over the worker's performance.
9. Complaints are more often than not created by conditions affecting the worker's status and self-concept.
10. Leadership that encourages cooperation and participation, rather than demanding obedience, promotes productivity and reduces employee turnover.

The work of the Harvard group is perhaps the most important single research study in the area of motivation. It is important not because it has given today's managers all the answers (it hasn't), but because it was the first real effort to study people at work. The whole experiment has deeply infuenced management thinking while serving as a stimulus for later research.

Two other points about the experiment:

○ The scientists conclusions have never been proved wrong. The findings of the group, published in the book *Management and the Worker*[3] in 1939 by Rothlisberger and Dixon, are as valid today as they were then.

○ The study contributed to the reaction against the scientific-management school, with its stopwatches, time-and-motion-analyses, quota incentives, programmed efficency, and the like. Unfortunately, many of the Hawthorne study's conclusions were interpreted to mean that management had to be "nice" to its employees. Thus the study helped give rise to the human relations period of management—the period of managerial softness, indulgence, paternalism, and the attempt to create "happy" workers.

[3] Cambridge, Mass.: Harvard University Press, 1939.

THEORIES X AND Y

Douglas McGregor, consultant, college president, and management professor, made many contributions to management thought. The best-known of these is what he called Theory X and Theory Y. Fundamentally, McGregor says that every manager has certain beliefs and assumptions about the people working for him. These assumptions have been developed over the years and result from his experiences, personal values, and training. As a consequence, he is likely to manage his people according to the traits and behavior patterns he assumes they possess.

These assumptions, McGregor suggests, can be categorized as Theory X and Theory Y. In proposing the two theories, he is not describing people as they *are* but how the manager *feels* about them.

Theory X

1. People have an inborn dislike of work, whether physical or mental. They will therefore do whatever they can to avoid it. They probably have to support themselves and their families, so being productively employed is essential. But as work is a necessary evil, they tolerate it to meet their physiological needs for food, shelter, and clothing.

2. Because of the inherent dislike of work, people will do enough to keep their jobs but no more. They have to be threatened and coerced to meet the minimum requirements and, unless an effective system of control exists, are unlikely to meet even those requirements. If they put forth enough effort to be reasonably productive, it's because management has exerted the necessary pressure on them.

3. The average person wants security above all. He thus avoids responsibility because of the risk it poses to his security. Responsibility implies the freedom to decide, to act, to be independent. Given this freedom, he could make wrong decisions or conduct himself in ways that, if discovered, might well threaten his personal security. He therefore prefers to be told what to do, when to do it, and how to do it. This way he avoids responsibility for mistakes or failures, and his security is not endangered.

Theory Y

1. Work is not foreign to man's nature. Instead it is as natural as rest, play, or engaging in social activities.

2. External pressures and controls do cause people to produce, but

they are not the only motivating influences. A person *will* exercise self-control to achieve certain goals and objectives if he is committed to them. The commitment produces an internal force that motivates him toward goal attainment. The rewards of attainment come in the forms of self-esteem and realization of his own potential.

3. People are not reluctant to accept responsibility. Indeed, if the climate is right in the business environment, they not only will accept it but will seek increased responsibility.

4. Given the opportunity and/or encouragement, the average human being will demonstrate a high degree of imagination and ingenuity. If permitted, he will make positive contributions to the solution of organizational problems and will develop better methods of doing the job.

To reemphasize, McGregor is not describing *people* in these theories. He is describing the *attitudes* that managers have about people. Most managers, when introduced to the theories, almost universally agree that people are far more Theory Y than Theory X. The same managers, says McGregor, then return to the job and supervise their subordinates as though every word of Theory X were gospel. Intellectually they accept Theory Y; their behavior, however, reflects deep-seated Theory X values.

Which brings us to the Pygmalion Effect, or the self-fulfilling prophecy. If a manager has Theory X values about people, he will treat them as though they were incompetent, would take advantage of him if given half a chance, and would do nothing unless specifically directed.

Being managed this way, the subordinates respond predictably. They do only what they're told, take every possible advantage of the manager, and give every possible indication of incompetence and disinterest.

Observing this behavior, the manager decides that the only thing to do is get tougher and tougher. As he does, his people resist more and more—so he continues to tighten the screws. And the struggle goes on until the inevitable moment when the group, with its numbers and common bond, wins out. This is a battle the manager is sure to lose. If his people aren't producing, it's very rare that the entire group will be fired. Instead, the manager is replaced.

Under the Pygmalion Effect, a person himself creates what he has imagined to be true. Here the manager was convinced his people were no good, he treated them accordingly, and because of that treatment, they behaved exactly as he had anticipated. His prophecy was fulfilled. Treat a person like a child, and a child he will be.

THE HIERARCHY OF NEEDS

Another approach to the study of human behavior and motivation that has had considerable influence on management thinking is the "hierarchy of needs" developed by Dr. Abraham H. Maslow. Pictured diagrammatically, the hierarchy is composed of five levels of needs in a topless triangle (see Figure 1). The lowest-level needs, which must be satisfied first, are the physiological—the needs for food, water, clothing, and protection from the elements.

Once these are basically satisfied, man moves up a step. He now wants to secure the Level 1 fundamentals without having to expose himself to undue risk or personal danger. Security and personal safety become important.

With these satisfied, according to his own standards, next comes the need for family, friends, and congenial associates—and for some other things that he doesn't *have* to have in order to sustain life. The latter, because they are not essential, are termed "luxuries."

Moving to Level 4, man now seeks satisfaction of the more intangible or internalized needs, such as *recognition* of who he is and what he has done; *opportunity* to learn, advance, grow, and achieve; *challenge;* the chance to *contribute;* and *involvement* in matters that affect him.

Finally, at Level 5 comes self-fulfillment, also called self-realization or self-actualization. At this stage, man's image of himself becomes a reality, the flower in full bloom. As Maslow has said, perhaps only 10 percent of the people in the world have advanced this far in the satisfaction of their needs.

Some observations or explanations are in order at this point:

1. *Man does not move from one level to the next until the needs of the*

FIGURE 1. Maslow's hierarchy of needs.

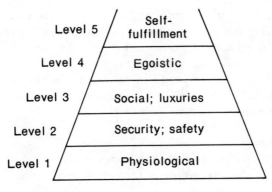

lower level have been met to his satisfaction. The trip up the hierarchy can be very slow for those born into a traditional or developing society. On the other hand, one born into wealth has the first two levels already secured for him. He really begins, then, at Level 3 or perhaps even Level 4.

The last point can explain, in part, why some of the younger generation seem to rebel against the ways of their parents and the old ethics of "starting at the bottom," "hard work," and "thrift." Securing the basics has never been a concern. They started life at Level 3 and probably moved fairly rapidly to 4, where they satisfied their egoistic needs in their own (to their elders, often mystifying) ways.

2. *The trip down the hierarchy can be very rapid.* If you are at Level 4 and suddenly find yourself without a job or any source of income, egoistic needs become most unimportant. You are likely to retreat quickly to Level 2.

3. *A satisfied need is never a motivator.* Say that a group or individual is seeking satisfaction of the Level 4 egoistic needs. This implies that the needs of the first three levels are no longer important concerns. It's Level 4 that counts and demands attention.

Many companies don't understand this simple fact. Employees, perhaps subconsciously and without directly communicating this, want from their jobs recognition, opportunity, challenge, and involvement. But management, in an effort to motivate them, provides an improved hospitalization program, a better retirement plan, a new cafeteria, or something else when the people *are already satisfied with what they have.* They'll take whatever the company offers, but improved fringe benefits or greater security is no longer the issue. What counts now are the unsatisfied needs of Level 4.

The results of the company's "generosity"? Higher personal costs, but not a whit more motivation or productivity. A satisfied need is never a motivator.

4. *People are never completely satisfied.* They always want something more, whether physical, intellectual, or emotional in nature. That's why there is no top to the hierarchy pyramid. Even the person at Level 5 cannot find total and lasting satisfaction.

Where do most of the people in the world stand today in the hierarchy? Obviously, generalizations have their risks, but the following may be a reasonably accurate summary:

The West and Japan

In the countries that have reached Rostow's Stage 5, the age of mass consumption, most people are at least at Maslow's third level, which means that the Level 4 needs are being felt. There are of course exceptions among the unemployed and the disadvantaged. Even then, however, government support programs, charities, and the like protect all but the smallest minority from the ravages of starvation, insufficient clothing, or inadequate protection against the elements. For the vast majority, the basic needs of life have been met and those of a higher order now prevail.

The Soviet Bloc

The countries in Rostow's Stage 3 (takeoff) or Stage 4 (drive to maturity) are generally at Maslow's third level, with many of the needs at that level still unsatisfied. This includes most of the Soviet bloc nations. While Soviet citizens are considered well-to-do by world standards, with a gross national product of more than $2,000 per person, luxuries and the nonnecessities of life are in short supply. People stand in lengthy queues for hours seeking to buy a staple or an appliance that we can find in quantity at any neighborhood shopping center. Housing is available, but how many years does one have to be on a waiting list to get a cramped flat in Moscow? The same holds true for automobiles. Even if the average Muscovite could afford one, just getting delivery is an interminable process.

Party heads, key military personnel, and those who have distinguished themselves in the arts or athletics are well-supported. Most members of the population, however, aren't concentrating on Level 4. Their concerns are primarily for a few of the nonessentials that make life a little more comfortable.

The Third World

The developing countries, particularly most of those in South America, Africa, India, and Southeast Asia, are at no more than Level 2, with several still at Level 1. Poverty is rampant, hunger is ever present, and disease, caused by water pollution and poor sanitation, takes a heavy toll. "Americans," says a report by the Overseas Development Council, "feed more to animals than all Indians and Chinese eat."[4]

Of course there are the wealthy and the well-fed in every country. But since it has been estimated[5] that 1.4 billion people received less than their minimum daily food requirements in 1975, it is safe to say that a major portion of the Third World is still seeking satisfaction of

[4] *U.S. News and World Report,* July 31, 1978, p. 58.
[5] *Ibid.*

the basic physiological needs. For an American working in such a setting, it is of little avail to talk about "recognition," challenge,"
"growth," and the like when the workers may not even be able to
provide adequately for their families on the salaries paid.

In the oil-producing countries of the Middle East, it's a different
story. There are the laborers, of course—such as the imported Yemenese, the Sudanese, the Indians, and the Pakistanis—who perform
the menial tasks and are compensated accordingly. For them, Level 2
is about as far as they have climbed. The typical plant or factory
worker is something else, as is the office clerk or secretary. Not that
they are wealthy, or even well-paid, by our standards, but they have
risen above the bare subsistence level. In fact, the majority are at
Level 3 and are now seeking satisfaction of the egoistic needs. This is
all too evident when one listens to Middle Eastern employees talk
about what they want from their jobs and the frustrating blocks management has placed in their way. They're seeking more from their
eight hours at work than just a paycheck or paternalistic fringe benefits. These they'll take, of course, but the more intangible needs of
Level 4 are gnawing at them now. Here is where the wise manager
creates a climate that satisfies those unsatisfied yearnings.

While there are exceptions everywhere, it is safe to assume that in
the well-to-do countries, most of the employees have reached Maslow's third level. For them, the unsatisfied needs of the fourth level—
growth, development, opportunity, recognition, and challenge—are
now important. When the job provides these, self-motivation is almost guaranteed. The manager stationed in a poorer part of the world
will probably have to concentrate (to the extent he has the authority)
on a proper pay structure, adequate health and dental care, and helping his people obtain more of the necessities of life. Motivation takes
on a different garb in an environment of poverty or semi-poverty.

SATISFIERS AND MOTIVATORS

Closely related to Maslow's hierarchy is Dr. Fredrick Herzberg's
concept of Satisfiers and Motivators (or Hygiene and Motivators, to
use his specific nomenclature).

Herzberg's fundamental thesis is diagrammed in Figure 2. Surrounding the job in the outer ring are the Satisfiers—the things the
company does to or for the people. Management provides the *physical*
working conditions, the *social* climate, and a certain level of company
and job *status*. It also ensures the proper *orientation* of its employees,
the necessary *security* measures, and *economic* policies and programs

FIGURE 2. The theory of Satisfiers and Motivators. (Adapted from M. Scott Myers, "Who Are Your Motivated Workers?" *Harvard Business Review,* January–February 1964, p. 86. Reprinted by permission of the *Harvard Business Review.* Copyright © 1964 by the President and Fellows of Harvard College.

that provide for a proper compensation structure as well as fringe benefits.

When an employee joins a company, he expects the Satisfiers to be healthy and competitive with those of other local firms in the same type of business. This is one aspect of the employment contract, as it were; it's part and parcel of a well-managed organization. No matter how healthy they may be, however, Satisfiers *don't motivate.* They're accepted for what they are, and perhaps they're even appreciated, but that's all. They merely allow reasonable satisfaction or prevent dissatisfaction. Satisfiers permit the employee to say, "I'm not *un*happy."

On the other hand, if any part of a Satisfier becomes unhealthy through inattention or because management takes something away from the people that has always been granted, considerable dissatisfaction is almost inevitable. While adding to the Satisfiers doesn't motivate, allowing a healthy condition to become unhealthy *demotivates*. How many times has a personnel policy been tightened up or revised downward only to be followed by an angry outburst from the people? And then the industrial relations manager wrings his hands in dismay.

The reaction was entirely predictable: something that had apparently been accepted as routine was taken away or reduced. Whether it was a large or a small thing matters little. A previously healthy condition was made less healthy. Why more personnel people haven't grasped this simple fact of human behavior is a mystery, but the mistakes go on and on.

If the Satisfiers don't motivate, what does? Obviously, the factors in the inner ring of the diagram in Figure 2. These represent the way the manager makes use of his people. He gives them jobs or assignments that provide the *opportunity* to do something of significance and *challenge* their capabilities. He increases their levels of *responsibility* to the maximum extent possible, he helps them *grow* and develop, and he provides prompt *recognition* for successes and *achievements*. What people want once the Satisfiers are healthy are the intangible benefits of the Motivators. The items listed in the inner ring are just a few of the tools the manager has at his disposal to establish a self-motivating work climate.

Note that merit increases, bonuses, and profit-sharing may sometimes be Motivators, in that they are forms of recognition for what an individual has accomplished over a year. Here is the power of money as motivator: it's something *I* got for what *I* did. I am now egged on to do more because my efforts don't go unappreciated or unrewarded. In this sort of climate, self-motivation takes over, with accomplishment and uncommon results the typical byproducts.

Relating Herzberg to Maslow, we see that the Satisfiers correspond to the lower levels of the hierarchy (1 through 3) while the Motivators relate to Level 4, the egoistic needs.

To the manager abroad: first study the Satisfiers. If they are healthy, keep them that way and then begin to create a climate that inspires self-motivation. Don't waste time and money trying to buy loyalty or bursts of productive energy by adding to conditions that are already hygienic. Look now to the more intangible aspects of the job, which only you can provide. *Do* things to and for people to prevent dissatisfaction; *use* people wisely to generate internal motivation. Just keep in mind that a Satisfier is never a Motivator.

The Hawthorne experiments, Theories X and Y, and the concepts of Maslow and Herzberg all tie together. Each uses different words, but when combined, they offer meaningful clues to how motivation really works.[6]

Do the Theories Work Overseas?

Historically, management practices in the United States moved from the scientific-management period (roughly the 1900s to the 1940s) through the human relations period (the 1940s to the 1960s). We are now in an era that is broadly called the period of participative management. What will come next, if anything, no one knows. The point is that we, and most of the industrialized West, have moved through a somewhat natural but often traumatic evolution as we progressed from one period to another. In advancing to industrial maturity, however, is this evolution a requirement? Is it an immutable law of nature, just as a baby becomes a child, then a teenager, and finally an adult? Or can the developing societies, with our help, bypass the first two periods and begin their drive to development by employing the participative-management methodologies?

The answer, predicated on a fair amount of experience abroad, is yes. The initial periods can be skipped; a gradual evolution is not required. Managements abroad can and should learn from our experiences and not commit the same errors of which we have been so guilty.

Everything depends, of course, on the economy of the country. But if a workforce exists that is reasonably well-fed, well-housed, and secure in the material things of life, the concept of motivation as outlined here will work. Specific efforts may be rejected at the beginning, such as increased delegation, but individualism in most countries is strong, and the people will respond to the granting of trust and responsibility. It takes training; it takes development. That, however, is what is expected of the U.S. manager who goes abroad as an operator/developer.

[6] Despite their current popularity, the Maslow and Herzberg theories are not without their critics. For a summary of the cases against both concepts, see Donald Sanzotta, *Motivational Theories and Applications for Managers* (New York: AMACOM, 1977), pp. 48–54.

A common tendency among newly arrived managers is to adopt one of two approaches in their management of the local employee:

1. *Treat the employee as though he were fully capable, trained, and skilled in Western business and production techniques.* This might be the case, but it is highly unlikely. Then if the local person fails (because the manager has assumed too much), the manager becomes impatient or intolerant, and often destroys whatever potential the employee may have had.

2. *Manage the employee as though he were a child, incapable of doing anything other than following strict and detailed instructions.* This is the other side of the coin and just as detrimental. The local person probably will need training, but he is teachable. He wants to be a part of the transition to industrialization. He will learn. To be accorded the status of man-child in his own land by a foreigner is a humiliation that built-in pride will not accept.

Between these extremes lies the middle road of patience and understanding. It is the road where great concern for the local employee's self-esteem is fundamental, where treatment of him as an individual is as basic as an interest in his physical well-being.

As has been noted before, individuals in developing societies typically respect power and authority. However, they do not react favorably to raw authoritative management. They expect their bosses to be visible and to be fair. This is especially true of locals who were educated in the United Kingdom or the United States. Their horizons have been broadened, and dictatorlike management is something they will not tolerate. Openness, honesty, and balance are what the local employee is looking for.

Is all this talk about motivation just theory? Not if the following has any validity. A recent survey conducted by the author among managers and nonmanagers alike in a developing country brought forth these direct quotes:

- "Management should generate more esprit de corps through example. People's enthusiasm will fade if those above display lack of interest." (A middle manager)
- "I wish they'd let us know what's going on." (An engineer)
- "*Work* is stressed, not the human factor." (A first-line supervisor)
- "There's a problem with favoritism. One group is favored more than another." (A mechanic)
- "Senior management should be seen. People work in isolation." (A first-line supervisor)

- "There's a slow reaction, if any, to recommendations we make to management." (A chemist)
- "We don't get much information on what the company wants to do." (A middle manager)
- "What objectives? I never heard of them." (A middle manager)
- "There's an undisciplined organization climate—too much 'What's in it for me?' " (A training specialist)
- "Managers are not exercising managerial responsibilities." (A senior engineer)
- "What authority? I don't have any, and I'm a supervisor." (A first-line supervisor)

This company, largely British- and American-managed, has a lot of work to do! The comments, however, are not isolated. They've been heard over and over in the United States, Latin America, Europe, and the Middle East. Perhaps you've heard them—or made them—yourself.

Despite the volumes that have been written about motivation, managers still aren't reading or listening. There's no deep mystery to it, and it costs little if any money. All it demands is attention by the manager to some common human traits. Nationality by itself does not make us different. Except for intelligence variations among individuals, it is only culture that separates us and that sometimes makes the understanding of others difficult.

The principles of motivation apply just about everywhere. The clue to successful management lies in adapting them to the local culture and work situation. If this is done intelligently, many of the obstacles to achievement will be brushed aside. Not all, to be sure, but the people problems so frequently encountered can be greatly minimized—at the very least. At the best, your people will perform as exceptionally as the Pakistani clerk described earlier.

A Test: "What Do You Want from Your Job?"

Do you want to test the validity of these conclusions regarding motivation, or assess the climate you're dealing with in your new job? Once you're in the job overseas, distribute the questionnaire at the end of this chapter to your people. Ask the supervisors or workers to select five of the items listed that are the most important to them in their jobs now. Then summarize the responses. Items that are frequently checked tend to be those most seriously lacking in the work situation. They stand out because the people don't have them. They're red flags signaling soft spots in your administration of the people. If the Satisfiers are healthy, the odds are that the checked items will be Motivators or, in Maslow's terminology, will fall in the area of egoistic needs.

Of perhaps passing interest, this questionnaire has been given to thousands of management personnel and nonsupervisory employees in Mexico, throughout the United States, in almost every European country, and in Arabian Gulf nations. All sorts of cultures and firms have been represented. The directions given were a little different, however: the people were asked to select *one* item, not five, that was most important to them in their jobs at that time.

In all the times the questionnaire has been administered, Item 8, "Fair (equitable) pay for the job being performed," has been checked *only eight times*—once in Mexico City, twice in the United States, once in Greece, once in Saudi Arabia, and three times in Kuwait. By inference, pay was the most important to those eight people because, at least in their opinion, it was not adequate for the job they were doing. It was *unhealthy* in comparison with the other items and thus stood out.

The balance of the number 1 selections have run the gamut. Almost without exception, however, they have been Motivators or at the egoistic level of needs. All of which clearly indicates that management is providing the necessary Satisfiers but isn't paying much attention to the real and current needs of its people. It's the same story regardless of the particular country.

The questionnaire isn't very scientific, but it's an attitude survey of sorts. Try it out. Your people will be telling you a lot without knowing what they're telling you.

In one brief sentence, a quote from an unknown source seems to sum up this whole matter of motivation most effectively: "The greatest motivator of all is the opportunity to attain ever-increasing mastery over one's own environment." That captures the essence of Mayo, McGregor, Maslow, Herzberg, and the host of other scientists who have studied the psychology of people at work. Think about the sentence. Doesn't it apply to you, too?

QUESTIONNAIRE

Several hundred managers and nonmanagers alike, when asked the question "What do you want from your job?", have listed items such as those suggested below. The list does not pretend to be complete, so if you feel that an important condition has been omitted, add it after Item 40. The sequence 1 through 40 is random and does not imply any degree of significance.

INSTRUCTIONS: Study the list and then select *five* items that are the *most* important to you in your job today. Check those items in the left margin.

Next, review your selections and rank them in order of importance to you (1 = the most important of the five, 2 = the next most, and down to 5 = the least important of your choices). Number 5 is still critical, however, because it is one of the 40 elements that is of significance to you.

Please return this questionnaire to me, *but do not sign your name.*

_____ 1. Opportunity for advancement.
_____ 2. Security.
_____ 3. A job with a challenge.
_____ 4. Chance to make a meaningful contribution to the job and the company.
_____ 5. Knowing what is going on.
_____ 6. Effective two-way communication channels.
_____ 7. Chance for self-development.
_____ 8. Fair (equitable) pay for the job being performed.
_____ 9. Good fringe benefits.
_____10. Fair, consistent supervision.
_____11. Involvement in job-related matters.
_____12. Being asked, not ordered.
_____13. My opinions asked by higher supervision.
_____14. Meaningful, purposeful work.
_____15. Reputable company to work for.
_____16. Honesty and integrity at all levels.
_____17. Respect of superiors.
_____18. Respect of subordinates.
_____19. Respect of peers.
_____20. Recognition of my performance.

____21. Being given credit when it is due.

____22. Good physical working conditions.

____23. Having the right to be wrong.

____24. Having responsibility in accordance with my experience and ability.

____25. Having authority equal to my responsibility.

____26. A good group to work with.

____27. Freedom to communicate upward differing points of view.

____28. Having clearly defined goals and objectives.

____29. Help with personal problems, when needed.

____30. Being trained and developed in company-sponsored programs.

____31. Results-oriented performance appraisals.

____32. Social organizations, such as employee clubs, sports groups, and special interest groups.

____33. A title that reflects prestige and/or status.

____34. Office location and furnishings in keeping with my position.

____35. A job-rotation plan for broadened experience and growth.

____36. A feeling of accomplishment.

____37. The opportunity to be creative or innovative.

____38. Realization of personal goals and objectives.

____39. Supervision that doesn't meddle, interfere, or constantly follow up.

____40. Feeling a part of the organization.

____41.

Rank your selections

Your ranking	Item number	Copy the exact wording of your selections
#1	_____	_____
#2	_____	_____
#3	_____	_____
#4	_____	_____
#5	_____	_____

7

Communicating with the Local National Employee

Of all the barriers to effective management, communication problems are usually listed as the most critical. Whether the communication is supposed to be going up, down, horizontally, or diagonally, and whether it is oral or written, messages just aren't getting through. Static of some sort distorts the message and affects its reception. The problem is universal.

Some Definitions

"Communication" comes from the Latin *communicare*, meaning "to share" or "to make common." When messages are shared and the information is "common" to both parties, it's fair to say that understanding now exists. Perhaps not acceptance, but at least understanding.

Communication, like motivation, has been defined or described in a multitude of ways. For example:

o Communication is a process by which all human interaction takes place.
o Communication is effective only when there is a meeting of minds, not merely an exchange of words.
o Communication in an organization may be downward, upward, or lateral—but no matter what level or channel, it is always a personal process.
o Communication is the establishment of mutual meaning that integrates people to produce the desired human interaction.

Suffice it to say that most organizations are not integrated, simply because there's no mutual meaning or understanding. Despite meetings, flows of paper, and attempts to explain, what senior management regards as important loses much of its impact as the message moves down the line. The meaning is distorted, the understanding diluted by the time the word gets to the target audience.

It's just as bad with the upward flow. Messages important to the employee are interpreted by management as griping or only further examples of labor's demand for more while giving less.

If it's hard to communicate effectively in an organization where everyone has the same mother tongue, the problem is magnified a hundredfold when there are two or more very different languages and cultures gathered under the same corporate roof. Whether management skills and technologies are being transferred or simple instructions are being given to a different-nationality subordinate, the barriers to mutual understanding are formidable.

The Common Barriers

If communications are to be improved, the blocks and barriers to a free flow have to be isolated and consciously attacked. The principal causes of failure include, but aren't limited to, these:

LANGUAGE—THE MOST OBVIOUS

This is the most obvious barrier and brings up an equally obvious initial question: Why do companies send their representatives to a foreign country without even a smattering of the local language?

Of all of the qualifications the manager abroad needs to be successful, language training is often the most important. With the ability to communicate in the host country's tongue, adaptation to the culture is infinitely easier; the subtleties of word meanings are more easily grasped; and the manager can transmit his messages with greater clarity. The logic behind language training is obvious, but we still send people overseas who can't read a menu, buy groceries, or even give a taxi driver directions at the airport.

If a manager has had a few years of high school or college Spanish or French, he might scrape by in South America, in Latin America, or on the Continent. He *might,* that is. His beginner's proficiency, however, would be meaningless in a business conference where English was not spoken.

In the Middle East or the Orient, he'd be completely lost. English, French, and Spanish have no identifiable relationship to the languages there. Not even the symbols and letter combinations can be distinguished. In most of the Western languages, at least an occasional word in print can be picked out, but not in Japanese or Arabic.

Even the Arabic numbers are different from ours, despite the fact that we use the "Arabic numeral system." Originally the numbers were constructed similarly, but today only the 1 and 9 can be clearly identified by one who has no knowledge of the language. The number 5 is somewhat oval in shape, 7 is a V, and 0 resembles a small diamond:

• ١ ٢ ٣ ٤ ٥ ٦ ٧ ٨ ٩ ١•
O I 2 3 4 5 6 7 8 9 IO

The excuses for not insisting on language training aren't very original, but they've been heard time and time again:

"He doesn't need to know it. They all speak English there, anyway."

"There isn't time. We need him there now."

"It would take too long."

"It costs too much."

"It wouldn't be a good investment. We don't know how long he'll be there."

"Teach both him *and* his wife? What are we, subsidizing Berlitz?"

"He'll learn it over there."

"I can't learn foreign languages" (statement by the manager in question).

In retort, the people there may indeed all speak English, but if they do the fluency will range from passable to complete, depending on educational level. And even if fluency is great, blocks to understanding remain, as will be discussed shortly.

With regard to time and cost, those are specious arguments. Admittedly, complete proficiency in any language takes time, but that level of skill isn't the issue here. With the availability of language labs, night-school or community-sponsored courses, cassette tapes, and books that teach conversational skills, any manager, with a little effort, can master at least the fundamentals. Cost and time are weak excuses.

". . . We don't know how long he'll be there." This poor manager has two strikes against him from the start. If management doesn't know how long he'll be there, maybe he shouldn't be sent at all. Something else is wrong when the future is that clouded.

It's almost a sure bet that he *won't* learn it over there. Oh, he'll pick up a few basic words or phrases, but it's a rare manager who enrolls himself in a formal course or program to master the language. Some who have been in the same post for 20 years know little more than "Good morning," "Good night," and "Where's the coffee?" The intention to learn it over there may be entirely sincere, but the road to hell is paved with too many such intentions.

What if the manager himself says, "I can't learn foreign languages"? That simply isn't true. Some may find it harder than others, and some may need more time than others, but if the person is worth sending to a responsible foreign post, he has what it takes to develop reasonable language proficiency. It's one thing taking a French course in college because it is a requirement. The only objective there is to pass or get a good grade; the student may never go to Paris anyway. It's another matter when the manager *knows* he's going to be based in Paris and that he *has* to know French if he hopes to communicate at all. The motivations are entirely different when the need to learn is based on career factors rather than just a desire to get a passable grade in French 1.

A plea to the company: Require the manager to learn the language. It will help him in countless ways in every business dealing.

A plea to the manager: Whether you are required to or not, learn the language. Your entire tour will be far more profitable if you can communicate with acceptable fluency with your co-workers, representatives from other companies, the butcher, the taxi driver, the doctor. And you will be surprised how you rise in the esteem of the nationals when you converse in their tongue. A simpatico feeling, or commonality, develops that is difficult to achieve otherwise.

Let's say the language isn't learned but most of the people in the plant or office speak English. Does that remove the barriers and ensure clear communications? Not at all. If words referred only to *things,* the problem of understanding would be less. Words, however, also establish relations *between* things and affect how those relationships are interpreted.

A simple example: Even the British and the Americans don't speak the same language when it comes to certain interpretations or meanings. Take the word "compromise." To the Britisher, it means to work out a good solution to a problem. To an American, it is a less-than-satisfactory solution in which some points of importance have been lost. In the United States, "trolley" arouses images of old streetcars or San Francisco's Powell Street. The Britisher thinks of a restaurant serving cart. A "bonnet" covers the engine of a car in London, while an American visualizes a baby's hat or the Fifth Avenue Easter parade.

Words that pass between people can't be trusted to assure mutual understanding. The relationship between what is said and the image conjured up in the receiver's mind is a function of experience, culture, and, in a broad sense, education.

Another problem is that some English words simply cannot be translated into certain foreign languages. No counterpart word exists. The only way the translation can be made is from word to phrase, not word to word.

Arabic is one such language. Listen to a group of Arabs talking in their tongue. Suddenly you may hear "engineer," "generator," "brake assembly," or "data processing." Unable to find just the right combination of words in Arabic, they find it easier to use the English term. This fact is especially important in technical training or technical publications where, let's say, a Kuwaiti is struggling to draw some parallel between what he is reading or hearing and similar meanings in his own language.

Even if direct translation is possible, the exact interpretations can differ. As cited earlier, the word "tomorrow" is a typical example. In many parts of the world, "tomorrow" doesn't literally mean *tomorrow*. It's just some time in the future. The Spanish *mañana* or the Arabic *bukrah* can mean several days or weeks after today.

Alison Lanier, in her briefing "Your Manager Abroad: How Prepared? How Welcome?",[1] illustrates the varying interpretations of words with the story of a Chinese official who was being challenged by an irate American. "Last month," the American blustered, "you said, 'Now all paperwork is finished.' Suddenly you give me ten more forms to fill out in quadruplicate. What did you mean by saying 'Now all paperwork is finished?' That was not true and you knew it." His face was red and angry. The Chinese official bowed gently. "That was last month," he said with dignity. "For the now that was then, that was true. For the now that is now, it is not true." As Lanier says—"a truly Asian reply."

The barrier of language is obvious to everyone. Yet it still is often disregarded by managers in a foreign culture. They know *they* have communicated, perhaps in very simple words. They then assume that the message was received as transmitted and understood as intended. A very dangerous assumption, at best.

[1] New York: American Management Associations, 1975, p. 12.

There's one other aspect of language that should be mentioned, but from a different perspective. It's the matter of profanity.

Local nationals typically resent the American's free use of four-letter words, "God damns," and swearing in general. If you hear a local resorting to such profanities, you can be reasonably sure he was educated in the United States. He slips easily into the vernacular, apparently thinking it's smart and shows how Westernized he is. Otherwise, local people don't like it, and it only downgrades the American in their eyes.

There's no need to curse and fume all the time, if you have any vocabulary at all. An occasional "damn" or "hell" isn't too bad, but anything more is out of bounds in most overseas locations.

RESISTANCE TO CHANGE

Do people really resist change? Yes—and no. Resistance arises only when change presents a threat to an individual's security. The installation of a new method, a new system, a different process, or a reorganized work flow is almost certain to meet resistance, simply because old habits and comfortable ways have to be discarded. The "new" is potentially threatening and thus a source of insecurity.

But when there is no threat, change is actually welcomed. People like variety; they try to avoid boring, repetitive patterns of living, doing the same thing day in and day out. Look what happens when the new model cars hit the showrooms. People await the first unveiling with considerable eagerness. The same is true of clothes and the latest fall fashions. These obviously present no threat, and there is generally acceptance of the change instead of resistance. If workers fight new ways of doing things, it's because of the way in which the new methods were introduced. To overcome this block to communications, the effective manager will:

1. Outline the "new."
2. Explain why it is being introduced.
3. Describe the benefits of the new way (it's faster, easier, less complicated, more efficient, less costly, or whatever).
4. Outline the training (if any is necessary) that will be given to help the worker master the "new."
5. Solicit questions and discussion to be sure the reasons for the change are understood.
6. Ask for feedback from the employee so that the effectiveness of the "new," once installed, can be evaluated and deficiencies corrected.

7. Follow up to ensure worker understanding and competence in the new way.

This takes time, but it's a lot better than announcing a change in an impersonal bulletin. A one-way meeting where the manager stands up and says, "Now, fellas, this is how we're going to do things in the future . . ." isn't much more productive. Remove the *cause* of resistance at the very outset and you remove the resistance itself. Then the communication gets through.

WANDERING ATTENTION

Typical of meetings, lectures, or other face-to-face communications is wandering attention. We listen for a while and then become distracted by:

o *Boredom.* The subject is dull; it doesn't pertain to me; it's the same old thing, I've heard it a hundred time before; why doesn't he get to the point? What the other person is saying *might* be of interest, but we'll never know. We've been off in another world.

o *The I-can't-wait-to-talk syndrome.* The speaker makes a point with which we don't agree. It triggers a mental rebuttal and we begin planning a counterargument. All listening stops as attention is turned inward. We only wait impatiently for him to shut up so we can start talking.

In a meeting, someone makes a long-drawn-out proposal. The idea has merit, but we suddenly think of a potential problem in it or of a way to improve the proposal. As we mull over what we want to say, listening ceases until we can capture the floor.

o *Physical distractions.* These are the obvious causes of inattention. Examples are a window view, pictures on the wall, a clock, noise, poor ventilation, uncomfortable chairs, poor or unreadable visual aids in a meeting or training class, an open door with passersby or people in another office visible, interruptions, or a ringing telephone in a conference room.

There are enough barriers to communications without adding to the problem by failing to eliminate those that can be controlled. Of all the barriers, physical distractions are usually the easiest to overcome.

WISHFUL HEARING

This is a common block in any communication process but even more so in interlanguage communications. If the conversation is in

English and the local person is unable to translate the spoken word literally, he tends to hear what he wants or expects to hear. As a result, he nods his head as though comprehension were complete when he really hasn't understood at all.

A group of disgruntled employees attend a meeting called by their supervisor. They hear in the words spoken what they expect to hear—confirmation of management's general unfairness. They are seeking only substantiation of their negative feelings, so no matter what the intent of the message is, they interpret it to fit their own moods and attitudes.

The boss has a complaining subordinate in his office. The boss knows him to be a chronic griper, so regardless of how valid the specific complaint may be, the boss hears only what he expects to hear—just another meaningless grievance from a Theory X employee.

And then manager and worker alike wonder: "Why can't we get the message across?"

ASSUMPTIONS

Assuming, in part, means taking something for granted. We attend a meeting in which a new system or method is introduced. As the explanation progresses, we *assume* we understand—only to find out later that we didn't understand at all. We had made certain assumptions and then stopped listening.

By the same token, the speaker or writer may assume that he has made his point crystal clear and that complete comprehension is automatic. He too may be fooled.

An expatriate instructor was working for an airline in a developing country. One of his jobs was to train the cargo-handlers, most of whom were uneducated local employees with only a minimum ability to read. The task was primarily to teach the proper handling of shipments, whether inbound or outbound, and to ensure that delicate shipments were accorded the appropriate care.

Crates or boxes requiring special care were usually identified as "Fragile" and marked with a large arrow indicating "this side up." In inspecting the cargo building one day, the instructor noticed with alarm that every shipment with an arrow was upside down, with the arrow pointing to the floor. When he got the cargo-handlers together, he explained again, through gestures and simple English words, that the arrow meant "up," not "down." The workers disagreed. "No," they were saying, "arrow means down. Box should be put right here"—and they pointed to a specific spot on the floor.

This misunderstanding had to be corrected, so the instructor got a large piece of paper and drew a picture of a house. It was a plain square house and over it he sketched in the roof, which intentionally resembled the tip or point of an arrow. Then he roughed in a door, windows, and a couple of scraggly trees. When he had finished, he turned to the group and asked them to tell him what the picture was. Nodding, they identified it as a "house."

"Right," said the instructor. Then he turned the paper upside down and looked at the people as if to ask, "Is this okay?" Shaking their heads, they indicated no. "Right," said the instructor again. Placing the paper in an upright position, he followed the contour of the peaked roof with his hands, saying, "Roof looks like arrow. Roof up, arrow up. Arrow not down. Everything fall out."

That was the last time any shipments were inverted in the cargo building.

A Western manager may mistakenly assume that everybody knows an arrow means up, especially when "This side up" is imprinted on the carton. But the cargo-handlers were just as right in their own thinking that the arrow meant down—"Put this right here"— especially since they couldn't read.

Assumptions also include the fact that a meaning can be read into a statement that wasn't intended. A particular word or expression may trigger an emotional response that blocks all further communication. Listening stops as the receiver reacts to what he *thought* the communicator had said or meant.

Half the battle against erroneous assumptions is to speak with the listener in mind and write with the reader in mind. Avoid jargon, in-house slang, complicated sentences, and unfamiliar technical terms. And then follow up with questions to be sure the message was accurately received.

THINKING SPEED VERSUS SPEAKING SPEED

Most people think in phrases or in flashes of whole thoughts. When broken down into separate words, the speed of thinking is 400–500 words a minute. The average speaker, however, talks at a rate of 125–150 words a minute. Even when both individuals speak the same language, this difference may cause the listener to decide what the speaker is going to say before the actual words come out. Listening then stops and the woolgathering begins. Of course, what the speaker *actually* says may be a far cry from what the listener *thought* was going to be said, but meanwhile the thrust of the message is lost.

In interlanguage communications, a different problem arises. The local employee may have considerable fluency in English, but does he *think* in English? This question came up during a recent seminar in Kuwait. Approximately 24 managers were attending the seminar, with the majority living and working in Kuwait but coming originally from Egypt, Palestine, Lebanon, and Syria. While Arabic was of course their native tongue, all but one or two were proficient in English and entirely capable of expressing themselves. During a discussion on communications, one of the Arabs asked: "Just out of curiosity, how many of us actually think in English?" Two participants raised their hands. The other 22, as good as their English was, indicated that they still had to make mental translations before the message received could be understood.

The American abroad is certain to lose at least 90 percent of the national listeners if he talks at his normal rate of 125–150 words a minute. He must learn to slow down to perhaps 75 or 80 words (at least until he has determined the language capabilities of the nationals). He must learn to speak succinctly and clearly, and to choose simple words as synonyms for more complicated terms or expressions.

"There's too much chaos around here," says the manager. His subordinates start looking under their chairs and sniffing the air. "Chaos" might be the exact word to describe the situation, but it means nothing to the average local national. Find a more common word that describes chaos, such as "noise," "confusion," or "disorder." Otherwise, the local employees will be struggling to make sense out of one term while the American barrels on. Communication is obviously lost.

MISTRUST

When one party mistrusts the other, communication channels are almost always blocked. Written words or spoken comments are viewed with suspicion. The reader/listener looks for clues that will support his mistrust. He interprets the communication in ways that may not have been intended but yet substantiate his feelings.

Mistrust is a common barrier. Anti-company unions sneer at and openly reject the most sincere management communiqué; management tosses off legitimate union requests as merely another symptom of the workers' "gimme" psychology; international peace is continually at stake because treaties and agreements are viewed as self-serving instruments, valid only until it is in one party's interest to break them. Mistrust is at the root, whether it's person-to-person, group-to-group, or nation-to-nation communication.

From a business point of view, eradication or prevention of mistrust is essential to a healthy communications climate. So long as mistrust prevails, even the most meaningful message will be twisted and distorted by the receiver to justify his own conclusions, be they about his boss, his peers, management, or the company as a whole.

EVALUATION

Evaluation is somewhat similar to wishful hearing and assumptions. A remark is made, and the listener concludes that the speaker was right or wrong. In either case, listening stops. If the listener agrees with what was said and has been of the same opinion, he sits back and reflects, "That's what I've always said" or "He's pretty smart—he agrees with me."

Conversely, if there is disagreement, the listener hears nothing more as he mentally prepares his arguments and rebuttal. The speaker *might* have something further to say that would cause the listener to change his mind or see things in a different light. But the evaluating listener will never know. His ears are closed.

SEMANTICS

The various meanings of words erect communication barriers everywhere. But the problem is even more acute when different mother tongues are involved and translation is required. The word "face," for example, has something close to 50 different meanings in English: the front of the head, disguise, presence, dignity, the front of something, an exposed surface of rock, an inscribed or marked side, the side of a building, to confront impudently, to make the surface of something flat or smooth, and so on.

Or take the words "rough," "value," "machine," "sink," "quarter," and "model." These are simple, common English words, and yet each has several meanings. When it's left up to the local employee to decide which interpretation the manager had in mind, the whole communication effort may be thrown off base. ("Off base"—there's another descriptive term Americans use, but how many non-Americans understand it? Baseball is hardly the favorite sport overseas, Japan excepted.)

A U.S. instructor was conducting a management training program in London. As part of his introduction, he said that one of the objectives of the program was "to help change the culture in the organization," meaning to help the managers create a more healthy working climate. On hearing the words, one Englishman became red in the face and exploded, "What do you mean, 'change the culture'? You mean from our culture to yours?"

In his mistrust of any American, he had heard "culture," misinterpreted its use, made some assumptions, and stopped listening. Many barriers appeared all at once, with a semantic difference as the trigger. Fortunately, his emotions had caused him to speak up, which then gave the instructor the opportunity to explain that he had been referring only to a change in work atmosphere.

Was the misunderstanding the fault of the listener? No, but it temporarily blocked communications. Was the instructor to blame? Yes. He assumed that his audience would interpret the term "culture" in the same way he had intended it. He was wrong—and this was an English-to-English dialogue. The outspokenness of one listener, however, permitted an explanation, and the program took on a new "culture" that allowed it to proceed without incident.

THE SILENT LANGUAGE

Spoken words are only noise, whereas the silent language of movements, gestures, and facial expressions is experienced visually. What is seen may communicate far more emphatically than what is heard. The silent language often tells a story that words don't convey. Boredom, relief, happiness, enthusiasm, irritation, approval, anxiety, fear—all can become most apparent by the slightest motion or expression.

Typical examples of the silent language are a nod, a smile, a frown, a furrowed brow, a raised eyebrow, shrugging the shoulders, crossed arms, tapping a pencil, leaning back in a chair, gazing out the window while in conversation, shuffling through desk drawers while "listening," and doodling. Each of these communicates a message; each is a symbol of a feeling or emotion that can either advance or block the communication process.

Also, before he ventures into the foreign scene, the U.S. manager should know what gestures or actions are culturally acceptable or objectionable in the society. Putting your feet in a position with the sole of the shoe toward an Arab is an insult; our finger symbol for "Okay" has a vulgar connotation to him. Throughout the world, there are body motions that have particular local meanings—some good, others bad. The American needs to be aware of what these are before he unwittingly creates erroneous impressions.

Related to the silent language is the instinct of space, or territoriality. All living things preserve for themselves a certain spatial separation. Alligators, for example, maintain a "flight" distance of about seven feet, hawks about 75 feet. Man's territoriality, often called his "intrusion distance," varies from one part of the world to another.

North Americans and northern Europeans normally insist on approximately a three-foot separation from other people in their everyday relations. Latin Americans and Asians tend to move closer together until they seem to be talking almost nose to nose. They may also mingle closely in the marketplace, crowd onto already-overloaded buses, or jam around an airline ticket counter. Pushing, shoving, and other types of physical contact are considered perfectly normal.

This behavior is neither discourteous nor disrespectful of others, which is what Americans often think at first. It's simply indicative of the small intrusion distance compared to that of the West. However, an American or a northern European reacts with discomfort as someone, during normal conversation, comes closer and closer to him. His territoriality is being violated and he edges backward until the "proper" separation is reestablished. This is not discourtesy either. The person is simply seeking to protect his accustomed "living room."

Recommended reading in this sensitive area is Edward T. Hall's *The Silent Language.*[2] Hall also wrote an article called "The Silent Language in Overseas Business"[3] in which he analyzed the languages of time, space, things, friendship, and agreements. He concluded with a case study of an American executive who failed to sell a multimillion-dollar communications network project to a Latin American republic simply because he didn't understand the silent language in business abroad. A recognized expert in the field, Hall makes very clear the importance to the American of the silent language and its effect on how business is done in a foreign culture.

FILTERS

A message communicated from speaker to receiver goes through four steps and two filters, as shown in Figure 3. Most messages have two parts: content-idea and emotion-idea. When interlaced with symbols, semantics, assumptions, and the rest, what the receiver *thought* he heard in the decoding process may have been affected by the emotions he *thought* he detected. The filtered message can thus be a far cry from what the speaker *thought* he sent. It's a long way from (1) to (4).

DILUTION/DISTORTION

Messages, especially those issued orally, have marvelous ways of becoming twisted and distorted as they move down the line. Key points are lost, new interpretations are added, and if five levels are in-

[2] New York: Doubleday & Company, 1959.
[3] *Harvard Business Review*, May–June 1960.

FIGURE 3. The filtering process in communication.

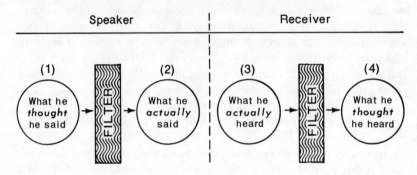

volved in the transmission, the fifth level gets only 10–15 percent of the original communication.

Try this sometime to test the loss ratio of a verbal message: Ask for five volunteers from a group. Send four of the volunteers out of the room. Then assume the role of president of a company and read a prepared message to the one remaining volunteer, who is your "vice president." The message can be anything you want, but there should be some positives as well as negatives in it. Here is one that the author has often used:

> (Name)____, I'd like to talk to you about your department. I had a call yesterday from Bob Howard of National Products and he had a few comments about our business with him. First, he wanted to compliment us on the way your people helped him with that emergency order he had. From what he said, we did a great job and got the shipment out on time. The only trouble was that the quantity was wrong. Two crates were missing, and yet our waybill showed the full order. He said this wasn't the first time this had happened, and he was pretty upset about the shortage.
>
> Now I don't know if Production just unproduced, the shipping department lost the crates, or whether somebody stole them, but we've got to stop messing up orders like this. I'd like you to pass this message down to the people on the line and tell them three things: One, National Products and I appreciate the extra work they went to to fill the emergency order; two, that two crates were missing because of carelessness somewhere or outright theft; three, that accuracy and security must be increased as of right now. We can't afford to lose a good customer like National—which is what will happen if we don't shape up. I don't want to scare our people, but if this is happening with a top account like National, it must be happening to other customers as well.

Don't repeat any part of the message, and allow no questions from the "vice president." Now call in one of the volunteers. He is the general manager of production, reporting to the vice president. From memory, the vice president relays your message to the general manager. Again allowing no questions, call in the next volunteer, the production superintendent. The general manager then relays the vice president's message as he remembers it.

Continue this process down through the next level, which might be the production and shipping supervisor, to the final level of production and shipping foreman. The foreman is then asked to repeat the message *he* received to the remainder of the group members, who are the "employees."

What the employees hear is, without exception, not more than 5 percent of the original story as told to the vice president. In one case, all the foreman could say to his employees was: "Where the hell are the two crates?" That was the sum total of his message. In another, a ship captain somehow got into the story, and the foreman's sole comment was that the captain had been lost overboard.

Never has the president's compliment about the good job that was done been passed on to the employees. The positive is always lost, while the negative remains. Figure 4 shows the approximate percentage of loss that occurs on a level-by-level basis as a verbal message originated by the president moves down the line to the employees.

Of course, this is merely an adaptation of the old parlor game of "gossip" and isn't really true to life because nothing is in writing and no questions are allowed at any time. Even so, it demonstrates the fallacy of memory as well as the distortion and dilution that take

FIGURE 4. Loss of message content in dilution/distortion test.

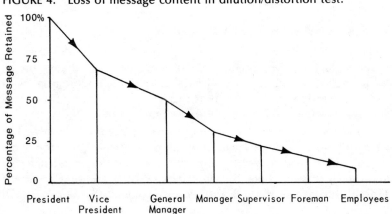

place as a message goes down the line. And the test represents only a slight exaggeration of what studies in business have factually revealed.

These, then, are some of the common barriers to effective communications: language, resistance to change, wandering attention, wishful hearing, assumptions, thinking versus speaking speeds, mistrust, evaluation, semantics, the silent language, and dilution/distortion. Overcoming them, or at least partially overcoming them, is the theme of the next section.

Some Basic Rules for Good Communications Abroad

LEARN THE NATIVE LANGUAGE

This has been stressed already. However, in the unlikely event that conditions make this impossible, at least the basic words and terms used in the shop or office can be mastered. If a technical expression can't be translated because it's untranslatable, learn the words the local employees use for it, and then use those words in future conversations.

The exhortation to learn the language doesn't mean that the manager is expected to be so conversationally fluent that English is discarded entirely. If the firm is American-owned and -managed, the locals in management positions will undoubtedly have reasonable English capabilities. However, the American who knows the language is that much further ahead, and he'll be infinitely more comfortable in his associations with local national executives from other companies and with people he meets socially.

TALK SLOWLY AND SIMPLIFY WORDS

These points have also been stressed, but are mentioned again for reemphasis. Cut your speaking speed almost in half and get in the habit of using a grammar school vocabulary in communications with most local nationals. Simple words that seem elementary to the manager may be just right for the other party.

It's also helpful to say something one way and then another. The repetition gives the national more time to think, and the same thought expressed somewhat differently increases his opportunity to find the right translation. Remember that all but the most proficient in English continue to think in their own tongue.

ASK FOR FEEDBACK

Regardless of the local's English skills, the manager should always ask for regular feedback to be sure his message is getting across. He can't depend on nods or yeses as indicators of comprehension. They often mean nothing. Out of pride or self-esteem, the local may not want to admit that he hasn't understood. He doesn't want to look stupid, so unless there is a strong relationship of trust between the two, he'll give every appearance of understanding. Only later will the manager discover that there had been no communication at all.

How to ask for feedback? First, *don't* say: "Do you understand?" This is almost certain to elicit a nod or a "yes." Not many locals (or Americans, for that matter) will respond to the boss with: "I'm completely lost. I didn't understand anything you said." Try some of these approaches instead:

- "I may not have made everything clear, so would you repeat the instructions as you understand them?"
- "Outline for me what we're going to do differently from here on."
- "Explain the method as though you were teaching me."
- "What problems do you see if we do things the way I've suggested?"
- "Now tell me what you're going to do."
- "Under what conditions would you do (this or that)?"
- "Review for me the action we've agreed on."
- "If you faced the same problem in the future, how do you think you would handle it after our talk today?"
- "Why did I say that this technique might be better?"
- "Now that we've talked about it, what were the reasons the method you were using wasn't quite as good?"
- "Tell me what you would do in (this or that) situation."

Above all, avoid yes-or-no questions. "Do you have any questions?" isn't any better than "Do you understand?" Meaningful feedback will result only from effective probing and questioning. Feedback is also a measure of how well the *manager* is getting his messages across. When a message isn't received accurately, it's possible the sender garbled the transmission. To paraphrase an old adage ("If the student hasn't learned, the teacher hasn't taught"), it might be that: "If the listener hasn't received, the sender hasn't sent."

SIMPLIFY SENTENCE STRUCTURE

In both oral and written instructions, keep your sentences short and uncluttered. Long, strung-out combinations of phrases and clauses only confuse. The best advice is to follow the Navy's admonition of KISS—Keep It Simple, Stupid.

USE VISUAL AIDS WHEN POSSIBLE

In any training situation, visual aids are essential. The picture is still worth a thousand words—or more, when there are language barriers to cross. Flip charts, flannel boards, and blackboards are relatively inexpensive but not always available locally. If reasonable carpentry skills exist in the area, or if the company has a carpenter shop, mockups can be constructed. Be certain, however, that the plans and dimensions are carefully delineated. Projection equipment of course costs money. If you use films, filmstrips, or slides, preview them thoroughly first to be sure the narrative is simple and clear and the visual aid is not too complex for the intended audience.

When the English skills of the audience are very limited, one technique that works is to buy a film that carries the visual message you want and have the narration translated into the local language on tape. Then turn the projector volume off and run the tape in conjunction with the film. If the tape and film have been properly synchronized, this system works well and is not difficult to produce. Just be sure that the translation is accurate and tells the story as it should be told.

In one-on-one meetings with a subordinate, try to use a pad to sketch out what is wanted. No matter how rough, drawings, schematics, layouts, floor plans, system flows, and the like help cement the message you are conveying.

OVERTEACH, OVEREXPLAIN

In communicating with and training nationals, it is generally advisable to do more teaching or explaining than would otherwise be necessary. Say something one way, then another, and then even another. It may seem that you're belaboring the point, but that is rarely the case. When the language barrier exists, repetition is essential. If instructions are then followed with well-chosen questions, the manager will know whether his message has been accurately received. Keep in mind that the local may be reluctant to admit that he hasn't understood. It's the manager's job to *know* that the subordinate *knows,* whether in the classroom or across the desk. Overexplaining and asking questions are the only ways to ensure understanding.

TRANSLATE WRITTEN MATERIALS

Bulletins, instructions, policy statements, and similar management communiqués should always be translated into the local language. This seems obvious but isn't always done, perhaps because of the time required or the cost involved. Both are sound investments, however, with the benefits far outweighing the costs in terms of communication clarity.

The only caution: Be sure the translator is qualified to do the particular job. Some translators speak fluent English but do not have sufficient expertise to accurately translate a technical document (see later discussion). After the translation has been made, someone should retranslate it into English for the manager, so he can be sure his message was transmitted as he sent it.

SPEAK AND WRITE IN THE EMPLOYEE'S "LANGUAGE"

"Language," as used here, doesn't mean Spanish, Japanese, or Arabic. Instead, it refers to what the employee listens for when management speaks.

Everyone recognizes that it's the boss's job to communicate to his subordinates in order to get the job done and achieve objectives. Messages are usually designed to elicit some sort of employee response in terms of doing more of something, doing less of something, or doing something differently. Occasionally they are merely for information, but these are comparatively infrequent. The desired result is usually action in some form.

Two languages, however, are involved in this process. One is management's, as it speaks in the language of *production;* the other is the employee's, as he listens in his language of *motivation.* In a lecture, William Oncken illustrated the difference between the two this way:

Management speaks in the *language of production* about:	BUT	People listen in the *language of motivation* for:
Planning		Opportunity
Organizing		Recognition
Directing		Belonging
Coordinating		Security (emotional
Controlling		and economic)

Management's job is to translate its production language into that of the people—to talk about planning, organizing, and the rest in ways that make it easy for the employees to find opportunity, recognition, or other benefits by doing what they are being asked.

Management is typically businesslike, production-oriented, and efficiency-centered. It also communicates that way. The subordinate receiver hears all the words but listens in a different language. He's trying to find in management's dictates the things that are important to *him*. When his search is successful, his response to the communication is usually positive. When it is unsuccessful, the most that can be expected is perfunctory obedience.

A not-uncommon type of message from above:

Effective immediately, all personnel will comply with heretofore published safety and on-job behavior policies. Violators will henceforth be summarily punished.

Signed: Your Boss

If all else has failed in the past, perhaps this is the only measure left that will produce the desired results. If so, fine. Otherwise, this threatening dictate offers little opportunity, recognition, belonging, or emotional security. Hence it provides little motivation—except to retain economic security until a more rewarding job can be found.

Management's language is typically cold, abrupt, and demanding rather than soliciting compliance. Yet managers will get much better results if they "translate" their messages in advance, talking and writing in ways that make it easy for people to find motivation in what they are being asked to do.

Why not make it easy for employees to *want* to respond as management has requested? This doesn't mean mollycoddling them or being wishy-washy. It just means taking a little more time to phrase a directive so it will appeal to the needs of employees. Their reactions may be both surprising and gratifying.

Working with Translators

There are three kinds of translations:

1. The literal, word-for-word translation, which is always distorted except when the two languages are very similar in structure and vocabulary.

2. The formally correct type, in which certain conventions to idiomatic expressions are respected.
3. The psychological type, in which the words produce approximately the same effects on the reader that the sender had in mind. This type usually requires free rendering, frequent explanations, and many circuitous routes to get the point across.

The last is the most common translating technique, as it almost has to be. When retranslated to the sender, the message may sound ungrammatical or even distorted. But if the translator has done the job well, the national will have understood, despite the difference in wording.

Interpreters or translators can be extremely helpful to the U.S. manager, whether they are professionals in the field or qualified English-speaking locals on his staff. The professional is usually scholarly and well-educated compared to others in the society. With his education, he's often critical of his country and its backwardness. However, should the American do more than merely agree with the criticism, the professional can become angry and defensive. In other words, "It's okay for me to say these things, but not you." If the American isn't careful, an interpersonal barrier could develop that would affect the usefulness of the translator. He might even undermine the manager by intentionally making minor translation errors or omissions. This has happened more than once.

If the manager decides to employ a nonprofessional, he should be very certain of the person's English ability before entrusting a translation to him. Many plans and directives have been seriously distorted because the translator *thought* he understood the English and the manager *thought* the translation was accurate. The American simply can't take anything for granted.

In one case, a local-language newspaper wanted a story on a particular program that was being introduced in a company. The reporter spoke no English, so the article was drafted in English and then turned over to a highly educated local national who was a graduate of a U.S. university. His language skills were impeccable, but he labored for hours in the effort to translate a 200–300 word draft. When he was finished, a third party who had equal fluency read the article back in English. He had had no part in the original effort, so the story was new to him. The retranslation was so full of distortions and misinterpretations—all unintentional—that the project had to be started over again, this time with the help of a professional.

Translators are invaluable to the American. He must, however, use them wisely and double-check their work. To assume that all has gone well can be very dangerous.

Conclusion

It's true that "nothing happens until somebody sells something." But it's also accurate to say: "nothing happens until somebody *buys* something." There have to be both a seller and a buyer for a transaction to be complete. The same principle applies in communications. The sender may send for all he's worth, but nothing happens until the receiver receives and then responds according to the intent of the message. At this point, the chain of communication is complete.

William Oncken defines communications as "the chain of understanding that integrates an organization from top to bottom, bottom to top, and from side to side." Inability to forge that chain is one of the biggest blocks in a foreign assignment. When the message doesn't get through to the local employees, they can't and don't perform as expected. The American, watching all the fumbling and foul-ups, becomes frustrated and autocratic, and the whole organization process begins to crumble.

It's a challenge to the U.S. manager to understand and to be understood, but it's a challenge he must meet if his tenure abroad is to be successful. Effective communication is obviously not the whole secret of success abroad. All else being equal, however, it is the foundation on which the "chain of understanding" is fashioned. Without it, little of significance is likely to be accomplished.

8

Developing Policies
Acceptable to the
Nationals

Abroad as at home, poor supervision and inappropriate policies produce negative responses. Labor strife isn't caused by people who are inherently disruptive and destructive; it comes from the way people are managed. Anti-company behavior is only the physical manifestation of employee dissatisfaction with things as they are.

Some Reasons for Anti-Company Behavior

Many reasons for anti-company behavior by local employees have already been discussed: poor supervision, cultural ignorance on the part of the U.S. manager, inability to communicate, intolerance, and so on. A few others, however, deserve mention.

LOW OPINION OF NATIONAL'S CAPABILITIES

Too many Americans view local people as incapable or untrainable. And rather than keeping their opinions to themselves, they may give themselves away through thoughtless comments or degrading observations.

A U.S. manager goes to another American's office. In the outer area, five or six local employees are working. Not seeing the American at his desk, the manager looks around, then comments to the local people: "Nobody here, I guess." Their reactions aren't hard to imagine.

Another manager, when asked to leave his office for a couple of hours, indicates he can't, with the observation that "I'm the only one here." His staff of local employees, overhearing the remark, are sure to be fired up with renewed vigor after that appraisal of their worth!

FAILURE TO PROVIDE TRAINING

Americans often don't take enough time to train the local employees. As a result, the locals, not being sure what is expected of them and fearful of making mistakes, do only what they're told—and perhaps don't do that very well.

The manager then becomes impatient and makes his impatience evident. The employees, becoming even more apprehensive, grow increasingly cautious in what they do; the manager gets tougher and tougher; and so it goes. Under such circumstances, the growth of anti-company feelings is not difficult to understand.

INEFFECTIVE COMPENSATION POLICIES

Often, pay and reward policies are badly designed. The belief that money is the primary concern of local employees may be prevalent. In a highly production-centered climate where the human factor is largely disregarded, this belief will be constantly reinforced. The people keep asking for higher wages, even though they may be incompetent in their present jobs, because they don't know any other way of expressing their dissatisfaction with the treatment they are receiving. When several wage increases fail to halt the demands for more and more, the real problem obviously lies elsewhere.

Firms new to the international scene occasionally make serious mistakes in establishing their wage and salary policies. Without adequate analysis of what other organizations in the area are paying for similar job responsibilities, management may set wages for the local employees either too high or too low. One company, several years ago, opened an operation in Greece. In its ignorance, it decided that the pay range for Job X should be identical to the range in the United States for the same job. The result was that the local employees in Job X were getting more money than the government ministers—and this was a skilled nonmanagement position. It wasn't long before the government took a hand in things and forced a restructuring of the whole compensation policy.

Mistakes of this magnitude aren't seen too often these days, but many discrepancies still exist. If the employees are overpaid, *they're* happy, but the business or government communities become upset. If the people are underpaid compared to employees in comparable industries, they're *unhappy*, but outsiders don't care—unless the government steps in because the pay scale is below the legal minimum.

An American company, especially if it's going international for the first time and is thus limited in foreign experience, should (1) find out the government standards, if any, affecting wages and salaries; and (2) conduct a survey of what private businesses are paying for the same general types of jobs. Don't compare titles—compare responsibilities. Titles mean little. A "superintendent" may be the top man in production in one company but a lower middle manager in another.

Another policy related to compensation is that affecting merit increases. This has already been discussed, but it warrants reemphasis. "Merit" raises should go to the few who have exceeded the established performance standards and deserve special recognition for their contributions. They should never be given to all employees once a year, even on a percentage basis, and referred to as "merit" increases. Their value as a self-motivator is destroyed when the below-average performer gets 2 percent, the average 5 percent, and the outstanding producer 10 percent.

A well-managed wage and salary program provides for cost-of-living increases, constant review of salary ranges to be sure they are equitable for the work being performed, and, perhaps, seniority increases that are granted just for being around another year. However, merit funds should be separate from all of these.

A SHORT TOUR OF DUTY

The policy affecting the duration of overseas tours can cause problems. Say a manager goes over on a two-year assignment. After that, he'll come home. Knowing that he just has two years to prove himself, he tends not to develop much interest in any aspects of the job other than day-to-day production. The long-range effects of his decisions and actions aren't paramount to him, nor are the feelings and future welfare of the local employees.

Therefore, his philosophy is: dive in, get the job done, impress the home office, and go back home to a promotion. Having such short-range objectives, the American concentrates on the work itself and avoids contact with the locals as much as possible. His attitudes are sensed by the locals, however, and do little to promote a pro-company spirit.

Few people want to go to some foreign assignment without any idea of the length of the tour. On the other hand, a flat "two-year contract" has its undesirable byproducts. Better than either extreme would be a two- or three-year firm assignment with a renewable "contract" for another two or three years, depending on the wishes of both the manager and the home office.

Many firms have this renewable or extension policy and find that it works well for all parties. The American is more careful in his long-range planning and the decisions he makes. He becomes more concerned about the training and development of his subordinates. His interest in the local growth of the enterprise is greater. He mixes more in the community life and becomes more attuned to the local culture. And his family has a sense of reasonable permanence, which encourages social involvement rather than an attitude of, "Why bother? I'll only be here a little while."

From the viewpoint of local employees, a reasonably long tenure means stability and continuity. Instead of a new manager darting in and out every two years, each bringing new ideas and different ways of doing things, a reassuring uniformity prevails. The locals know where they stand and, under the right manager, are being progressively developed for further responsibilities.

Tenure is also important to government officials and business executives in other firms with whom the manager might have to deal. The government doesn't have to reorient a new expatriate every couple of years, and external executives can anticipate future relations with the company with some measure of confidence. The longer (within reason) the right U.S. manager holds his office, the more everyone benefits. If he's not the right person to begin with, even one month is too long.

POLICIES THAT INFRINGE ON TRADITIONS

Any policy or practice that affects traditional local customs is sure to arouse anti-company reactions. Infringements on religious obligations or family responsibilities produce only rebellion. No policy should be installed until its potential effect on cultural or social traditions has been researched. Recall the U.S. manager, cited earlier, who demanded that his Moslem subordinates put in a full day's work during Ramadan despite the prevailing policy of shortening working hours during the holy month. You don't win many friends with decisons like that.

Hiring Third-Country Nationals

First, what is a "third-country national"? Definitions vary, but for our purposes here, he is this:

Individuals from Country A own or are responsible for managing a company in Country B. For whatever reason, employees are hired from Country C. These are the third-country nationals. Because they are natives of neither Country A nor Country B, a potential for conflict exists.

The local nationals (the natives of Country B) may already hold anti-company attitudes because of their growing ambition. They often feel that the overseas managers are trying to protect their own jobs and are thus intentionally holding the nationals back. The larger the foreign staff, the more pronounced is this feeling. The nationals' concern is not without foundation. As one American observed during a meeting at which several local people were present, "Why should I develop a Saudi who would just take my job away?" And yet, parenthetically, that's exactly what he was there to do, only he didn't recognize his responsibility. He was not a developer but an operator—in every sense.

When a third-country national is hired, the feeling is only reinforced. Usually, the third-country employee is multilingual and possesses skills not yet developed by the locals. If he is of management caliber, he is then often placed in an intermediate position between the U.S. manager and the local workforce.

When this happens, the locals see him as another obstacle they must overcome if they are to advance. At the same time, the third-country employee knows that his own potential is limited, since he is working in an American-owned or -managed firm in a country that is not his own. If he develops the locals reporting to him, he places his own future in jeopardy.

So the impasse grows. The local is unhappy because he has two barriers to overcome—the third-country national and the U.S. manager—before he can advance. The third-country national, if he's a supervisor, sees his job threatened if he develops the local employees. The U.S. manager becomes frustrated when production standards, for which he is responsible, aren't met because of untrained subordinates. From all of this can come time-consuming grievances filed by the workers, inferior work, and a growing move toward unionization.

Two policies should prevail: (1) reduce the U.S. staff to the minimum as rapidly as possible, but not until the local nationals have been developed to take over; (2) employ third-country nationals only when absolutely essential, as for manual labor, secretarial skills, or specific technical or managerial requirements. Local employees should be trained to move up and occupy the jobs now held by foreigners. When this policy is practiced, many of the personnel and production problems that occupy so much of the manager's time will disappear.

Sharing Responsibility

Keep in mind that conditions for conflict are ever present in a U.S. company abroad. Both it and the manager are foreigners in the host country. Wrongs, or imagined wrongs, become intensified in the cross-cultural relationships. Unless great care is exercised, labor strife is a very real possibility.

One way to help reduce the potential for strife is to share some of the operating responsibilities with the local workforce and have a policy of open problem-solving. For example, an employee committee could be established to run the cafeteria, including the selection of the caterer and the monitoring of his service. If there is a social club, let the local people run it and take responsibility for its maintenance. Another group might be responsible for company housing and the enforcement of occupancy rules. A safety committee is another obvious possibility, as well as a committee designed to represent the workforce in personnel matters.

The point is to get the people involved as much as possible. The more they are a functioning part of the operation, the faster problems will surface and the more rapidly management will be able to act.

It doesn't take much to become anti-company when management is a faceless, intangible entity. Conversely, it's not hard to be pro-company in an environment that encourages direct contact between management and employees, the airing of problems, and an atmosphere of mutual respect. When subordinates know that they can communicate freely with management, conflict is much less likely.

Promoting Local Nationals

The importance of developing local employees has already been stressed, but the coin has another side to it. "When do I get promoted?" is a common question of the local. Certainly this is understandable. Exposure to the new industrialized life creates rising expectations, which in turn generate a desire for increased responsibility, greater prestige, and more material comforts.

Frequently, however, the local isn't fully aware of his present level of competence or how much he doesn't know. This is the fault of the manager, but that doesn't change the fact. Along with this lack of awareness, most local employees don't realize how much time would be required for them to master the new technologies or methodologies. The result may be an unrealistic demand for more money or for promotion.

Other things that contribute to the employee's lack of realism about himself include:

1. Some U.S. managers advance a local employee too rapidly, primarily to satisfy the latter's desires and to keep peace in the family—even though the person is not qualified for the higher position. The advancement is observed by the other employees, and unreasonable expectations are further fueled.

2. Pressure from a higher source, either internal or external, may be exerted. The word goes out to "take care of so-and-so." "So-and-so" may be completely unqualified, but the manager has little choice. Nepotism or the societal tradition of "watching out for our own" is in play, with ability secondary to familial protectionism. Meanwhile the rest of the people see what is happening, perhaps without appreciating the pressure being exerted on the manager, and they demand their cut of the pie.

3. In a rapidly expanding organization, jobs have to be filled. Because of the need to get "a body" into a particular position, a local may be promoted even though he's unprepared. The result is that unqualified people frequently occupy positions of authority. Most of the other locals will tend to overlook the individual's lack of qualifications and the fact that he will probably fail in his new job. All they know is that one or more of their peers got better jobs—"So why not me?"

4. The misuse of merit funds (we're back to that again) plays its role in the problem too. When merit money is dispersed across the board, the logic is this: "I got a merit increase. Therefore, I have been doing a good job. If I have been doing a good job, I should get promoted." The rationale makes sense, and the local employee can't really be blamed. The fault is either in the merit policy itself or in the way the manager administers the merit funds. In either case, corrective action should be taken—now.

5. A fifth contributor enters the picture when the locals are not trained and developed. Frustration sets in, and, not realizing how much they don't know, loyal employees may demand escape through advancement.

6. Tenure in a position is often equated with qualification for promotion. "I've been in this job for five years. Why haven't you promoted me?" In itself, tenure or seniority means little. Someone may have been in a job for five years, but that doesn't necessarily rep-

resent five years of experience. It could be one year of experience five times over. However, the claim that tenure should mean promotion is frequent, and needs to be brought into perspective by the manager.

Obviously local employees should be promoted—when they are qualified. Getting them qualified, however, is a long-term process requiring planning, training, and conscious development. It also demands honesty on the part of the U.S. manager. He has to evaluate the local's present performance objectively on the basis of predetermined standards. Next, he must determine what gaps have to be filled through development so that the local meets all the standards of the job today. Then he has to make an objective appraisal review of the employee's performance so that the latter knows without a doubt where he stands.

Finally, a "development" review should be held during which the manager and his subordinate agree on the following: (1) what the manager will do to help the subordinate became more proficient in his present job; (2) what the subordinate will do to develop himself in his present job; (3) what the manager will do to help develop the subordinate for a higher position; and (4) what the subordinate will do to develop himself for that higher position. Of course, if the subordinate isn't remotely qualified today for promotional consideration, Steps 3 and 4 are superfluous and not subjects for discussion.

A development policy of this nature removes the emotions and the guesswork from the "Why haven't I been promoted?" issue. It won't eliminate those forced promotions where a relative or a government authority lets it be known that: "My good friend So-and-so should really be in a much higher position than he is. You'll see what you can do, won't you?" Such pressure isn't easy to overcome, especially when it's a common cultural practice.

Barring this, a well-designed development program, marked by managerial honesty and candor, will go a long way toward helping the local employee become realistically objective about himself. He will know where he stands *now*, what is being done to train him *now*, where he might go in the future, and what will be done to prepare him for that future. That's about all anyone could ask.

The Dangers of Paternalism

Keep in mind what has been said about corporate paternalism. In some parts of the world, such as Japan, it's the normal relationship between employer and employee. Elsewhere, a certain degree of it is in line with local habits, and an American-owned or -managed company may have to be more generous than one owned by nationals. There are dangers, however, in going too far. Loyalty and performance can't be bought. People still like to do things on their own.

Keep Herzberg's Satisfiers healthy, but don't try to be Santa Claus. If the employees honestly want a swimming pool, build it for them. If they want a social club, help them organize one. Comply, if possible, with their voiced requests—and then shut up about it. Management shouldn't go around patting itself on the back saying, "Look what we've done for you. Now be grateful and go to work." The people probably won't be any more grateful, and they probably won't work any harder.

The amenities given must attempt to meet only real needs. Benefits that are dispensed gratuitously will perpetuate dependence on the one hand, and on the other will often be accepted with nonchalance or even criticism. The U.S. company may indeed have to offer more than a native firm if it's going to lure good people away from what might be a much more secure job. But going too far beyond what is habitual and customary in the host country is both unnecessary and counterproductive.

The only policy the U.S. firm should have is to be competitive while keeping the Satisfiers at a healthy level, Excessive generosity is neither respected nor rewarded. People just aren't made that way, as the United States has so sadly learned in the arena of international politics.

PART II

Selecting, Training, and Developing the Local National Manager

9

The Significance of Development

Note that the following chapters are addressed to the manager who has a dual role abroad: (1) to head up a function and assume responsibility for the production of a product or a service; and (2) to develop one or more local employees for advancement within the management ranks. Some techniques will be presented that have proved successful in the areas of selection, orientation, training, and development. At the same time, these chapters discuss certain issues or conditions the manager might encounter that could either simplify or complicate the selection-and-development process.

While Part II is primarily designed to help the U.S. manager, it is suggested that he train his local subordinates in the same techniques of selection, orientation, and the like. If the methods outlined produce results for the U.S. manager, they should be imparted to the local subordinate so that he will be just as adept in hiring and developing those who report to him.

The same is true of the principles of human relations, motivation, and communication that were discussed in Part I. What applies to the American applies equally to the local manager in the supervision of his own subordinates. That's how the links of continuity are forged. The U.S. manager sets the pace; the local person, if he sees the techniques are working, follows.

What Does "Development" Mean?

Basically, development is a planned and conscious program of training, assisting, coaching, and counseling that prepares the subordinate:

- ° To act independently.
- ° To act with understanding and intelligence.
- ° To perform his assigned duties and responsibilities at a level that meets at least the expected standards for the job.
- ° To advance, either vertically or diagonally, to a higher management position.

Development is thus considerably more than mere "training." Not that training isn't critical—it is, but it's only a step in the growth process. Training provides the technical and managerial knowledge required; it sharpens skills; it teaches the what, when, where, why, and how, and is thus essential to competence in any line of work.

Development, however, goes beyond this. Its purpose is to build on knowledge and broaden the subordinate's skills and abilities so that he can gradually assume increased responsibility—either in his present position or in a higher capacity.

Some typical actions that result in development are:

- ° Delegation.
- ° Granting of increased responsibility and commensurate authority.
- ° Vertical job-building.
- ° Job rotation.
- ° Having the subordinate function in an "acting" capacity.
- ° Involvement in higher-level activities, such as objective-setting, budget preparation, project development, and staff meetings.
- ° Committee or task-force assignments.
- ° Reading and self-study programs.
- ° Management development seminars and courses.
- ° Frequent and open manager-subordinate communications.
- ° Plant tours, visits to the home office or to other sites.

Unlike training, development is a long-range program. Transference of knowledge and hard facts can be accomplished relatively rapidly; so can the honing of the skills essential for performing a task. This is "training" in the accustomed sense. Development, however, implies the gradual growth of an individual through a variety of processes that expand his horizons and broaden his potential. We typically train a worker. The supervisor, however, is both trained and developed—not only in his present job but to prepare him for further advancement within management.

The Development Demands on the U.S. Manager

The job of an operator abroad is relatively simple: get the work out, finish the project, and go home. This requires high technical talent, some managerial skill, and a little human skill—enough to get the desired level of worker performance today. The future is unimportant. At a given point in time, the project will be completed, which is all that was contracted for.

It's a different set of demands, however, for the operator/developer. Yes, he has to get the work out, but at the same time he needs to groom one or more local nationals to replace him and continue to function at maximum efficiency after he is gone. To be successful at this grooming process, he must have considerable self-control. There will be times when he will be tempted to do—but must avoid doing—the following:

- Display anger over inferior performance by local people. ("Oh, come on now. I've told you a hundred times how to do that. Can't you remember *anything?*")
- Make derogatory remarks about local nationals that they may overhear or find out about. ("My God! These people are impossible.")
- Convey a feeling that local employees are slow, stupid, careless, or backward. (With a sigh: "Okay, I'll go over it one more time. Now try to learn it—if you can.")
- Delegate tasks and then recall the assignments without explanation because the local isn't producing fast enough, meeting the desired standard, or doing the job exactly as the manager would do it.

When a manager loses his self-control, he only shakes the local person's self-confidence and self-esteem. It is then quite natural for the employee to do only what he is told and to exercise every precaution in the process. He knows full well that the sword of scoldings and abusive recriminations is dangling perilously over his head. People don't learn in this type of atmosphere. Thinking ability dries up under stress and tension, with the trainee fearful of making a move on his own lest the chastisements flood forth again. Security becomes more important than learning or taking risks. Or, if security isn't important to the individual, he may simply quit.

Some overseas managers think they can head off these problems by delegating as little as possible. But if a manager, all by himself, could do everything required of the function he is supervising, his unit would be grossly overstaffed. Because of his human limitations, he has subordinates who are extensions of himself—subordinates who, under his leadership, collectively do what is beyond the physical capabilities of any one person. The manager, then, *must* rely on those who report to him if the full purpose of the organization is to be achieved.

This isn't easy, however, especially when the subordinate staff lacks the necessary experience or competence. The challenge to the manager, then, is that much greater. It means that he will have to arrange his priorities so production standards are maintained at the same time that development is pursued. Only by a division of efforts will a manager's staff grow in skills and abilities. Without that growth, the manager will find himself in a whirlwind of activities as he tries to do his own work and take up the slack created by incompetence below him. It's just about an impossible situation, with ultimate failure practically assured. Technical skills are a must for the operator. The operator/developer, however, has to have equal strength in technical, managerial, and human skills. This places demands on him that test his every professional talent.

Development—Not Just Something "Nice" to Do

Development of the local employee, especially if he's in the management ranks, is not just a nice gesture or something to do only when there is time. If a manager has that philosophy, there will never be enough time. Development is essential from three points of view:

Economically. Unless the company is overseas on a one-shot, in-and-out contract, it is very costly to maintain a full staff of Americans to manage an organization. Not only that, but the cost of shuttling managers and their families back and forth as one tour ends and another begins can become exorbitant.

Merely from a dollar-and-cents standpoint, few organizations can afford the luxury of an all-American, nonlocal staff of managers. But even if that were possible, there's another aspect to consider. Local firms, with which the American company might do business, usually prefer to deal with their own people. The commonalities of language and customs make communications both easier and more effective. Of course those firms are willing to transact business with an American, but in day-to-day intercompany relations, two people of the same nationality generally accomplish more in less time. Likes, in this case, tend to attract.

Organizationally. If the management ranks are composed chiefly or exclusively of local nationals, there is more of a oneness throughout the organization. Keep in mind that a local person working for an American company may be looked on as a bit of a traitor—especially if locally owned competing firms are in the marketplace. It's as though a Frenchman in Paris were employed by Pan American or TWA. The more Americans on the scene, the less the employee feels that it is "his" company.

When the firm is managed largely by his fellow countrymen, a different psychology emerges, and with it, a different set of loyalties. Further, having a primarily local management elevates the company in the business and social communities. The fact of foreign ownership is dimmed as recognition grows that the firm is really home-managed and dedicated to local needs.

Morally. If the foreign-owned firm has hired local nationals, is paying them, and is assuming responsibility for their economic as well as psychological well-being, it has an obligation to develop them. It has no moral right to keep them in organizational servitude—to teach them just enough to perform a series of tasks and then neglect their further growth. That is like cracking the door to better things but then chaining the door from the other side. Development is an obligation to the local employee, not a privilege bestowed on him when there's nothing else to do.

This is especially true if the company has been commissioned by the local government to perform a specific service for the country. For example, say American expertise is imported to establish or manage the country's national airline. The first thing the Americans should do, of course, is get the airline organized and operating. Once it is a going concern, with as many American or third-country flight and ground personnel as necessary, the next thrust should be the development of local people to man the aircraft, maintain them, and perform the myriad of technical and management responsibilities. Little by little, the Americans should phase themselves out and be replaced by qualified nationals. It may take years, but eventually the airline will be fully nationalized, with local people exercising control over who does what. The moral obligation will then be satisfied.

There's nothing worse than a staff of Americans hanging on to ensure job perpetuation when the nationals are ready and eager to take over. Too many Americans avoid subordinate development because "somebody will come along and take my job." The fear of a rising subordinate is one of the primary causes of development-avoidance, whether overseas or right here at home. By the same token, it's just as bad for the Americans to say about local people: "They can't learn." They will learn. It may take more time, but if there has been no learning, there has been no teaching.

Conclusion

From every viewpoint—economically, organizationally, morally—development is the only path if the company is anticipating a long-term tenure overseas. Don't worry too much about it if it's a one-shot, in-and-out contract. But in most other cases it is indispensable to the reputation of the organization.

Although nondevelopment is still much in evidence, it is self-defeating and usually stems from the U.S. manager's own insecurity. It's easier, in his opinion, to keep a tight rein on things and claim indispensability to the home office. "They're not ready to take over yet, but maybe in a couple of years. . . ." That way the job is assured as the subordinate staff turns over several times in frustration. With each resignation, the manager's "indispensability" increases. It's the easy way to create job security. It's the wrong way by any ethical standard.

Perhaps the importance of development has been belabored. If so, it's only because too little of it, on a planned and conscious basis, is taking place abroad. The reasons may be many, but certainly one of the most pronounced is the failure of the home office to define what it expects of the manager before he departs for the foreign post.

The operator role is normally assumed, with development given a low or nonexistent priority. Then if things aren't going well, the home office gets excited, demands better production, and puts the manager even more squarely in the operator's seat. When the pressure is on, it's natural to assume tighter control, become more deeply involved in the operation, and adopt the attitude that "the only way to get things done right is to do them myself." Development is most unimportant then.

Just possibly, however, if the subordinate staff had been better prepared, things wouldn't have begun to go badly in the first place. But the manager will never know. He is the product of the very die he has cast.

10

Beginning
at the Beginning –
Job Definition

In these chapters, the assumption is made that the manager is concerned with the selection, training, and development of national *management* employees. The job title is of no significance. It could be supervisor, chief (as chief chemist, chief engineer), foreman, superintendent, assistant superintendent, manager, or whatever. Regardless of title, the employee is in a position that the company identifies as "management."

To try to discuss the development of a worker and a manager at the same time would only confuse the issue. While some of the suggestions in Part II relate to both, it's not logical to mix the training of a laborer with the development of a manager. The objectives as well as the processes involved are entirely different.

Another assumption is in order: when the U.S. manager arrives on the scene, he either has no subordinate staff or has one that is inadequate in numbers to do the job. Because of the shortage, he will have to hire and train one or more supervisors to meet his head-count needs. Should a full staff be on hand, perhaps one inherited from his predecessor, his initial task is of course eased considerably. To cover the full range of required activities, however, it is assumed here that the manager is building an organization from the start and will *have* to be an operator/developer if he is to succeed in the foreign assignment.

The First Step: Defining the Job

It's surprising to discover how many managers can't answer with any degree of positiveness these questions about their jobs:

1. Do you know exactly what duties and responsibilities you are expected to fulfill, for which your boss holds you accountable?
2. Do you know, without question, what conditions will exist when each duty has been performed *well?*
3. Do you know exactly what authority has been delegated to you to carry out your duties and responsibilities?
4. Do you know what yardsticks or measurements your boss is using to evaluate your performance?

A positive answer to any one of these questions is rare—extremely rare. All of which is a serious indictment of the manager's boss, who hasn't defined what he expects of his subordinate or clarified the job. Except for a broad outline, the subordinate is in the dark. He's a victim of ignorance, through no fault of his own. And then the manager wonders when the boss says, "But you should have known!" or "That's your job—you handle it" or "Why didn't you check with me first?" Uncertainty, buck-passing, and overstepping of authority are the products of lack of job definition. Clarifying the jobs under him should be the first responsibility of the new U.S. manager in a foreign assignment.

Job definition means:

1. Determination of the basic duties and responsibilities to be carried out by the job incumbent.
2. Establishment of performance standards for each duty—standards that a well-trained, experienced incumbent should meet.
3. Clear-cut statements of delegation that delineate the authority granted to the incumbent to carry out his various duties and responsibilities.

When the job has been properly defined, the appropriate salary range and grade can then be determined.

Job definition eliminates the uncertainties common to so many employees—managers and workers alike. Whatever his position, the employee now has a clear idea of what the job entails. And, with the proper pay grade and scale established, he no longer wallows in ignorance about his relationship with his superior, his peers, and his own subordinates.

But—how is all of this accomplished? What tools or instruments can the manager use to ensure that jobs are clarified? The following three-step process of job definition has generally proved successful.

Step 1. The Job Description

This is the initial and essential first document. In broad terms, and on one or two sheets of paper, what are the basic responsibilities of the job? What authority for planning and decision-making is being assigned to the position? What are the required internal (in-company) and external (out-of-company) relations?

The typical job description establishes the parameters and is thus a fundamental document for purposes of job evaluation and wage and salary administration. Formats do vary, but the example in Figure 5 is representative of a typical job description. Rarely, however, is a job description sufficiently detailed to inform the job occupant of exactly what his manager expects of him. As Figure 5 shows, it should be a general, broad-brush summary designed primarily for job-evaluation purposes. It creates the framework but leaves out most of the pieces that make up the whole picture. The result is an instrument that is inadequate for communicating the details of the job. Furthermore, many employees have never even seen their job descriptions. What they know has been gleaned from conversations with the boss—and too often he can't specifically describe the details. He's never really thought about it to that extent.

Relying on the job description alone leaves many gaps. Ignorance is rife when it's the sole instrument for job definition. Nevertheless, development of the description is still the essential first step.

Step 2. The Job Performance Guide (JPG)

Working from the job description, the manager next prepares what is called the Job Performance Guide, or JPG. This fills in the pieces and provides details that are neither feasible nor practical to include in the job description.

THE STRUCTURE OF THE JPG

As illustrated in Figure 6, the JPG contains two columns: the one on the left outlines the various duties and responsibilities of the job, while the right column describes the conditions that will exist when each duty has been performed *well*—the standards of performance. Note that Figure 6 represents a partially completed version of a JPG.

In organizing the various duties and responsibilities, the manager must first settle on six to eight major areas of responsibility (MARs) or, as some term them, the key-result areas. These are the basic re-

(Text continues p. 158.)

FIGURE 5. Sample job description.

47231	**JOB DESCRIPTION** Management, Professional, and Office Positions	Grade 37

Job Title Head of Design and Drafting   Date _____

Unit or function ___ as assigned ___   Department ___ as assigned ___

Basic Function

Supervise the group which provides drafting and mechanical design services for the division. Prepare design layouts, make mechanical designs and coordinate drafting and design activity for various projects as required.

Scope

Responsibilities include providing any drafting or mechanical design service requested by the R&D group, the engineering department, or the manufacturing department of the division.

Work Performed	Percentage of Time
1. Perform all supervisory functions of the group including hiring, making recommendations of salary changes where appropriate, and taking disciplinary action when necessary.	(varies)
2. Assign drafting and design jobs to members of the group, balancing the factors of time availability, project priority, individual ability, and personnel training.	
3. Train the people assigned to the drafting group in all phases of their work. Continually strive to improve the technical competence of the individuals in the group.	
4. Search for ways to improve the quality of service provided and to reduce the cost of such service.	
5. Prepare the drafting group budgets for capital equipment expenditures and for operating expenses.	
6. Check all drawings produced by the drafting group for technical completeness accuracy.	
7. Prepare project/product design layouts.	
8. Select materials and components for product design.	
9. Use knowledge to coordinate the efforts of those working in the group to complete, on schedule, drawings which display a practical and workable solution to design problems.	

Incumbent's supervisor   Incumbent

_____   _____
Signature   Date   Signature   Date

FIGURE 6.   Sample Job Performance Guide.

Job title <u>Supervisor, Dept. 111, Sec. 3, Unit 2</u>

Reports to <u>Manager, Dept. 111, Sec. 3</u>

Brief job description:

(Summarized from the current job description.)

The following has been mutually discussed and agreed upon as descriptive of the duties and performance standards of the above position.

Incumbent's signature   Supervisor's signature

Date   Date

Duties/Responsibilities	Performance Standards *This duty has been performed well when:*
I. Common Major Areas	
A. *Financial Control* Control unit costs	Costs never exceed approved budget limitations (unless higher approval is granted). Cost reductions are effected wherever possible but with no loss of product/ service quality or quantity.
Control petty cash	All procedures are followed, and no shortage or overage ever occurs that cannot be explained and justified.
Prepare unit budgets	The budget reflects realistic needs, is mathematically accurate, can be justified without exception, and is submitted to the designated authority on or before the due date.

(Figure continues through p. 157.)

Duties/Responsibilities	Performance Standards *This duty has been performed well when:*
Approve and/or prepare expense reports	All reports are mathematically correct and reflect expenses as agreed upon (per diem or reasonable/actual). Reports are submitted to the appropriate higher authority no later than the date established by policy.
Protect negotiable instruments	All cash, checks, and other negotiable papers are accounted for with 100 percent accuracy and are securely safeguarded. No loss or misappropriation ever occurs. Bank deposits are made daily.
B. *Material and facilities control* Requisition materials and capital equipment	The need for materials and equipment has been analyzed, the most practical type of material or equipment has been researched, and essential requirements have been budgeted accordingly. Upon purchase approval, requisitions are initiated per policy and established lead times adhered to.
Ensure cleanliness and organization of work areas	Work areas are physically arranged and equipped to permit maximum employee efficiency. Cleanliness and organization are such that no complaints from any personnel are received relative to this aspect of housekeeping.
Ensure maintenance of the physical facility.	All equipment and utilities are in good repair, and breakdowns are immediately reported. Painting and structural repair needs are anticipated and budgeted.
C. *Subordinate relations* Interview and hire new personnel	At least 90 percent of the people hired meet all job-performance standards within the predetermined time required to master the job. No complaint from any candidate is received concerning the courtesy or professionalism of the interviewer.

Duties/Responsibilities	Performance Standards
	This duty has been performed well when:
Conduct a new-employee orientation program	A thorough orientation program is initiated the first day the employee reports for work and is continued until the employee is indoctrinated to his or her satisfaction. No employee terminates within the first 90 days because of inadequate orientation to the organization and the job.
Train subordinates	After the prescribed training program, no employee errors occur because of knowledge deficiencies or instructional inadequacies. Voluntary terminations within the first 90 days of employment because of training-program failures are zero.
Ensure proper day-to-day position coverage	The necessary staff members are scheduled to be on duty each day, and there are no instances of personnel shortages at any time because of faulty planning.
Control absenteeism and turnover	Absenteeism is no more than 2 percent a month, and voluntary turnover through termination does not exceed 10 percent per year.
Keep subordinates informed	All immediate subordinates are continually made aware of matters that concern them on the job by whatever means are most practical at the moment. Rumors are at an absolute minimum, and no questions are asked about matters that should already have been communicated by the supervisor.
Train and develop a replacement	At least one immediate subordinate has been trained and developed to assume the position to which he or she currently reports. The designated replacement has also been approved by the next higher authority.

Duties/Responsibilities	Performance Standards *This duty has been performed well when:*
Maintain a disciplined work group	All personnel know what is expected of them and conform to established rules and standards. Disciplinary action, when required, is administered fairly and in accordance with current rules and policies.
Handle complaints and grievances	Employee complaints are received and promptly acted on so as to minimize the person's dissatisfaction and the need to resort to the formal grievance procedure. When submitted, grievances are handled strictly according to policy.
Conduct performance appraisals	Quarterly and annual appraisals are conducted for each subordinate. The interview focuses on the subordinate's performance and leaves no doubt as to how well he or she has carried out the prescribed duties and met the established standards. No complaints are received by a higher authority concerning the quality of the interviews.
Grant merit increases	Merit increases are granted only to those subordinates who have continually exceeded their job-performance standards. Merit funds are never used to compensate for cost-of-living increases or to control salaries.
D. *Administration* Safeguard accountable forms, confidential files, records, and correspondence	There is no instance of loss, pilferage, or unauthorized access to confidential materials.
Maintain required forms, stationery, and office supplies	No instance of shortage occurs because of a faulty inventory system or failure to monitor current supplies.

Duties/Responsibilities	Performance Standards *This duty has been performed well when:*
Maintain departmental performance records and statistics	Records and statistics reflecting agreed-upon areas of performance are current and 100 percent accurate.
Submit operating reports	All required reports are prepared according to existing standards and are submitted to the appropriate authority on or before the due date.
Prepare and issue local policy or procedure bulletins, letters, reminders, and the like	Written instructions are clear and to the point, and include explanations as to *what* and *why*. Bulletins, etc., are kept to a minimum and relate to essential performance or operating matters that must be recorded in writing.
Write letters	All letters, either internal or external, are grammatically correct, accurate, and free of erasures or typographical errors. Correspondence received requiring a reply is either answered or acknowledged within a maximum of three days following receipt.
E. *Internal relations* (Responsibilities that relate to this position, such as coordinate with planning, consult with industrial relations, keep marketing informed of production delays, cooperate with public relations in plant tours and publicity, and so on.)	(Corresponding performance standards)
II. **Functional Major Areas** (Duties and responsibilities that relate specifically to *this* position)	(Corresponding performance standards)

sponsibilities for which the occupant of the job is being paid. For managerial positions, there are usually at least five common MARs:

o *Financial control.* Most managers have some responsibility for budget planning, preparation, and control. Many have certain operating or capital expenditure authority. They approve subordinate expense reports. They may have a petty cash fund or have to account for negotiable documents. It's a rare manager who has absolutely no type of financial responsibility.

o *Material and facilities control.* Again, most managers have some control over the type, quantity, and quality of the materials they use, the facilities in which they work, the maintenance of the facilities, and the equipment, furniture, and machines required in the operation. Requisitioning, purchasing, and maintaining the materials and facilities are all part of the job.

o *Subordinate relations.* Only the manager who has no one reporting to him is exempt from this MAR. All others have responsibility for hiring or screening job applicants, training subordinates, communicating with them, delegating authority, developing morale, coaching and counseling, conducting performance appraisals, discipline and taking disciplinary action, and so on. For practically every manager, this is a key MAR.

o *Administration.* Again, an almost universal MAR. Included here is the responsibility for records, files, correspondence, establishing departmental policies, typing, secretarial services, and the like.

o *Internal relations.* No manager exists in isolation. He has to work with other units within the organization that either affect his operation or he theirs. There must be coordination of efforts and compatibility of objectives, which means open channels of communication among all concerned parties. There should be a working-together climate where collaboration among units prevails and departmental chauvinism is at a minimum.

These are MARs common to most managerial positions. In addition, each manager will have his own *functional* MARs—those that relate peculiarly to his specific job title. Depending, of course, on the specific nature of the job, some typical MARs include customer satisfaction, safety and good housekeeping, market penetration, production, quality control, inventory control, purchasing, warehousing, sales, advertising, public relations, external relations, accounting, disbursements, accounts receivable, self-development.

In analyzing a given job, a manager should add the functional

MARs to the common ones. The typical position will end up with a total of perhaps eight or ten MARs.

Once the common and functional MARs have been determined, the manager decides what duties or responsibilities should be listed under each. These are brief statements in sentence form, such as "Control unit costs," "Prepare budgets," "Interview and hire new personnel," "Train subordinates," "Control absenteeism and turnover," "Provide adequate staffing," or "Conduct performance appraisals."

After stating the duty/responsibility, the manager next establishes the standard—the conditions that will exist when that duty has been performed well. A standard does not represent perfection. Instead, it is par for the course, a performance level that an experienced, well-trained employee should be able to attain.

A properly constructed standard meets six characteristics. It is:

Measurable.
Attainable.
Realistic.
Challenging.
Results-oriented.
Understandable—to those who need to understand it.

Additionally, the standard does not describe activities. If the duty is "Make sales calls," the standard should *not* be something like "Call on eight customers a day." That's an activity, not a *result* of the calls.

A better standard for the duty might be: "(This duty has been performed well when:) a sales revenue of at least $X is realized per month from established customers and a minimum of Y new customers are created." Whether one or twenty calls a day are made is unimportant. What counts are the results of the calls and the salesperson's effectiveness in marketing his or her product.

One other point: neither the duty nor the standard tells *how* something is to be done. The "how" is a function of training. To include it in an instrument of this nature would only duplicate manuals, procedure bulletins, and other instructional media. The JPG states only *what* will be done and *when* it will have been done well.

HOW THE JPG IS DEVELOPED

First: If the job is new *or* if no one is currently occupying the position, the JPG has to be written by the manager. Once the position is filled, he then discusses the duties/responsibilities and standards in detail with the incumbent, as well as what training the latter will be given so that he can meet the standards.

Second: If the job is currently filled by one or more subordinates, the manager meets with him or them. He begins by outlining the purpose of the JPG. Then he and the subordinate collectively develop the common and functional MARs, the duties and responsibilities under each MAR, and the performance standards for each duty or responsibility. The final product is then typed and each subordinate given a copy.

At this point, three of the four questions asked earlier can now be answered. The subordinate knows what his boss expects of him, when each duty will have been performed well, and what yardsticks his boss is using to evaluate his performance. The JPG does *not* spell out the authority delegated to him to carry out his various responsibilities, so one of the four questions still remains unanswered. That, however, will be clarified by another instrument to be outlined a little later.

If at all possible, the JPG should be developed with the participation of the person in the job. When it is the product of mutual agreement, there is commitment on the part of the subordinate to the duties and standards. A genuine desire to meet the standards is a natural outgrowth of this commitment. On the other hand, when standards are dictated, there is no involvement, hence no commitment.

The same thing happens when objectives are dictated to the subordinate. Under this pseudo management-by-objectives system, the boss tells his subordinate: "These are your objectives for the new year." "Baloney," says the subordinate to himself. "They're not my objectives. They're yours." And then managers wonder why MBO doesn't work the way it should or why imposed standards don't motivate their people to higher performance levels.

SOME USES OF THE JOB PERFORMANCE GUIDE

Screening Job Applicants

Once completed, the JPG is an excellent screening device for the hiring of new personnel. Many applicants apply for jobs they know nothing about. All they want is work, and they are willing to do "anything." If a copy of the JPG for the position under consideration can be given to the candidates and time allowed them to read it over, a good percentage will screen themselves out of contention. Once they see in writing the duties and standards, some will decide the job isn't right for them. Others may say just the opposite—the job is what they're looking for and they have a clear picture of what will be expected of them. They still may not be accepted, but they can at least come to the interviews as viable candidates.

The same applies when promoting from within. Employees often want promotions, so when, let's say, a supervisory position opens up, the bidders may be numerous. The only trouble is they know little about the job, and, especially in the developing countries, the primary interest is more money and increased prestige. If they can study the JPG, a fair percentage will return with a "Thanks, but no thanks." They have screened themselves out when the position details are laid out before them in black and white. Those who return for further consideration know what they're getting into if accepted and, again, are viable candidates.

Coaching, Guidance, and Training

Another advantage of the JPG is that it keeps the manager in touch with how the subordinate is doing, the progress he is making. Having specific statements of duties and standards, the manager knows what duties are being performed and whether the standards are being met. When deficiencies exist, he's in a position to provide the necessary coaching, guidance, or training.

Here the manager is not developing his people in a vacuum or on a hit-or-miss basis. He's not making subjective judgments of strengths and weaknesses but rather objective evaluations of how effectively his people are meeting concrete standards.

Self-Evaluation

In a similar vein, the subordinate knows how he stands in terms of the JPG. He knows whether he's fulfilling his various responsibilities and whether he is below, at, or above the standards. Through self-evaluation, he can, if so motivated, upgrade his own performance where improvement is necessary. He needs no one to remind him of where he is succeeding or failing. It's all there for him to see.

Performance Appraisals

The JPG is a vehicle that opens the door to more effective and objective performance appraisals. Instead of the archaic trait-rating system where the manager evaluates intangibles such as quality of work, loyalty, learning ability, courtesy, attitude, and other unmeasurable characteristics, he has an instrument that measures the individual against agreed-upon standards. The standards are being met or not met. It's that simple.

The actual interview (which should be conducted at least quarterly) now presents no unpleasant surprises for the subordinate. There are no arguments over subjective criticisms, such as: "Your attitude isn't good. You have to change your attitude." Instead, the interview becomes a discussion of what the subordinate *did,* not what he *is.* It focuses on performance, not personality. And needless to say, it's much less traumatic for both parties to discuss man against job than man against unmeasurable and often meaningless behavioral traits. The difference between the two approaches is dramatic.

Merit Reviews

If the company has a genuine merit program, the JPG is a material aid in deciding who gets how much. Figure 7 presents some examples, which are discussed here.

FIGURE 7. Examples of merit-increase decisions.

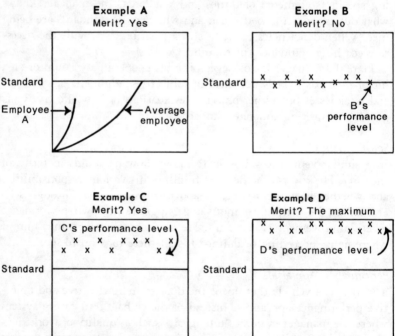

Example A. Experience has indicated that it takes the average new employee about one year to meet the various job-performance standards. Employee A enters the job and in six months has progressed considerably more rapidly than the average over the same period of time. He still is not at the established standards, but it's now merit-review time. Should he be given a merit increase? Yes, probably. He is exceeding the learning-curve standard, and a small, perhaps 3 or 4 percent, increase would reinforce his better-than-average performance. This situation is illustrated in Figure 7(A).

Example B. Employee B has been on the job for some time and is performing just at standard. See Figure 7(B). A merit raise? No. He's been paid all year to do his job well. Further recognition for doing that only encourages continuation of the same level of performance.

Example C. Employee C is above standard but not outstanding. See Figure 7(C). If the maximum allowable increase is 10 percent, perhaps one in the range of 5–7 percent is in order for this employee.

Example D. Employee D is outstanding in every respect. His performance meets the highest expectations. See Figure 7(D). His merit increase? The maximum company policy allows. If it's 10 percent, then he gets it.

Among its other advantages, the JPG takes the mystery out of appraisals and merit allocations. It isn't 100 percent objective, but it comes as close as possible.

THE JPG—FOR THE JOB, NOT THE INCUMBENT

Regardless of how the Job Performance Guide is developed—whether by the manager himself or in concert with his subordinates—it delineates what is required of the *job*. It should not be distorted to conform to the likes or dislikes, the skills or lack thereof, of those occupying the job. The incumbents must be trained, developed, and evaluated according to the needs of the job.

If this principle prevails, the JPG, once completed, remains unchanged *unless* the job duties change or experience indicates that the standards are too loose or too stringent. Then minor revisions are made. Otherwise, it is a static document. The incumbent meets the requirements of the job; the requirements aren't diluted to accommodate the capabilities of the incumbent.

But suppose the incumbent is capable of doing more than the job demands? Fine. That's the time to delegate new short- or long-term assignments. These take advantage of the person's talents and contribute to his or her development.

It should be understood, however, that the assignments can be recalled at any time because they were delegated to the individual and are not permanent elements of the job. Should they ever become permanent, the position would be subject to reevaluation and possible upgrading. It's bigger than it was and may be worth more money.

ADVANTAGES OF THE JOB PERFORMANCE GUIDE

Broad Applicability

The JPG works at almost every level. Perhaps the very top executives don't need it or would consider it too confining, but it has been utilized most successfully in all other organization echelons.

And, it's not just for management personnel. Those in the lower ranks have seen its benefits and have profited just from the dialogue with their supervisors. As one union janitor remarked, "This is the first time anyone ever talked to me about my job." The area for which he was responsible was never cleaner than after his JPG was developed.

In the developing countries, there is almost no limit to the guide's application. It won't mean anything to the illiterate laborer, but that group is about the only exception. If the guide is prepared in English and then translated into the local language for those whose English is marginal, it will be a useful instrument throughout the organization.

Long Life of Each JPG

Some managers, when introduced to the JPG, feel that it's too much paperwork. Admittedly, it *is* longer than the usual job description, which may be only one or two pages. The typical JPG for a supervisory position has perhaps seven or eight pages, with three to four pages for a nonmanagement job. But it should be kept in mind that once completed, most JPGs don't change unless the duties are changed or the standards need adjustment. When they're done, they're done, so the fear of excessive paperwork is unfounded.

Relatively Small Time Investment

Managers also occasionally object to the concept because of the concern that it would take too much time to develop guides for everyone below them. Two points: (1) A manager develops JPGs only for the positions reporting directly to him. His subordinates do the same for those reporting to them, and so on down the line. (2) Completing a JPG for a group of managers, all with the same basic responsibilities, requires about eight hours. Typing, editing, and a final review with the managers take another full day. So, in the equivalent of two working days, a very useful instrument is produced. That's not much of a time investment, considering the returns.

THE RELATIONSHIP BETWEEN JPGS AND MBO

While the concept of performance standards is hardly new, few managements have adopted anything similar to the suggested JPG. If they have, a form of management by objectives is often inserted, which means that the JPG has to be revised every year or whenever new objectives are added. This only complicates the system and produces unnecessary work. Consequently, in most organizations, either nothing exists to define jobs, except perhaps a vague position description, or there's an excessively bulky version of the JPG that is periodically altered to reflect new objectives and target dates.

If both JPGs and MBO are being used, how should they be harmonized? The JPG should be used to delineate the routine, everyday duties and responsibilities of the job. Objectives will come later; first the basic job must be performed and at the agreed-upon standard. Under MBO, the incumbent will usually have five to seven objectives on which he has agreed. These are *in addition to* his routine duties. The job, as set forth in the JPG, is the foundation; objectives are set to solve problems or find better, faster, easier, less costly, more productive ways of doing things. The two should never be combined in a single document, nor should more emphasis be placed on attainment of the objectives than on the job itself. When that happens, the manager knows where his reward lies and he quite logically focuses his efforts on the objectives while allowing his routine duties to go by the wayside. As things fall apart on the job, MBO gets the blame and is allowed to die an unmourned death.

This discussion has placed considerable emphasis on the Job Performance Guide because of its proven value as a working managerial tool. Its advantages are many, its shortcomings few. For the local national supervisor, who is likely to be new to the ways and demands of Western business practices, it can be a most important instrument in clarifying what is expected of him and what constitutes a job well done. It removes the guesswork while providing a tool that the subordinate can use to develop himself, and that the manager can use as he coaches and guides his subordinate to his full potential.

Step 3. The Job Delegation Guide (JDG)

Once the Job Performance Guide has been completed, the manager is better prepared to clarify the degrees of authority he wishes to dele-

FIGURE 8. Sample Job Delegation Guide.

Issued to: _____(name)_____

Job title: Supervisor, Dept. 111, Sec. 3, Unit 2

This guide is designed to clarify the authority delegated to you to carry out your assigned responsibilities. It is not intended to curb or restrain your judgment or initiative.

Your decisions are, of course, subject to established policy. If doubtful on any matter, follow normal reporting channels in seeking guidance or approval of your intended actions.

_____ _____
Incumbent's signature   Supervisor's signature

_____ _____
Date   Date

KEY

Column 1 You are fully responsible for these matters. Take final action without consulting me.

Column 2 You are free to take final action on these matters, but advise me of action taken.

Column 3 Keep me informed on these matters and seek my approval before taking action.

Column 4 Prepare for my approval (A) or signature (S).

Column A Authority granted to full-time incumbent.

Column B Authority granted to "acting" incumbent.

"C" Copy to manager.

Responsibilities	1		2		3		4	
	A	B	A	B	A	B	A	B
A. Financial control								
Approve operating expenses up to:								
$100	X							
$101-500			X					
$501-___					X			
Purchase capital equipment up to:								
$250	X							
$251-___					X			
Approve subordinates' expense reports	X							
B. Material and facilities control								
Keep all equipment in good repair	X							
Insure cleanliness and organization of work areas...................................	X							
Establish and monitor a preventive maintenance program.....................	X							
Authorize installation of fire prevention and detection devices, as needed......					X			

Responsibilities	1 A	1 B	2 A	2 B	3 A	3 B	4 A	4 B
Authorize correction of lighting, heating, or cooling problems	X							
Correct equipment and utilities breakdowns: Minor	X							
Major					X			
Authorize painting and structural repairs: Budgeted			X					
Not budgeted					X			
Establish safety and housekeeping policies			X					
C. Subordinate relations								
Hire new personnel: Non-management	X							
Management					X			
Schedule personnel for training	X							
Request development of training courses to meet specific needs — technical, clerical, supervisory, etc.			X					
Establish working schedules	X							
Institute and monitor personnel development programs			X					
Promote personnel: Nonmanagement within your unit	X							
Management within your unit					X			
Nonmanagement to management within your unit					X			
Schedule vacations	X							
Authorize vacation carryovers	X							
Authorize excused absences: 1-3 days	X							
4 days or more							XA	
Take disciplinary action Oral warning	X							
Written warning			XC					
Suspension without pay					X			
Demotion (in your unit)			XC					
Termination					X			
Prepare written performance appraisals							XA	
Conduct appraisal interviews			X					
Handle first-step complaints and grievances			X					
Grant merit increases							XS	
D. Administration								
Establish proper security measures	X							
Requisition office and stationery supplies	X							
Establish record-keeping and filing systems	X							
Write interoffice letters, memos to peers	X							
Write letters, memos to other managers			XC					
Write letters, memos to the general manager or above							XS	
Publish unit policy and procedure bulletins			XC					
Write out-of-company letters: Routine matters	X							
Nonroutine matters					X			

Responsibilities	1		2		3		4	
	A	B	A	B	A	B	A	B
E. Internal relations								
Contact any other department on:								
Routine matters............................	X							
Unusual situations or problems					X			
Emergency matters			X					
Coordinate activities with and assist other departments as requested in:								
Normal, routine matters	X							
Unusual or nonroutine matters.........					X			
Keep other departments advised of problems within your unit that would affect their production or performance..			X					
Discuss with other departments problems they are causing you in meeting your production or performance standards					X			
Resolve any conflict between your unit and other groups or departments..........			X					
F. Other								

gate to the subordinate so that he may carry out the various duties and responsibilities. This can be done, of course, without the benefit of a Job Performance Guide, but the task is more difficult and often less thorough.

As illustrated in Figure 8, the Job Delegation Guide (JDG) lists the responsibilities *for which authority is needed* on the left side of the page. On the right are four columns that indicate the amount of freedom, or authority, being granted.

Each column is divided into two subcolumns, identified as A and B. The first is used to establish the authority delegated to the full-time incumbent, while B specifies the authority granted to an acting or part-time replacement, as when the permanent occupant goes on vacation and someone sits in for him during his absence. An X or check mark in one of the four primary columns identifies the degree of authority the manager is delegating to the subordinate.

HOW THE JOB DELEGATION GUIDE IS PREPARED

The first step in preparing the JDG is for the manager and the individual subordinate to review together the latter's Job Performance Guide. In going over each duty, they discuss whether specific authority is required or whether the very statement of the duty/responsibility implies authority.

For example, consider the duty "Control unit costs." This probably involves certain expenditure authority, within the approved budget. How much can the subordinate spend for operating purposes or for capital equipment? At what point does unilateral action end and his superior's approval begin?

After discussion, the two might agree (unless corporate policy dictates otherwise) that the subordinate can spend up to $100 without any communication with his manager. An X then goes in Column 1. For expenditures of $101–500, he can spend the money but is to advise the manager of what he has done. An X is entered in Column 2. For anything over $500, he must talk with the manager first, and an X in Column 3 establishes that limitation.

Now take another duty: "Train subordinates." No delegated authority is needed here. The duty says it all, so no entry is made on the JDG. However, should the supervisor want to send one of his subordinates to an outside course, he has to be guided by his expense authority and how far he can go in committing funds for tuition fees, travel, and the like.

Each duty is reviewed in the same manner until the JDG is completed to the satisfaction of both the manager and his subordinate.

THE DELEGATION GUIDE: FOR THE INDIVIDUAL

The Job Performance Guide is for the *job*. The Job Delegation Guide is for the *occupant* of the job. There's logic to this for the simple reason that individual judgment, experience, and job tenure differ. To delegate the identical authority to all subordinates in a given job at the same time without regard for these variables might prove very costly.

To illustrate: Supervisor A has been in the job a long time. He's proved himself, and his manager has placed as many X's in Columns 1 and 2 as possible. But he leaves or is promoted and Supervisor B moves up the line to replace him. The manager would be foolish to grant B the same authority at the outset that he had given A. B is new, unproven, and inexperienced, so the manager would probably put most of the X's in Columns 3 and 2. As time goes on, however, and B masters the job, more and more X's would be placed in Columns 2 and 1—until, at some point, B had all the authority the manager could legally or safely delegate. Even then, B might never have as much as A had, or he might have more—depending on his proven track record.

The Job Is Now Defined

With a valid job description and complete Job Performance and Job Delegation Guides, job definition has become a fact. The mystery is removed. The uncertainty of "I *think* I'm responsible for that" or "I'm not sure whether I have the authority to do that" is dispelled. The incumbent now knows exactly what his duties are, where he stands in relation to the job, and what and where performance improvement is necessary. By the same token, so does the manager, who is thus better equipped to provide training or coaching that will ensure the subordinate's continuing development.

With job definition, both parties avoid dealing in generalities, operating under assumptions, and viewing the job from different, perhaps conflicting, points of view. In an overseas position, job definition is essential. The local supervisor *must* know what is expected of him and how he is progressing. He wants something like the JPG, which answers so many questions for him. He wants some sort of delegation guide, even though he may at first resist some levels of authority.

The manager, for his part, needs the JPG and JDG if he is to have any sort of organized development program. Combined, these make clear the local employee's deficiencies that have to be overcome and the strengths on which he should build. Otherwise, development occurs more by accident, if indeed there is any development at all.

Job definition—the first step for the U.S. manager. It may take a little time, but it is an essential investment that will pay rewarding dividends.

11

Recruiting and Hiring the Local Manager

Let's assume that when the manager arrives abroad, he finds, for whatever reason, that he has a supervisory position to fill. The position may be new or one that has existed but is now vacant. Let's further assume that both a job description and a Job Performance Guide have been completed. Now where does he turn to find the subordinate he wants?

Sources of Managerial Candidates

Basically, there are four sources: the present workforce, local and foreign university graduates, government agencies, and local businesses. Some previously filed application forms may be on hand, and there is the possibility of the casual drop-in who just happens to call the Employment Office to see if anything is available. These last two, however, aren't particularly prolific sources and shouldn't usually be relied on with much confidence.

THE PRESENT WORKFORCE

This is the first and most obvious place to look—if a workforce already exists. It's also the best source, if there has been any sort of ongoing development program. Someone should be ready to move up, either from the nonmanagement ranks, from a lower supervisory position, or from another department.

Should any such individuals be available, the manager would be foolish to look elsewhere. Hiring from the outside when the potential talent is there to be tapped is just as morale-destroying to local nationals as it is to us here at home. An outsider might have more of the needed technical skills, but that advantage can be short-lived in view of the negative spinoff from failure to promote from within.

There is an additional point to consider when evaluating the present workforce. Many developing countries insist that native-born employees be given preference, whenever possible, over employees of any other nationality for job opportunities. If a third-country national is promoted over a local national, the manager may be called on by a representative of a government agency or ministry and asked to justify his choice. If he cannot establish the clear superiority of one over the other, his decision stands a good chance of being reversed.

The U.S. manager has to remember that the social and economic welfare of its citizens are often far more important to the government than the efficiency or managerial competence of a business enterprise. This is why it's so difficult to fire or demote, and why local people are often put into positions they are not yet qualified to occupy.

LOCAL UNIVERSITY GRADUATES

This source has possibilities, but overoptimism about the recent graduate's immediate potential should be avoided.

University teaching in the developing countries is changing, but many of the traditional patterns of education remain. Students, for instance, have been taught to listen and memorize, with little encouragement of open discussion, argument, or debate. They have learned to be more conformists than individuals. Not that they don't want to speak up or disagree, but traditional ways of life—involving respect for authority and age—are still powerful influences. In Saudi Arabia, for example, Richard Nyrop and his co-authors describe the education process this way: "Instruction at all levels emphasizes rote learning and memorization of lectures and assigned reading. Students reportedly show little curiosity, initiative, or creative ability; libraries, for example, are said to be little used." [1]

The causes, Nyrop *et al.* conclude, are three: (1) traditional Islamic training; (2) the importance of written examinations prepared at the Ministry of Education and their determination of the student's progress and the teacher's evaluation; and (3) inadequately trained teachers (many from Egypt and Jordan). The typical graduate, straight from the halls of learning, may be more of a "yes man" than a creative, dynamic leader. He may have the potential to become such a leader, but that role is not always compatible with the education process he has undergone.

[1] Richard F. Nyrop *et al.*, *Area Handbook for Saudi Arabia* (American University, Foreign Area Studies, 1977), pp. 111–112.

GRADUATES OF U.S. OR U.K. UNIVERSITIES

Some foreign-owned or -managed companies have student programs whereby a qualified high school graduate is hired and then sent to the States or England for his college education. The company pays his expenses and tuition, and he is expected to return to a position in the organization for which his education qualifies him.

In other instances, the company, assisted by government funding, sponsors a local national as a "trainee" and sends him to a U.S. or U.K. university but does not consider him to be an "employee" in the literal sense. Once he graduates, he can shop for a job in the open market and is not indentured to the company that sponsored him.

Both systems exist, especially when a country is developing rapidly and the government wants as many locals as possible not only employed but in increasingly responsible positions of authority. It's a desire to nationalize and assure the economic welfare of the citizens.

Western-educated graduates should be a good source of management candidates, and in many cases they are. There's a problem, however. These students seldom attend the best colleges or universities. This is not because of financial limitations but rather because of their precollege educational level, with language ability another factor. Consequently, colleges little known even to Americans are often chosen. That in itself is no criticism, but the quality of the education is often subject to question.

And then there is this: pressure is often placed on the colleges, and thus on the faculty members, to pass Jose or Ahmed, regardless of grades or accomplishments. So Jose or Ahmed gets a C or 2.0, graduates with a bachelor's degree, and returns home "educated." He has a piece of paper; he's spent four years abroad, and that's about it.

As always, there are marked exceptions. Graduates of technical institutions, such as those specializing in petroleum, electronics, or the hard sciences, usually come back with excellent technical qualifications. Many develop an almost accent-free English fluency. Almost without exception, they return with a broad appreciation of Western life and an understanding of Western thinking. These are pluses the typical graduate offers.

The U.S. manager, however, shouldn't expect every returning graduate to be that Western in his thinking. He may appreciate us and understand us, but four years abroad don't necessarily change a lifetime of entrenched habits and mores. The author personally knows a number of graduates who speak excellent English, are intelligent, use the current jargon skillfully, and are Western in dress and actions, but still cling to their cultural traditions. They are highly sensitive; they resist added responsibility; they say "yes" when they should say "no"; they often ask what they should do before acting. Old ways are not easily discarded, and the Westernized veneer should be recognized for what it is—just a veneer.

All of which is entirely natural and understandable. Furthermore, the graduate is now back home. He has to work and live with his fellow countrymen. To flaunt a foreign culture would be self-destructive. He *is* one of them, and he has to act like one of them. If he did otherwise, social isolation would be his lot.

The point is that the American manager shouldn't believe the veneer and assume that the graduate is now "Americanized" or "Anglicized." He isn't, nor should he be. It is unrealistic to expect that he will immediately adapt to Western ways of doing business.

GOVERNMENT AGENCIES

This is a productive source, but a few warnings are necessary. In some countries, where there has been a concerted effort to build local universities and educate the people, there aren't enough jobs to go around for the graduates. The government then hires them and provides reasonable pay, and they sit around with nothing to do. The economy is improved, but the educated workers are stagnating. Five years of experience in a government ministry may be one year's experience five times over.

Also if a government employee is hired, the possibility of autocratic behavior exists. He may have learned this mode from his peers and superiors because autocracy is typical in a government role. It's a hard behavior pattern to break, but it can be done by a competent manager who coaches and guides with patient leadership.

On the more positive side, assuming that the government employee really did something of significance in his position, he is usually educated and attuned to business, commerce, and organizational life. He knows what responsibility means, he's typically knowledgable, and presumably he has displayed a history of dependability. Another plus can be his contacts within the government structure and, because of the contacts, his ability to cut through some of the inevitable bureaucratic red tape.

The value of this type of candidate is further increased if his government work relates in any way to the company's product or service. An oil company, for instance, could benefit materially by hiring someone who had been in the Ministry of Petroleum (or whatever the agency might be called). A former employee of the Ministry of Transportation might be important to an airline, as would one from the government health agency be to a hospital or clinic. These people know people and can help get things done.

The government in every developing country is a powerful force. Doing business in those countries means establishing and maintaining a healthy relationship. Here is where former government employees can be influential agents for the organization.

LOCAL BUSINESSES

Private businesses and government-owned firms, such as airlines or oil companies, offer perhaps the best sources for potential management candidates. The experience has probably produced a work orientation in which profit, or at least the quality of a product or service, has been paramount. All other things being equal, candidates from these sources usually fit into the scheme of things with the least difficulty of all.

A point to keep in mind, however: the salary, fringe benefits, working conditions, advancement opportunities, and the like must be comparable to or better than those offered by the local firm. Working for a foreign-owned or -managed organization poses certain security threats as well as limited promotional possibilities. The attraction must be enough to justify making a somewhat risky employment change.

Related to this, and as mentioned before, is the fact that a local national working for a foreign company is just a bit of an economic traitor—especially if the company is in competition with a national firm. It's like a Brazilian being employed by Braniff Airways instead of Varig, his country's flag carrier. He is directly helping an American company rather than one of his own country.

Transferring loyalties isn't always easy, especially when strong nationalistic feelings are part of the culture. All of which means (in the terminology of Chapter 6) that the Satisfiers offered must be at least as healthy as those in the local firm, and the Motivators should be superior. If not, local businesses as a recruiting source will soon dry up.

The Difficulties of Staffing

No American should underrate the difficulty of staffing his organization. Finding the right person for a specific job is not easy. Skills and experience are usually limited, as is the personnel market itself. People don't jump from job to job with the same facility as here at home.

Finding laborers or semiskilled workers is not much of a problem. Also, many manual or even technical jobs can be contracted out if the company doesn't want to build up a permanent, full-time workforce.

For management positions, however, it's a different story. Filling these jobs, from first-level supervision on up, demands a set of skills that the average line manager hasn't developed or in which he's been given little training. Effective selection techniques are important everywhere, regardless of geography, but they seem to be particularly critical in an overseas assignment because . . .

The Stakes Are High

From just a cost point of view, putting a new employee on the payroll is an expensive proposition. There's the advertising, the screening of X number of candidates, and the hours the manager may spend conducting interviews, doing paperwork, and processing the selected candidate. Then add reference checking, and sending notifications to the rejected candidates, and you have a fair idea of both the time and out-of-pocket costs involved. When time is translated into money, it's probably not unrealistic to estimate a $5,000 price tag to fill one supervisory position. And, depending on the market and the technical qualifications desired, that may be a very low figure.

Then a supervisor is hired, but the choice turns out to be a poor one. For whatever reason, he can't handle the job. We now have the costs of wasted training, wages paid that weren't earned, perhaps spoilage or damage, mistakes, rework, and the time of the manager that is expended in trying to force a square peg into a round hole.

Finally, keep in mind how difficult, if not impossible, it is to terminate even the incompetents in most developing countries. Except for the most extreme violations, such as criminal activities or repeated intoxication on the job, a state of indentureship exists, with the employee practically guaranteed a job for life. Either powerful unions, such as those in Belgium, or stringent government regulations like those of Kuwait may deprive the manager of justified recourse when an employee proves unsuited for a given job.

Demotions in position or pay, without the express consent of the employee, are equally difficult. In most developing countries, once a certain level is attained, going backward involuntarily is prohibited.

Given these built-in restrictions, the importance of thorough screening and professional interviewing is obvious. Which is another reason why promoting from within is the safest route. Despite the

Peter Principle, one of the best indicators of what a person will do is what he or she has done previously.

The Employment Interview

The construction of a strong subordinate staff begins with the interview. Effective interviewing, however, is a learned art. It requires preparation, practice, and the ability to judge the potential of another individual who is probably a complete stranger. These skills aren't developed overnight, nor are they the inherited ability some interviewers claim of "being able to size up a candidate the minute he walks through the door." That's hogwash, as any professional interviewer will tell you.

The art and techniques of interviewing warrant a full-length book in themselves. There are some basic considerations, however, that can be summarized, with special concern for the hiring and promoting of local national candidates. While the principles are the same for filling any job, keep in mind that we're talking primarily about staffing a management position.

PREPARATION

Step 1. Be sure a job description exists, along with a Job Performance Guide or something similar to it. The latter, particularly, should be in both English and the local language to avoid any chance of misunderstanding.

Step 2. On the basis of the Job Performance Guide, develop a clear picture of what qualities and qualifications are required. These may include technical knowledge; technical skills; education; experience; managerial skills (planning, organizing, directing, coordinating, controlling); human skills (the ability to work well with others, personality, empathy, concern for others); creativity; imagination; and so on.

Step 3. Consider whether the future is important. In other words, is the job to be filled a foundation for later advancement, or is someone needed for this position alone without regard for his advancement potential?

If the hiring is for this job and this job alone, that's one thing. But if the successful candidate needs to have the ability to grow and advance through the organization, the interview process needs to probe into the candidates' motivations, ambitions, goals, emotional stability, communicating abilities, desire to manage, and philosophy of managing.

Obviously, no interview can or will reveal the whole person. If it is properly conducted, however, even the inexperienced interviewer will emerge with a reasonably clear picture of each candidate's assets and liabilities.

Step 4. Review the application form before conducting the interview. This is obvious, but the completed form carries a message beyond the bare facts about the candidate. For example:

- Have all questions been answered or blanks filled in?
- Have directions been followed?
- Are there frequent erasures or corrections?
- Are there any periods of time not accounted for, as in education or employment?
- What do the handwriting and spelling reveal about the candidate's English proficiency?

How the form is filled out may indicate that the candidate:

- Does or does not follow instructions.
- Is neat, exact, and careful—or careless and sloppy.
- May have something to hide, if certain questions aren't answered or time blanks appear in his education or employment record.

Step 5. Prepare questions that will encourage the candidate to tell you what you want to know. If he's typical, the local candidate will give you the answers he thinks you want to hear. The question "Did you like your last supervisor?" will probably produce a not very meaningful "yes." A more response-encouraging approach: "Tell me about your last supervisor." It's hard to answer "yes" or "no" to that.

On the other hand, be alert to the types of questions most local nationals tend to resent. Probing into a person's family, hobbies, parents, the parents' education, what the father does for a living, or religious convictions is generally taboo. The same applies with employees already in the workforce. These areas are considered private and not subject to inquiry by a stranger. If the newly arrived manager has any doubts about what areas can and cannot be explored, he should seek counsel from a knowledgeable local. Overstepping accepted cultural limits will be a serious mistake.

Step 6. Find a location where the interview can be conducted privately and without interruption. Any interview demands these conditions, and one in which a job is at stake is no exception. The candidate is revealing himself; he's trying to sell himself to another person. He thus needs to feel that it is a one-to-one conversation and not something that may be overheard by a staff of workers in an adjacent area.

This is true anywhere but especially in the developing countries. By his very upbringing, the local is reluctant to talk too personally about himself. If strict privacy does not exist, his answers are likely to be terse, uninformative, superficial, and designed solely to satisfy the interviewer.

Interruptions should be prevented by any means possible. No interview can be conducted effectively if the telephone is constantly ringing or people are traipsing in with problems and questions, or just to pass the time of day. The closed door is not always respected by the local employee. He often feels that he can walk into anybody's office at any time, sit down, and take over the conversation. In much of the developing world, this is the custom, the tradition. Asking the intruder to leave is considered discourteous and damaging to his self-esteem.

Consequently, the only way to ensure privacy is to have a secretary or clerk challenge the would-be visitor and prevent his entrance. If that's not practical, mask-tape a sign on the door, in both English and the local language, that a meeting is in session and "Please don't interrupt." Even this may not be 100 percent effective, but it will discourage all but the most persistent and the illiterate.

THE INTERVIEW ITSELF

While the local national is usually reluctant to reveal personal family matters, he will talk freely about himself if he's treated with courtesy and respect. When he feels that the interviewer is honestly interested in him as a person, he is very likely to respond openly and candidly.

This means that the interview should be a dialogue with the candidate, rather than the interviewer taking the role of "the star." The interviewer should know how to create a relaxed, informal atmosphere and have the ability to ask questions. It all starts with . . .

The Opening

A trite but still valid admonition: put the candidate at ease as quickly as possible. Do it naturally, however, and in a way that reduces his probable feelings of tension and uncertainty. Not likely to be very helpful is something like this: "I see your name is Abdulla Said. Tell me why I should hire you."

Whether it's Abdulla Said or Tom Smith, that opening starts

things off on a sorry footing. This type of opening is more effective: "It's a pleasure to meet you, Mr. Said. Please make yourself comfortable. Tell me, did you have any trouble finding my office?"

Even though you may not smoke, have an ashtray handy and make it clear that the candidate is free to smoke if he so chooses. Also an offer of coffee or tea is an appreciated gesture that, more often than not, will be accepted. To refuse is considered discourteous. At the same time, it's an icebreaker that promotes a more relaxed conversation.

The Body

Having begun with a comfortable opening, the interviewer can move easily into the main portion of the interview. Again with informality in mind, here is one approach: "I'm glad you've given us the opportunity to talk with you about joining our company as an accounting supervisor. In looking over your application, I see that you have worked for Khalil Construction. Would you tell me a little about the work you did there?"

From here on, the conversation can proceed and take whatever direction the interviewer chooses. To discuss all the techniques of interviewing would be out of place here, but a few of the basics do merit passing attention:

Listen—listen—listen. A rule of thumb: aim for the 30/70 ratio—talk 30 percent of the time, listen 70 percent. You may not make it, but if you end up 50/50, you'll be way ahead of most managers. The best advice to an interviewer is to *shut up.* You never learned a thing while you were talking.

Ask questions. Rely on the "W" and "H" questions:
"What did you do after that?"
"What happened then?"
"When did you begin to feel that way?"
"Why did you feel that way?"
"How did that affect you?"
"Which of your university courses were the easiest for you?"
Use statements—to change the pace. For example:
"Tell me what you did after that."
"Compare the two jobs for me, if you can."
"Describe your reactions to that situation."
"Outline for me the career path you have in mind."
Use reflections, as another technique. A reflection is a repetition of a comment the other person has made in which approximately the same words are used but the words are in the form of a question.

Applicant: "I just got bored with the job."
Interviewer: "You got bored with it?"
Applicant: "Oh, I got along with him pretty well."
Interviewer: "You had a good relationship?"

Give encouragement. Many remarks can be used to encourage the applicant to keep talking. For example: "That's interesting," "Tell me more," "I see; good point," "Uh huh," "And . . . ?" and "Go on."

Keep the silent language in mind. Physical behavior communicates volumes, either positively or negatively. The professional interviewer is alert to facial expressions, gestures, and body movements—whether his or the other party's—because of the messages they may be conveying. Examples are raising an eyebrow, shrugging one's shoulders, crossing one's arms, strumming one's fingers on the desk, doodling, tapping a pencil, frowning, smiling, or looking at one's watch.

The silent language encourages or discourages talk. Use it, but use it for positive purposes and to learn more about the candidate.

Avoid moralizing, preaching, or scolding. These are excellent ways to *destroy* an interview. For example:

"That wasn't a very smart decision."
"Well, I hope you learned a lesson from that."
"You certainly don't seem to know where you're going, do you?"
"What makes you think you could possibly meet our requirements?"

Encourage questions from the applicant. Toward the end of the interview, give the applicant every opportunity to ask questions. For instance:

"What more could I tell you about the work?"
"What have I not made clear enough for you as we've gone along?"
"What other questions might you have about the job or the company?"
"To what extent do you think you understand our pay policy?"

The local candidate may be reluctant to ask questions for fear of embarrassing himself. The reluctance will usually disappear, however, if a friendly climate exists and he is encouraged to clear up any doubts in his mind.

Make sure you've gotten the needed information. Before moving to the close, be sure *your* questions have been answered. Have you found out what you wanted to find out? Have you found out enough to make an intelligent decision about the candidate? Do you have an uneasy feeling that you've missed something or haven't gotten a clear enough picture of him?

If you aren't satisfied, go back and try to fill in the gaps. The person in front of you may be the best candidate you'll see, so you owe it to him and to yourself to be absolutely certain you have the essential facts to make the wisest decision possible.

Most American managers are aware of the limitations in this country on questions that can be asked of a job applicant during an interview. The Civil Rights Act of 1964, and as amended in 1972, specifies the areas that cannot be investigated. Few developing countries have anything comparable to the Act or the Equal Employment Opportunity Commission. Thus, questions that are illegal here are perfectly legitimate elsewhere.

While there are cultural taboos abroad, such as taboos on questions about family and parents, such inquiries are not unlawful. And it's entirely acceptable to ask about the candidate's willingness to work weekends or on religious holidays, and to find out who will care for the children if his wife is ill, whether he has a car, how he will get to work, how his family would manage if he were sent out of town on a business trip, and the like. Prohibited under EEOC regulations, questions of this nature are in order in most societies, whether the applicant is male or female.

However, the U.S. manager should investigate local restrictions before he launches into an interviewing program. He's probably legally safe in asking almost any question, but he ought to be sure— just as he should be aware of the culturally unacceptable areas that are to be avoided.

The Close

Some interviewers find this difficult, but it shouldn't be. If the right rapport has been established and both parties are satisfied with the information they have received, a smooth, unforced close is natural. Example: "Well, Mr. Said, we've covered a lot of ground, and I think you've given me a very clear picture of yourself. Before we end, are there any other questions you would like to ask?"

If the candidate has none, the interviewer can conclude along these lines: "It's been an interesting meeting, Mr. Said, and thank you for coming in. As we are interviewing several candidates, I'm not in a position right now to give you a decision, but I will be in touch with you by next Wednesday. Meanwhile, if you think of any other questions before then, don't hesitate to call me."

The final words should be "Thank you" and "Goodbye." And say them in *his* language, if at all possible.

What about Tests?

Tests are perfectly legal in most developing countries, whereas many types are barred in the United States because the results bear no direct relationship to the requirements of the job. There are two special difficulties with tests in the developing countries: the language barrier, and the educational level of most candidates.

If the candidate is a graduate of an American university and speaks fluent English, the typical I.Q. and psychological tests (Otis, Wonderlic, Minnesota Multiphasic, Rorschach, etc.) might be valid measuring instruments. Even then, the results should be evaluated cautiously by a professional in the field. The applicant's language, and thus his interpretive skills, may not be that well developed. For example, here is a true-false question from the George Washington Series Social Intelligence Test: "One of the most efficient ways to succeed in the world is through an inviolate fidelity to friends." It's unlikely that the average local national college graduate would understand "inviolate" or "fidelity." It's possible but not probable. A question on the Otis Employment I.Q. test offers this multiple-choice item:

A man's influence in a community should depend upon his (?)

(1) wealth (2) dignity (3) wisdom (4) ambition (5) political power.

Most Easterners would probably choose "wisdom." Would an American? And what emphasis ought to be placed on the word "should"? What *is* and what *should be* can be two different things.

Few, if any, of the current nontechnical tests would be applicable in a developing country or in instances where English ability is less than fluent. If any psychological or intelligence test is used, it should be translated and then scored by a qualified local national.

Technical and pure skill assessment tests are another matter. Tests of typing, dictation, driving, manual dexterity, welding ability, and other types of job proficiency will weed out the unqualified. The same is true of tests that measure mathematical skills, accounting knowledge, or mechanical abilities. Barring those, however, tests available today in English are likely to be of little value. The most they may do is reveal language limitations, which may not be that important anyway.

The Rejected Candidate

Above all, tell the rejected candidate he has been rejected! It's the worst sort of public relations to fill a job and never say a word to those who didn't qualify. This goes for applicants outside the company as well as for employees who were seeking a promotion.

Every candidate should be contacted by phone or letter and given the news. The employment interview is a highly personal experience where the candidate is putting his self-esteem on the line. He is offering his qualifications, ability, and personality for sale in the marketplace. To fail to "sell" and hence be rejected is hard to take, despite our awareness that life is full of disappointments and setbacks.

The rejected candidate must be told, but in a way that allows him to maintain his self-respect. Saying "no" gracefully isn't easy, but it can be done if some of these "don'ts" are avoided:

○ *Don't compare candidates.* To tell the rejected candidate that "We selected someone better than you" accomplishes nothing. Not only will it damage the local person's self-esteem, but it could put you on the defensive if he asks you to justify your decision.

○ *Don't get philosophical.* Little is gained by urging the rejected candidate to be brave and stoical about the bad news. Observations that "Somebody wins, somebody loses" or "The best man wins" are unlikely to change the feelings of the person who lost.

○ *Don't get hard-nosed.* Avoid any indication that you don't give a darn about the unsuccessful applicant so long as you've gotten the person you want. A cold, disinterested rejection is the worst one of all and almost inevitably reflects back on the manager and the reputation of his company.

If you have to discuss why the candidate was rejected, focus on the *requirements* of the job and his *qualifications*. This is far less personal and helps the candidate to be more objective about the reality of things. Be specific, if necessary, about the areas in which the person's qualifications didn't precisely meet the position requirements. Above all, *never* criticize the candidate on a personal level for anything.

These may seem like obvious admonitions, but the author has encountered many examples of job applicants who were eventually rejected and then told in brutally personal terms why they had failed to measure up. And in many cases, the interviewing manager was a local national himself. In his position of authority, he had lost sight of the sensitivity of his fellow countrymen and had tried to create something akin to a master-slave relationship. Which isn't too surprising, because that sort of relationship between the haves and have-nots is only slowly being buried as traditional societies move into industrialization.

In defense of these local managers it can be said that their behavior was both natural and the result of lack of training in the field of interviewing and selection. And in most cases they had worked for either American or British expatriates who had quite obviously done nothing to prepare them for higher management responsibilities.

The "don'ts" still apply when the rejected candidate is notified by letter. The letter should be brief and to the point, somewhat along these lines:

Dear _____ :

I appreciated the time we had together last Tuesday when we discussed your interest in _____ position.

I am sorry to have to tell you that you were not selected for the position. Unfortunately, your experience and technical qualifications did not meet the requirements of the job we reviewed in some detail. I am grateful to you, however, for giving us the opportunity to become acquainted with you and for your interest in joining our organization.

Please accept my best wishes for your future.

Sincerely,

Whether this wording is followed or not is secondary. The goal of the rejection letter should be to get the message across in the most graceful way possible and still have the applicant think favorably of the company. If, when it's all over, he can say, "That *would* have been a good place to work," the odds are that the manager has done his job well.

Some Reasons Why Interviews Fail

The causes of failure are many. Some of the more common ones are discussed briefly below.

FAILURE TO PREPARE

One interview is finished and in walks another candidate. The interviewer has no time to review the application form or prepare questions based on the information before him. Ill-equipped, he conducts the interview in a robot-like fashion as he practically reads the entries and makes meaningless remarks:

"I see you were born in 1951."

"You say you can start anytime?"

"And then you went to the university."

"I notice that you majored in political science. Did you like it?"

"And then you worked for Bechtel for two years. Did you like it?"

Never rush from one interview directly into another. Take time to analyze the pluses and minuses of the first applicant and to get ready for the next. Lack of preparation leads to a stilted session with poor questions and a lot of "yes" and "no" answers. This isn't fair to either party and makes it very difficult to arrive at a wise selection decision.

TOO MUCH TALKING BY THE INTERVIEWER

Because of inadequate preparation and lack of interviewing skills, interviewers tend to talk too much. It's the 30/70 ratio in reverse. The result: the candidate knows far more about the interviewer and the company than the interviewer knows about the candidate.

VARIOUS "EFFECTS" ON THE INTERVIEWER

The halo effect. This is a tendency to base the evaluation on one or two conspicuous or impressive characteristics. For example:

- ○ The candidate is friendly and a good conversationalist. Conclusion: he's intelligent.
- ○ He is reserved and ill-at-ease. Conclusion: he's either insecure or lacks ability.
- ○ He speaks excellent English. Conclusion: he's educated and thoroughly Westernized.

The extension effect. The manager may allow a few limited experiences with the candidate to predetermine his opinion of what the person will do in the future. If the candidate failed in one area, it is felt he will fail in others. If he succeeded in one area, it is felt he will succeed in others.

The superficiality effect. This is a tendency to form judgments on the basis of mere superficial evidence. As an example, one interviewer summed up a candidate in this manner: "That man carries himself well, he's energetic, calm, and ambitious. Hire him." The man turned out to be stupid, lazy, corrupt, and incompetent—none of which could be detected by superficial investigation.

The projection effect. Here the manager projects his own associations or prejudices into the interview. Say a candidate has long hair, a full mustache, close-set eyes, and a large nose. You knew and disliked someone 10 years ago who looked very much like the candidate. Result: You don't like or trust the man.

Or say the candidate has a background similar to yours. He also reminds you of a good friend back home. Conclusion: He's a great candidate.

The insignificant question (I.Q.) effect. Some interviewers will attach profound significance to meaningless or unanswerable questions. For example:

"Are you honest?"

"Have you ever lied?"

"Do you like your job?"

"What do you want to be?"

"What do you want to be doing when you retire?" (45 years from now)

The assumption effect. Here the interviewer makes unwarranted assumptions, such as the following:

Experienced people are automatically superior to the inexperienced.

Older people are better leaders than younger ones.

A highly extroverted person is a better leader than one who is quiet and reserved.

All redheads have hot tempers.

A bulldog jaw is a sign of determination and courage.

Conclusion

Interviewing skills and the ability to make wise decisions in the selection of management personnel are important qualities, regardless of geography. If anything, however, they are more critical in an overseas assignment for the reasons stated earlier. The market is not that plentiful, and the caliber of the candidates, in terms of education and experience, is often lower than what the U.S. manager has experienced at home. The choice is thus more difficult.

Adding to the importance of the selection process is the fact that the local manager hired today should usually be capable of advancing and assuming increased responsibilities. He is the one, among others, who eventually should replace the expatriates. If the wrong locals are hired, the entire nationalization program is retarded, with the company paying the inevitable price in costs and reputation. Plus, the "wrong" locals probably can't be demoted or released, so the organization is stuck with people who aren't very competent in their present jobs and have no potential for advancement. Everyone loses when the interviewing and selection process is performed at an amateurish level.

It's a challenging responsibility, but it's one every manager can master. The techniques are learnable, and the skills required to conduct an effective interview can be polished. Even the most highly professional interviewer will still need to exercise judgment in making his selection decisions. But the goal is to reduce judgment as much as possible so that objectivity and facts minimize the tendency to rely on feelings and intuition.

Perhaps the ultimate goal of the interview is to find a candidate who:

o Neither falls below nor exceeds the standards that have been set for the position.
o Does not possess a shortcoming so serious that it outweighs his positive qualifications.
o Will be capable in the job after reasonable and proper training.
o Evokes an automatic "yes" to the question: "Will we be safe in his hands?"

12

Orientation of
the New Employee

First, a case study:

Mohammed Abdul Wahab walked toward the new and impressive office building with a touch of excitement and a growing anticipation. He had just been hired by a well-known international company, and today was the start of a new career for him.

It was a short distance from his home to the office, and today the passing traffic, the auto horns, the scenes along the route merged into vague and indistinct impressions. None of the surrounding sights and sounds caught his attention. He was turning inward to his thoughts and emotions.

Wahab was ordinarily a calm, steady individual who revealed little of his feelings to others. If he suffered, he tried to control his anguish; if he was happy, he could conceal his joy. But despite an unemotional exterior, he was deeply sensitive and alert to the world around him.

This morning, approaching the office, the expectations, the excitement over what lay ahead were mixed with anxiety, a touch of fear, and a feeling of uncertainty. He wanted to do well; he wanted to succeed; he wanted to be accepted. But would he? Would he receive enough training? Would he be able to do what was asked of him? Would he be given a chance to prove himself? How would those with whom he worked react to him? The day was starting with promise. How would it end?

Not that this was Wahab's first job. For three years he had been an accountant in a medium-sized, locally owned department store. The work had been interesting but the potential for advancement very limited. When a friend told him that a similar position was open in the international firm, he immediately applied. He was interviewed by an American named Bryant and then told he would be notified about the

job in a few days. Finally, the letter came informing him that he had
been hired and telling him to report today to a Mr. Makki. Apparently
Makki would be his new supervisor, but he wasn't sure.

Wahab entered the building, took the elevator to the right floor,
and, after a moment of confusion, found his way to Makki's office.

"Good morning," he said to someone sitting behind a desk near the
door. "Could I please see Mr. Makki?"

"Mr. Makki isn't here," was the reply. "What's your name and what
do you want?"

"I'm Mohammed Abdul Wahab, and I'm to start working here today.
Mr. Bryant told me to report to Mr. Makki."

"Start working here? Doing what?" The man was hardly friendly.

"I'm to be an accountant," Wahab answered slowly.

"I thought we had enough of those around here already," muttered
the man behind the desk. "Well, I don't know what to tell you. Mr.
Makki isn't here and I don't know when he'll be back. He had an important meeting upstairs, I heard. But sit down over there. You can wait for
him."

Wahab thanked the man and seated himself in an armless, uncomfortable chair. The time, he noted, was 8:10.

Wahab watched the surrounding activity with interest. A great many
people seemed to come and go; the telephone was ringing constantly;
clerks brought files in and took files out; coffee and tea appeared, and
the empty cups were later removed; hurried conferences took place at
desks; and casual conversations were held in the entry office where
Wahab sat. It all looked busy and probably important but, to Wahab,
not very businesslike.

The time passed, the chair became increasingly uncomfortable. He
stood and tried to stretch without attracting too much attention. He
walked around a little, not wanting to go too far away from the man at
the desk who would introduce him to Mr. Makki.

At 10:45, a short, rather plump man walked briskly into the office
and stopped at the desk.

"Any messages?" he asked.

"Yes, Mr. Makki," the man said as he handed over several slips of
paper. "Also, that new accountant is here—Mohammed . . . what's
your name?" The question was directed to Wahab, who was watching
the two men.

He rose, went to the desk, and replied, "Mohammed Abdul Wahab.
W-A-H-A-B."

"A new accountant?" asked Makki. "Oh yes, I remember. You were
supposed to report today. Did you just get here?"

Wahab was about to answer when Makki interrupted. "Never mind. Come with me and I'll get you started."

Makki led the way into a large office filled with desks, typewriters, file cabinets, and people. Entering Makki's private office, Wahab sat down at Makki's invitation.

"So you're the new accountant. Bryant, Mr. Bryant, that is, told me he'd hired you. Let's see, where is that file on you?"

A few seconds of fumbling under various stacks of paper produced the file.

"Yes, here it is. A department store accountant, eh? Well, things are a little different around here. . . . But, let's get you started. I guess you know something about the company. It's not too big now, but we're growing and have lots of plans for the future. Now if you have any questions about sick leave or vacations or company policies, read this over and then if you're not sure, ask someone out there or see me. We want you to feel at home around here, so don't hesitate to ask questions."

Makki handed a pamphlet to Wahab over the desk, and then stood up. Pointing out the door, he said: "Take that empty desk over there by the window. At first, you'll be typing some of the reports the other accountants will give you and you'll do some filing. That way, you'll get familiar with the way we do things. So, if you don't have any questions, go to your desk and we'll give you some work as soon as we can. Since you're already an accountant, there won't be much need to train you."

Somewhat confused and a bit unhappy, Wahab rose, thanked Makki, and made his way to his desk. A few people looked as he passed, one or two nodded, but no one spoke. He assumed they were too busy.

Lunchtime came and went, but Wahab stayed at his desk, although he was hungry. He'd had little for breakfast that morning, but now he didn't know where to go to eat or exactly when the lunch period was.

It wasn't that he was busy, though. In fact, he had nothing to do. Every time Makki left his office, Wahab watched him with the hope that he'd be given some assignment. Each time he was disappointed.

At 4:30, everybody put things away and left the office. Wahab sat there, wondering if he too should leave. Seeing no reason to stay, he rose, passed Makki's door, cautiously said "Good night" to his supervisor (whose desk was still piled high with papers), and found his way to the street.

And so ended Wahab's first day. The next morning, he arrived promptly at 8:00 and again went home at 4:30 after an unproductive eight hours of sitting and waiting. It wasn't much better the next day, or the next, or the next.

Not that he had *nothing* to do. Occasionally some work floated his way, but the unfilled hours far exceeded his few busy minutes.

As one week passed and then another, Wahab became less and less punctual. He found that if he appeared at 9:00 or so, nobody paid any attention or said anything to him about it. "So why get here at 8:00 and have another hour sitting around doing nothing?" he rationalized to himself.

One morning, about a month after he had started, he arrived at the office 20 minutes late. Nearing Makki's office, he heard Makki talking with someone he didn't know.

"Take Wahab, for example. He's never here on time—hasn't been since his first day. We can't depend on him, so we just ignore him."

Wahab didn't hear the rest of the conversation as he quickly walked away in anger and embarrassment. At that moment he made his decision. In a few minutes, he was at the retail store talking to his old manager. Wahab was lucky. The manager hadn't been able to fill his position because he hadn't found anyone whom he thought would be able to do the job as well as Wahab.

The next Saturday, Wahab was excited as he entered the store. He was going back to work again.

An exaggerated situation? Not really. Things like this go on every day—and then management wonders why it has a high rate of early turnover. Just a few of the obvious mistakes in the case:

○ Bryant had interviewed and hired Wahab without involving Makki in any way. The immediate supervisor of the new employee should *always* interview the applicant and be the one to tell him: "You have the job." When that is done, the employee knows that it's his supervisor he has to please, not personnel or some higher-level manager, because it was the supervisor who actually did the hiring. A Bryant and a Makki can discuss the various applicants, but regardless of who makes the final decision, the Makkis should be the ones who notify the successful candidate.

○ Makki was completely unprepared for Wahab's arrival. Although he eventually found Wahab's file, he knew nothing about him and obviously hadn't even reviewed it. Ignorance of the new employee on the part of the supervisor does little to build the employee's self-esteem.

○ Bryant had given Makki no training or guidance on how to orient a new employee. To Makki, Wahab was just a bothersome interruption to be dispensed with as rapidly as possible. Makki's understanding of how a new employee feels on Day 1 was nonexistent. Perhaps the absence of empathy was his fault; on the other hand, it might have been Bryant's and his failure to train Makki properly in the entire orientation process.

○ The orientation was, of course, no orientation at all. When this is coupled with the lack of any training program or work of any significance to be performed, it's little wonder that Mohammed Abdul Wahab lasted only a few weeks on the job.

Early turnover—that is, turnover within the first 60–90 days on the job—is usually caused by a failure in one of three responsibilities, or a combination thereof: (1) faulty interviewing and selection techniques, (2) inadequate or nonexistent orientation programs, (3) incomplete job training. When the right person for the right job has been selected, the orientation has been gradual and thorough, and the training is complete, not many people are going to make an early departure from an organization that has shown so much concern for their welfare.

Studies have revealed that voluntary turnover is greatest on two specific days: either the very first day on the job, or the day the employee is released from training to do the job by himself. In extreme but not unusual cases, workers have been known to report at 8:00, check out at noon for lunch, and never return. The first few hours were enough for them.

In terms of orientation, a little managerial empathy combined with memory is needed. Most of us can recall quite vividly our first day on the job with a new company. Our feelings and emotions were mixed. On the one hand, there were excitement and optimism. We looked forward to the job. We wanted to succeed. We hoped that a good training program would get us started right and that the benefits and promotional opportunities would ensure our future. We wanted to make friends. We wanted to be successful. The last thing we wanted to do was fail.

At the same time, there probably were tension, nervousness, and perhaps a little fear. Our self-confidence wasn't all it should have been. Anxious and uncertain, we walked into a strange environment, hoping for the best.

Has it been so long ago that that first day has faded from memory? Just as a U.S. manager feels apprehension when he first moves into a different country and a different culture, so does the new employee when he enters a work situation foreign to his experience. This can be especially true when the company is American-owned or American-managed. The people, the work, and the work processes may be foreign to the employee in more respects than one. No wonder tension and anxiety are close to the surface.

The first few days on a new job are difficult for anyone. They're much more difficult if the initial introduction is marked by casualness or indifference. Conversely, these days can be productive and painless when someone takes an honest interest in us and in our emotional well-being.

A few employees, of course, only want "a job" and a paycheck. They don't expect to be around long and usually aren't. Such people do exist, and getting them on the payroll is the fault of interviewing. Also, as has been said, there are cases where the manager is practically ordered to hire someone who is "a nephew of a cousin of my sister's husband." Or a prominent government official suggests that it would be nice "if you could find a place for my wife's stepbrother's son." These pressures are difficult to ignore, and it may well be that the "nephew" or the "son" will prove to be an A-1 employee. But there are those who can offer little, or want to offer little, and are seeking only a sinecure.

These are the exceptions, however. The average person doesn't start out on Day 1 hoping to fail, planning to cause trouble, expecting to be disliked. That just isn't human nature. He begins *wanting* to succeed. And with any luck he will.

So—if the right person has been hired, the first day is the time to begin shaping and developing the individual into the constructive employee every organization wants. This is where orientation enters the picture.

What is "orientation"? Webster defines it as "the determination or sense of one's position with relation to environment or to some particular person, thing, or field of knowledge." In the work situation, the definition translates into the following:

- *Environment:* the physical facilities of the plant, the machines, the general atmosphere that prevails, benefits, pay, rules, and the like.
- *Person:* the immediate supervisor, fellow employees, who is who in the organization.
- *Thing:* the tools or equipment used to do the job, forms, materials, and so on.
- *Field of knowledge:* what the employee needs to know to do the job as expected and required.

A Seven-Step Orientation Program

To bring the definition to life, the following seven-step program has been found to be both thorough and rewarding—to the supervisor as well as the employee. Before it is presented, however, a couple of observations are in order.

First, the orientation program should be conducted by the employee's immediate supervisor, not the industrial relations manager or some disinterested personnel officer. That's not to say personnel can't be involved. It can and perhaps should be, especially during the review of some of the fringe benefits. Otherwise, it's the supervisor's job to get the employee started right, and it's his job to establish the strongest possible relationship with the employee at the earliest possible minute. The employee should know that he is to go to his supervisor *first* when any question on any matter arises. The supervisor is his boss in every respect, not merely in specific work direction.

Second, orientation is more than a one-hour or one-day process. The heavy dose comes at the beginning, of course, but some aspects can't be covered effectively all at one time. Some need to be discussed now, some perhaps in a week or two, and others even after that. Overwhelming the employee with facts, figures, and a lengthy dissertation on pay scales, the merit program, hospitalization, the retirement plan, and perquisites with seniority will only confuse him and invite a flood of questions down the road. Gradually conveying the information is more practical and productive.

STEP 1. CREATE A GOOD FIRST IMPRESSION

This is an old and obvious admonition, but it's so often violated. To begin, the employee should know to whom he is to report the first morning and where the individual can be located. There won't be any problem with this if the person (presumably his immediate supervisor) was involved in the interviewing. Otherwise, and without clear directions, he may find himself wandering around a strange building trying to follow confusing instructions given by an overworked receptionist. That's not a very confidence-building initial impression.

At the same time, the supervisor should be expecting the employee. He should have the employee's file and other pertinent data at hand, his desk cleared, and his schedule arranged to allow complete attention to the task of getting the new employee started on the right foot. A warm welcome and immediately putting the employee at ease will create that important favorable first impression.

STEP 2. BEGIN THE BUILDING OF SELF-CONFIDENCE

As was suggested earlier, the typical new employee doesn't have a large measure of self-confidence at this stage—particularly if he's moving into a different line of work. What little confidence there is needs to be strengthened.

One way to accomplish this is to show personal interest in the employee through questions and comments. The employee is on firm ground when talking about himself. Providing the opportunity for this eases initial tensions while helping him gain confidence in both the supervisor and himself.

Another technique is for the supervisor to express his personal confidence in the employee and the latter's ability to do the work for which he was hired. Something like this is beneficial: "We had several applicants for this position, but we selected you because we believe you are the most qualified. We have no doubts about your ability to succeed."

The challenge of the job, however, shouldn't be minimized or its importance denigrated. "Anybody can do this" may build confidence but it can destroy interest. The employee should recognize that he'll be facing a challenge, but with his education or experience and a sound training program, the responsibilities of the job can be mastered.

Confidence (not overconfidence) works wonders. The beginning— the very first day—is the time to start building it.

STEP 3. BEGIN BUILDING CONFIDENCE IN THE COMPANY

If he's typical, the new employee knows little or nothing about the company he's joining. It's the supervisor's job, then, to communicate some facts and information, such as:

A brief review of the company's history.
Its major products or services.
Its size in terms of installations and employees.
Its position and reputation in the industry, in the United States, and in foreign markets.
Basic company organization (general).
Department or unit organization (specific).
Future plans for new products, expansion, and so forth.
The company's purpose and role in the local community.

The reviews of these areas should be concise, organized, and presented in a way that will cause the employee to feel he has joined a stable, progressive organization—that the decision to select *this* company was a wise one. What better opportunity than right now to plant the first seed of corporate pride?

STEP 4. CREATE INTEREST IN THE JOB

This is orientation, not training. But before the training even begins, a brief overview of the employee's job should be given. For example:

What is the job?
What is the specific title or nomenclature given to the position?
Where is the work performed?
What does it involve?
What are some of the responsibilities?
How many people perform the same kind of work?
What is its importance and role in the final product?

Here's where the Job Performance Guide comes in again. If it wasn't reviewed or a copy given to the employee when he was interviewed, now is a good time to summarize it and discuss what will be expected once the employee is trained and has gained some experience. This is especially important when orienting new management personnel, primarily because their responsibilities are less easily defined than those of a welder or a file clerk.

The overview shouldn't stop with the immediate job, however. People like to know where they fit in the scheme of things. They want to know what happens before they become involved and what happens afterward. For orientation purposes, this brings in the *general–specific–general* formula.

Each job is obviously different, so every manager has to work out his own explanation. In broad terms, however, the explanation would include:

- *General:* a brief review of what takes place before the employee becomes involved—the work that precedes and the flow of people, processes, or parts.
- *Specific:* the employee's specific role and responsibilities in the entire operation—a summary of the work performed, what happens if the work isn't done properly, how the work is moved on to the next step.
- *General:* what happens after the employee has completed his portion of the job—where the work goes, who does what, how and when the product or service is completed, what the final output should look like or be.

For some types of work, an overview of this nature is unnecessary because the employee's role is clearly defined (as in the case of a secretary, an accountant, or a mailroom clerk). In most jobs, however, including even those just cited, there is a flow. Something happens before the job in question comes into the picture, and something happens afterward.

No job exists in isolation; each is a link in some larger chain. The general–specific–general formula, then, will help the employee understand his role in the total scheme of things. Job interest begins with this orientation of "where *I* fit in."

STEP 5. BEGIN BUILDING A FEELING OF SECURITY

Security has a variety of nuances. It can mean that the employee has a sense of safety, physical or otherwise; that the benefits provided by the company will guard against major financial loss in the event of family or personal illness; that the pay and privileges are equitable for the job being performed.

Basically, security means being able to plan ahead with confidence. At this point in the orientation, it should be made clear to the new employee that he can do so with reasonable faith and assurance.

To assist in this step—and in some of the others as well—an employee orientation checksheet (see Figure 9) lists a number of items in the "What We Offer You" section. Additionally, another section, "Some Specifics Affecting You," covers the rules, regulations, and policies with which the employee must be familiar.

This is the step in the orientation process that takes time. To try to do it all in one brief meeting would only cause confusion. The basic rules and regulations the employee must know *now* have to be covered, but the broad range of personnel policies and fringe benefits should be reviewed over a period of time. As said before, orientation isn't either a one-hour or one-day affair. While it may be fairly concentrated at first, subsequent periodic meetings should be programmed so that, little by little, all of the key issues are discussed.

Building a sense of security is of no passing importance. The new employee, regardless of title, has every right to know what benefits the company offers. He has a right to know whom he should see when personal problems arise—and that person ought to be the immediate supervisor *first*. He has a right to know what medical services are available, the vacation policy, how often and when he gets paid, and the working hours and schedule. These items, plus others, deserve full disclosure. The manager who slides over them is being unfair to the employee and to the company itself.

STEP 6. CREATE A FEELING OF BELONGING

The need to belong is important to everyone. The desire to become part of a group or be socially accepted is a strong emotion that shapes behavior and performance in the work situation.

Obviously, the new employee on the first day on the job has no sense of being a part of anything. The surroundings are foreign, the people with whom he will work unknown quantities. Being a stranger on unfamiliar ground and in the midst of people one has never met often produces a discomforting insecurity. "Psychosocial isolation" is one way of putting it. The U.S. manager can probably identify with this emotion if his own orientation was poorly done when he arrived at his overseas post.

Putting the new employee's natural concerns to rest is one of the supervisor's first responsibilities, and it can be initiated almost immediately. One step that is usually appreciated is to prepare an envelope, with the employee's name on it, that the supervisor gives him during the initial meeting. Included in the envelope might be items such as:

- A simple, hand-drawn map of the building or facility in which the employee will work. His own work area would be marked with an X and related organizations or functions identified. The map can also indicate lunchroom areas, washrooms, bulletin boards, parking areas, and the like. In Moslem countries, the room or space reserved for prayer should be clearly identified, if provisions have been made for such an area.
- A booklet or brochure that describes the history and growth of the company.
- Two organization charts: one of the company as a whole, but in skeleton form, and one of the employee's department in detail, with the titles and names of the people with whom the employee will work directly.
- A copy of the latest company newspaper or house organ.
- A copy of the latest stockholders' report—especially for those entering management positions.
- Samples of advertising materials, brochures, giveaways for customers, and similar items of general interest.
- A copy of key personnel benefits and regulations, whether in prepared booklet form (as many of the larger organizations provide) or merely reproductions from the company's personnel manual.

Whatever is in the envelope, the contents should be assembled with these objectives in mind: (1) to communicate, and (2) to make the employee feel that he was expected, he is welcome, and the supervisor is interested in helping him get started on the right foot. Small things, but they do pay off.

Next in this step is the actual physical orientation. This means tours of the work areas and offices related to the employee's job, plus indications of where facilities such as restrooms, snack bars, parking areas, bulletin boards, and telephones are located.

FIGURE 9. Employee orientation checksheet.

The following are to be discussed with all new employees. Do not attempt to cover every item in detail during the initial meeting. "Who We Are" and "What We Offer You" should be reviewed generally and supported by company literature, followed later by a more in-depth orientation. Check off each item when fully discussed. The completed form is then inserted in the employee's personal file.

WHO WE ARE

— 1. Company products or services.
— 2. Number of employees.
— 3. Basic company organization (general).
— 4. Department or unit organization (specific).

— 5. Brief history of the company.
— 6. Outstanding achievements/contributions.
— 7. Future plans for new products, expansion, etc.
— 8. Role in *this* country.

WHAT WE OFFER YOU

— 9. Medical services available.
—10. Sick leave policy.
—11. Holidays.
—12. Salary programs (automatic, merit, CLD adjustments).
—13. Insurance programs (eligibility, coverage, and so on).
—14. Retirement plans (eligibility, deductions, and so on).
—15. Vacations.

—16. Special privileges, discounts, and so on.
—17. Social groups, clubs, sports.
—18. Company newspaper, newsletters, and so on.
—19. Grievance procedure.
—20. Suggestion plan.
—21. Promotional opportunities.
—22. Service emblems, company pins, awards.

This phase should be a relaxed, walking-talking tour that gives the employee a sense of physical direction. There is no substitute for a few minutes spent going through the plant or offices. It eases the uncertainty of "being here but not knowing where 'here' is."

The last part of Step 6 is the personal introductions to fellow workers. These shouldn't be long-winded conversations. In fact, brevity is favored—just a few words about the new employee, some comments about the old employee being introduced, and a description of what the latter does. That's all that's necessary. As the rounds are made,

---

SOME SPECIFICS AFFECTING YOU

__23. Identification card, if required.
__24. Uniform or special work clothes.
__25. Lockers, wash-up areas.
__26. Conveniences (lunchrooms, restrooms, transportation).
__27. Information sources (bulletins, bulletin boards).
__28. Fire precautions (signals, ways of reporting fires, drills).

__29. Safety rules and precautions.
__30. Company manuals of direct concern.
__31. Disciplinary action—causes for.
__32. Personal conduct standards—smoking, drinking, appearance, wage attachments, use of company materials, and so on.

HELPING YOU GET STARTED

__33. Work schedule.
__34. Training plan.
__35. Questions—who to see.

__36. Introductions—supervisors, co-workers.
__37. Tour of facilities.

The items checked on this form have been reviewed and discussed with the employee.

_____   _____
Supervisor's signature   Title

_____   _____
Employee's signature   Title

_____
Date

the feeling of being a complete stranger will gradually diminish. Such a tour, when coupled with the other actions taken, will foster a sense of belonging. It's only a start, but an all-important start.

STEP 7. CONTINUE TO SHOW PERSONAL INTEREST

The initial orientation is over. Perhaps three or four weeks have elapsed. How is the new employee doing now?

Some supervisors haven't the slightest idea and care even less. If the first few days of orientation were done well and the employee had the feeling of really being a part of the organization, the supervisor's failure to show any further interest can be deflating and disturbing.

For one thing, the employee may begin to wonder whether he's failing or has somehow dissatisfied the boss. Or he may become disillusioned and decide that the orientation was just a sham—a routine the supervisor was required to go through—and the welcome only veneer.

Not all employees react this way, but many do. It is less likely when the new employee is in a managerial position because the very nature of his work will probably keep him in close contact with his immediate superior. When it comes to the nonmanagement employee, disinterest is more common. Perhaps this is because of the number of people under the supervisor; perhaps it's because the supervisor feels somebody else can easily be hired if this individual doesn't work out.

A more dangerous cause of this attitude may be the manager's belief that the semiskilled or laboring class is concerned only with a paycheck and isn't particularly sensitive to slights or managerial disinterest in its welfare. This is a blatant misconception. And if translated into behavior, it is likely to destroy the new employee's performance and whatever positive feelings he may have had initially.

Personal interest during the orientation process simply means a continuing demonstration of concern for the employee. It doesn't mean babysitting, mothering, or isolating the employee for special attention to the neglect of others. It just means good human relations and evident empathy for one who is trying to become an accepted, productive member of the organization.

Conclusion

Does an effective orientation take time? *Yes.* Is it worth the time? *Yes.* Will it always work? *No.* People are people, but in 90 percent of the cases, it *will* produce the results you want in performance, more rapid assimilation into the work group, and greater job and company interest. It will also reduce questions about pay, fringe benefits, and regulations. Finally, if the right employee has been hired in the first place, a sound orientation program will minimize the potential of early but very costly turnover.

These are fairly substantial returns on the supervisor's investment of his time. If the U.S. manager orients his immediate subordinates well and then trains them in the same techniques, the kind of program that produces results will soon become part and parcel of the organization's approach to the human element. When this is followed by an effective training program, the new employee—manager or worker—is off to the best possible start.

13

Training — the Next Step

The typical countries in transition are a far cry from what they were in 1970 or even 1975. The developing world is advancing rapidly as the wealth of oil and astute capital investments rush it into the twentieth century. It has the money and some of the hardware, but, by its own admission, technical and managerial expertise is in short supply. Help from the industrialized West is essential—not only in terms of materials, products, and know-how, but in helping the local employee learn what has to be learned so that he can function autonomously in whatever position he finds himself.

A well-managed training program is a basic element of a foreign enterprise. It is one of the best and most readily recognized demonstrations of the enterprise's willingness and desire to develop local employees. An effective training program can serve two functions: develop an effective work force and establish a favorable relationship with the local community.

Local societies look with favor on a foreign enterprise when it provides employment for local workers, when the jobs entail responsibility and offer pay comparable to those of jobs in other societies, and when the enterprise reduces the number of foreign specialists it employs as quickly as possible.[1]

All of which means that training is an expected segment of the work experience. Many U.S. managers, however, don't see it as *their* responsibility. That's up to the training department or somebody

---

[1] Robert H. Wilson, "Training in International Cultures," in *Training and Development Handbook,* ed. Robert L. Craig (New York: McGraw-Hill, 1976), p. 30-11.

else. Few rank it high on their list of priorities or even consider that they should be involved in it at all. "I'm no trainer; I'm a manager" is a common psychology. The very personal responsibility for the development of subordinates seems to escape a large percentage of our people abroad.

Another frequently voiced observation is that: "I don't have time to train—even if I wanted to." Watch these same managers, however, and see what they're doing most of every day. Among their various activities, you'll find them:

Correcting subordinates' mistakes.
Putting out fires.
Issuing orders.
Redoing work submitted by their subordinates.
Answering questions.
Solving minor problems.
Coping with crises.
Monitoring the work being performed.
Following up on deadlines, assignments, and the details of the operation.

Of course they don't have time! They haven't taken time in the first place to do the necessary training. Now, caught up in busyness and activities, they're reaping the harvest of their neglect.

The training department, if one even exists at all in the foreign location, has a role to play, but there's no way it can follow up on what each "graduate" is or isn't doing on the job. Nor can it be available to answer every question, solve the problems that inevitably arise, or hone the skills of its trainees. Those are the responsibilities of the employee's immediate superior, be he foreman or managing director.

When there is no training department on the site, which is more often the case, only the manager himself can fill the void. If he wants eventual performance from a probably unskilled labor or management force, the training responsibility is his—and only his.

Assuming the manager has selected the right subordinate, oriented him properly, and then trained him as he should be trained, the best possible beginning has been made to ensure employee competence. The foundation for the whole development process has been laid. Without the foundation, development is equivalent to building a house on sand.

When and When Not to Train

Don't jump to conclusions about training. There are times when it is essential and times when it's not the answer to performance problems. It is essential when:

1. The employee is new and knows nothing about the job. (This is obvious.)
2. The employee, experienced or not, cannot perform some task because of a knowledge or skill deficiency. This deficiency may have been identified through observation, quality or quantity of the end product, questions, monitoring, feedback, or mistakes in the work.
3. The employee is doing the work incorrectly because he has developed bad habits or thinks certain shortcuts would get the job done just as well.
4. The employee is being reassigned to a job or task he has not performed for a period of months. In such a case, he is likely to need some degree of refresher training, especially in the knowledge area.

On the other hand, training isn't the answer to *all* employee performance failures. When the cause of employee failure does not lie in one of the four factors listed above, the manager had better analyze his own shop and his personal supervisory techniques. There is where the fault probably lies. Training will have little effect when any of these conditions exist:

Poor supervision.
Incomplete or inadequate instructions, information, or directives.
Lack of proper tools, materials, or equipment.
Poor working conditions.
Inadequate staffing.
Conflicting instructions.
Failure to break down the language barrier.

If one or more of these conditions is the cause of performance deficiencies, a classroom or on-the-job training program is hardly the solution. That's only attacking the disease with the wrong cure.

If we disregard that possibility for now, the need for a planned, well-organized training program for local employees can't be overstressed. The odds are great that they won't know the Western ways of working, whether the field be technical, managerial, or whatever. Plus, they can't know how *this* company operates. Patient, thorough training is essential. The learning may take a little longer than the manager is accustomed to at home, but the local person will learn—if the manager will only teach.

Why Adults Learn

A number of basic factors enter into the adult learning process, many of which are accentuated because of the traditions and culture of the developing society:

○ *Fear*—of not knowing or of being caught short—creates an emotional force that says, "I *must* learn."

○ *Anxiety*, not as penetrating as fear, causes people to seek out further information or knowledge. "I'm not afraid of failing at my job, but I don't feel as secure as I'd like. I need to know more."

○ *Self-satisfaction* moves people to want to become more professional in their work, to do things well, to gain an inner sense of achievement and competence.

○ *Self-esteem*, so important in the developing societies, creates the drive to seek assistance that will allow them to appear favorably in the eyes of their family, friends, and co-workers. Failure, or anything resembling it, is to be avoided at all cost. The self-esteem of the local makes him a ready candidate for any learning experience.

○ *Family pressure* is a force more predominant abroad than in the United States. If the father has been successful, or if brothers or cousins hold responsible positions in some profession, the family name and its status in society are at stake. Pressure from male relatives can drive the employee to learn whatever is required so that he will reflect favorably on the family.

○ *Economic ambition* is an obvious contributor to the desire to learn. Without learning and knowledge, advancement to a more financially secure way of life is unlikely.

In many instances, however, this is not a strong motivator, especially in the oil-rich countries of the Middle East or in countries where promotions up the ladder are more through nepotism, paternalism, or tenure than ability. In areas of high per capita wealth, such as the Emirates, Kuwait, Saudi Arabia, and Venezuela, the local employee, particularly one in a managerial position, may come from a family in which money is of little consequence. Financial security is the least of concerns. Thus, appeals to the employee to learn on the basis of earning more money will have little effect. Instead, his motivating force will be self-esteem or family pressures.

○ *Reward,* either tangible or intangible, is another reason why people learn. "Reward" has various meanings, depending on the individual. It can mean a pay increase, a merit raise, a promotion, a commendation, or merely a favorable letter in the personnel file. Whatever it represents, it usually relates to financial benefits, self-esteem, or self-satisfaction. The potential for a reward of some nature sharpens the desire to learn as well as the learning process itself.

The challenge for the U.S. manager is to find out what factor is most likely to trigger the local employee's motivation to learn. For some, it could well be the appeal of money; others might respond more to family pride and maintaining the family name; the majority will probably react most positively when they can see the opportunity for greater self-satisfaction and increased self-esteem. Trying to force learning by creating a climate that breeds anxiety or fear is usually the least successful approach.

Why Adults Don't Learn

Even with strong motivation, adults may fail to learn when any of the following conditions exist:

○ *The working situation makes good performance impossible.* This is often the case when the manager finds his people not performing as they should. Rather than analyze the real causes, such as lack of materials, poor working conditions, or his own style of leadership, he sets up a training program. Because training, or the lack of it, isn't the problem, the results produce no changes—and the manager wonders why.

○ *What is being taught is too theoretical or impractical.* It doesn't pertain to real life and what goes on in the real world. Roaming in the clouds of the ideal, it fails to confront facts as they are. The material being presented must relate directly to what the employee will be expected to do on the job. Otherwise, he will turn off his listening and learning mechanisms.

○ *The training isn't relevant or job-related.* There should be no "training for training's sake," as occurred in one Middle Eastern company. A consultant was hired to teach Job Instruction Training (the old JIT from World War II days) to all management personnel except those at the executive level. The course was sound and well-presented, but many of those attending had no subordinates and probably wouldn't have any within the foreseeable future. So they sat through two days of classes in boredom and disinterest. A natural reaction, since the material taught had no practical application for them.

○ *The instructor is dull or uninspiring.* People need inspiration. They'll respond when the material is presented with a practical level of enthusiasm. Nearly everyone has experienced the plodding monotones of a robot-like instructor as he drones through his canned and rehearsed presentation. Maybe the motivation to learn was there, but heavy-lidded drowsiness soon dulled whatever desire once existed.

○ *The instruction is disorganized.* The subject may be relevant, the instructor enthusiastic, the jokes and stories scintillating. But if the material is presented in a labyrinthian manner, the trainee will be lost right after the introduction.

Organization is essential in training local employees. Use the approach of, "Tell 'em what you're going to tell 'em; tell 'em; tell 'em what you've told 'em." In other words, preview—body—review. First give them a verbal or written road map of where they're going. Then, step by step and little by little, cover the material in a logical, sequential order. With the probable combination of inexperience and language difficulties, anything but a highly organized presentation will produce confusion, and little or no learning will occur.

○ *The purpose of the training isn't defined.* If the local employee is to develop a desire to learn, he must know why he is being assigned to a training class and why the training is being conducted. For the new employee, the purpose is apparent. But someone who has been on the job a while may become suspicious or concerned. As one local said at the beginning of a management training course, "I was told to report here, but I don't know why. What have I done wrong? Has my supervisor said anything to you?" He was plainly ill at ease—a not uncommon condition when the whys and whats haven't been explained in advance.

○ *The end results (terminal behavior) are not stated.* The employee should know what the training will produce—what he'll be able to *do* once he's back on the job. "Understanding" or "having an appreciation of . . ." isn't enough by itself. As anyone familiar with programmed instruction knows, the ability to do something, on the basis of understanding, is what counts.

○ *The subject is too complicated or too basic.* In either case, the employee loses interest. Of the two, the first is the more common error in training local nationals. Not fully appreciating their relative lack of sophistication, the U.S. manager assumes that systems or processes which are routine to him will be grasped with equal facility by the local employees. When the results aren't what he expected, frustration sets in, and, at least mentally, he accuses the employees of "just not having what it takes."

If the subject matter is too basic, or is presented with funny-paper simplicity, the local person feels he's being talked down to, without adequate consideration for his intelligence. Being treated like a child is demeaning to his self-esteem, as indeed it is to anyone's. In his case, however, he's likely to be more resentful than an American subordinate because he detects the lack of sensitivity of the manager and a failure to accord him the respect he deserves.

   o *There is too much lecturing and not enough trainee involvement.* Americans have often been told that local employees won't question the instructor and will shy away from efforts to generate group discussion. In the author's experience, that simply isn't so. Admittedly, an informal climate of freedom and lack of risk has to be created. But, given that climate, a group of local trainees will talk, discuss, and argue with all the fervor anyone could ask.

The fault of U.S. managers is that they slip too easily into the "tell" mode. The tendency is to lecture, preach, and avoid the potential for controversy that a give-and-take exchange presents. So the training becomes a one-way monologue, with employee interest dwindling as the instructor plods on—and on—and on.

Involvement is the answer. Being allowed to ask questions at any time, becoming engrossed in case studies or simulated situations, role-playing—these and similar instructional techniques maintain interest and enhance the learning process.

Other factors that adversely affect people's ability to learn could be added. Poor lighting, uncomfortable chairs, not enough working space, not enough stretch or coffee breaks, a long lecture right after a heavy lunch, poorly prepared visual aids—these all militate against a healthy learning environment. Perhaps the instructor can't do anything about the lighting, the chairs, or other physical conditions, but he certainly can do something about the conditions over which he has control. A brief glance at reasons why people don't learn will indicate that each is within the manager's area of responsibility. It's up to him to plan, organize, and present his material in such a way that none of the reasons is allowed to affect the employees he is teaching.

A Suggested Instructional Sequence

The author's experience in training overseas managers has revealed what seems to be the most effective instructional sequence or organization:

STEP 1. ESTABLISH THE PRINCIPLES FIRST

It makes little difference whether the subject is welding, accounting, or how to conduct performance appraisals. The principles or theories should be established first. To do so is especially important in countries where the basics of technical or managerial work are strange to the society and represent new disciplines.

STEP 2. ASSIGN REALISTIC PROBLEMS OR SITUATIONS

On either a group or individual basis, involve the trainees in realistic, job-related exercises that are to be discussed, solved, or completed. The resolution of each exercise should require the trainees to apply the principles already established.

STEP 3. REVIEW AND EVALUATE RESULTS

Provide the opportunity for the trainees to present their solutions for group and instructor evaluation and then give them feedback on how well they attacked the problem or situation contained in the exercise. The feedback must be handled carefully, however. Wrong answers or wrong solutions have to be discussed most diplomatically. Any critique that would cause a trainee to feel inferior or incapable could have serious repercussions on his self-esteem.

The most successful technique in this situation is to give credit for the effort exerted and then, through questions, help the trainee analyze where he went wrong and how he might have resolved the issue by another approach. In other words, don't tell him what he did incorrectly. Help him discover his errors—whether mental, manual, or judgmental—so that he can intelligently avoid them in the future. Also, don't tell him what he should do if he faces the same situation again. Make him think of what he would do by using questions:

"What would you do next time?"
"Why would you do that?"
"What would happen if you did that?"
"If you did that, what could go wrong?"
"When would you take that step?"
"How might that affect the results?"
"Why do you think that's the best approach?"
"What other information do you need?"
"How practical is your solution?"

Without any doubt, the U.S. manager has to teach. That's his role in Step 1, when he establishes the principles and techniques. In so doing, he's primarily a "teller." The role is reversed, however, during the evaluation-and-feedback stage. Here, using questions, he tries to get the trainee thinking so that he can act with understanding and intelligence in real-life situations. The trainee should not be a robot, doing only what he was told in mechanical, unthinking ways.

Avoidance of a robot-like behavior mode is another reason why feedback is a delicate matter, whether in the training session or on the job. If the trainee has learned to fear his boss, he will do only what the boss tells him and do it in the way he was instructed. If, at some later time, he forgets any step in the instructions, he'll be at the boss's doorstep asking what he should do now. Independent action— taking the action he thinks is best under the circumstances—won't be one of his behavior traits.

Then, as so often happens, the U.S. manager becomes irritated and eventually concludes that "you can't teach these people anything." In frustration, he decides that "the only way to get things done right around here is to do them myself." So he does—and one more potentially effective local employee fades into the background of the also-rans.

STEP 4. RESTATE THE PRINCIPLES

After the evaluation, summarize the principles as they relate to the problem or situation. If additional instruction is necessary because the assignment wasn't well-handled, this is the time to provide it. In cases where the principles were clearly not grasped, more in-depth instruction may be required, followed by the assignment of another exercise. In summary, the sequence is (1) establish principles; (2) assign tasks, cases, problems, or situations; (3) evaluate results and provide feedback; (4) summarize principles or, if necessary, instruct further.

The Role of Experience in the Learning Process

Herein lies one of the more difficult problems in training local nationals. For adults, experience affects the rapidity with which they learn and the depth of comprehension. However, the local employee's experience is often not in harmony with what he is being asked to learn. Whether mechanic or manager, the local person isn't likely to have been exposed to American technology or methodology. Thus he sometimes finds it difficult to relate new knowledge to the accumulated experiences of a lifetime.

There is another reason why the local employee should be trained in a climate that encourages him to talk, interrupt, question, disagree, and think actively. He and his fellow workers aren't schoolchildren; they are adults who are trying to master concepts and practices that may be foreign to anything they have known. They must be allowed to become involved and not merely memorize the preachments of the instructor/manager.

Another aspect of experience is that what the local is being asked to learn must be in concert with his cultural habits, beliefs, and prejudices. If there is conflict, not only will learning fail to take place but what is taught will be rejected—perhaps quite vehemently. All of which means that the policies and practices of the U.S. firm must harmonize with, or at least not grate against, the local way of life.

Reward and Punishment in the Training Milieu

Reward and punishment, as elements of the Law of Effect, were discussed back in Chapter 5, and again they enter the picture in the matter of training. Generally speaking, children in the learning situation tend to react more positively to external forces, such as threats or promises of reward. The carrot-stick technique can also motivate the adult learner, but not to the same extent. His is more of an internal motivation to master, to achieve, to accomplish. Then if his successes are recognized and his failures delicately treated, the desire to learn is enhanced.

In the developing countries, threatening an employee, whether in training or on the job, is of little value. You must remember that you probably can't fire him or demote him. And material rewards, such as more money or a promotion, sometimes are empty promises that the manager can't keep.

So what's left? Nothing—except to conduct the training in a way that causes the employee to *want* to learn—not for the sake of some extrinsic reward, but for intrinsic satisfaction and increased emotional security. Then, when learning occurs and mastery of the subject is demonstrated, comes the time for congratulations, commendations, removal from probation, or promotion. The reward follows the act; it does not inspire it. The difference is subtle, but it's a very real difference in the training process. The promise of extrinsic rewards or the threat of extrinsic punishment rarely moves adults to learn, especially in the developing societies. If you can't punish to any measurable degree, it's foolish to offer only rewards—and how many rewards can you keep offering? The well soon runs dry.

Informality and Its Effect on Learning

The advantages of informality have been mentioned before, but they are still worth reemphasizing. The strict formality of the classroom, where the instructor is the star, is out of place in the industrial training environment. An atmosphere of coldness, one in which fear of failure is the dominant emotion, simply won't do the job. The trainee won't think; he'll merely memorize and parrot back the same words the instructor has used. He'll be a robot, with avoidance of failure his primary concern.

If your classroom has those miserable tablet armchairs, so common in most classrooms, get rid of them. Relegate them to the closest source of destruction. Then substitute tables and arrange them in a U so that the trainees can see and talk to one another face to face, not to the back of someone's head.

The visual aids (which will be discussed later) should be pertinent to the subject and well-designed. If a film is shown, be sure that it supports the subject and isn't used for entertainment or diversion. At the same time, don't just show it and then move on. A well-chosen film should generate an hour or two of profitable discussion, if the instructor uses it wisely.

Informality assumes the trainee's freedom to talk, argue, and disagree. When he feels free to say what's on his mind, the fear of failing is replaced by the desire to learn for the pleasure and benefit of learning. At that point, the local employee will be well on his way to mastering the new ideas or techniques being presented.

Tips on Making Instruction Easier

The foregoing has established a foundation for the instructional process. Below are a few additional tips that will make it easier for the U.S. manager, who in all probability is not a professional trainer.

START WITH THE KNOWN, LEAD TO THE UNKNOWN

At the very beginning of a training program that is to introduce something new, it helps to establish a relationship between something the trainee already knows and what will be taught. To illustrate: a manager wants to teach the principles and application of job-performance standards. He next intends to develop, with the subordinate, the latter's Job Performance Guide. Finally, the subordinate is to go through the same process with his own subordinates.

Instead of jumping into the subject feet first, the manager begins something like this: "Ramon, you've read your job description, and you know that it outlines, in broad terms, your responsibilities for planning, decision-making, supervising others, and so on. Now, what we're going to do is build on that job description. We're going to define your job more specifically by agreeing on your duties and then working out a standard of performance for each duty. What we finally develop will be another job description, but one that is more detailed and helpful to you in your day-to-day work."

Relating the known to the unknown provides a framework for thinking. It makes it easier for the trainee to comprehend the "new" because he can see a relationship between it and something he already knows.

TEACH THE SIMPLE FIRST, LEAD TO THE COMPLICATED

Or—crawl before you walk; walk before you run. This is an accepted principle that professional trainers follow but one that might not be practiced by the typical manager who is placed in a training position.

The lead-in is important. It mustn't overwhelm the trainee with confusing complexities. This will only create concern and so confound the trainee that he might easily surrender in frustration. An airline ticket agent finds it much easier to begin by learning that LHR is the designation for London Heathrow Airport than by jumping into interline ticketing and rate computations. A manager needs to know the basic functions of management before he is introduced to the techniques of problem-solving and decision-making.

In this respect, training is similar to the typical I.Q. test. The easy questions come at the beginning, the more difficult ones later.

KEEP EXPLANATIONS TO THE POINT

Even experienced instructors tend to be led astray at times. It's easy to get off the track. One question can do it, if the instructor isn't careful.

There is also the danger of the "That reminds me. . . ." What the instructor is reminded of may take him far afield into some unrelated area. The danger is that the trainee may not realize the digression is far afield. He may therefore learn, or try to learn, needless information.

With the local national, unidentified detours can be particularly harmful. Trained to take copious notes on whatever the instructor says, he could write pages on subjects that have no bearing whatsoever on the basic course material. In the process, he's learning the irrelevant and the trivial, which he may find difficult to separate from the essential.

If digression is necessary, make it clear that what is about to be discussed is indeed a digression. Tell the trainees when you're off course and tell them when you're back on the subject. Don't leave it up to them to determine when the detour starts and when it ends. They have enough problems without trying to make sense out of the instructor's wanderings.

GIVE REASONS FOR EACH STEP

This is simply a matter of explaining *why* something is to be done in a certain way or a certain sequence. The need for such explanations is apparent, but even experienced trainers occasionally fail to provide them.

The problem is that the better they know a job or an operation, the more they tend to make assumptions. They assume that the local employee understands the rationale behind a certain step in the process; they assume that he knows why this step comes first and that second; they assume that he grasps the relationship between steps and how one depends on another. The more thoroughly a manager knows a given job, the more likely he is to skip over key elements in the operation as well as the little tricks or knacks that help move the operation ahead.

It's somewhat like the instructor who was teaching a group of local instrument technicians how to re-solder electronic components that had separated from their original connections. Everything was going along fine until the trainees were told to go ahead and practice soldering a broken connection. Nothing happened. The instructor had forgotten to tell the trainees to plug in their electric soldering irons. It was such an obvious step that he had completely overlooked even mentioning it and had further assumed that *anyone* ought to know that's the first thing you have to do in such an operation.

Assuming is dangerous, particularly when training local nationals. The process, procedure, or method may be foreign to anything they've known before. To comprehend the logic behind what they are learning without explanation is asking too much of them. Lacking comprehension, all they can do is memorize the sequence and perform the task in robot-like fashion. Reduced to a formula:

Why = Understanding = Intelligent action

ENCOURAGE DISCUSSION

The value of trainee involvement has already been emphasized. Case studies, problems, subgroup tasks, and role-playing practically force the trainee's participation and response. When these are not on the immediate agenda, well-phrased questions and statements will arouse a lively discussion.

One of the most useless questions is, "Do you have any questions?" Close to it is, "Do you understand?" These beg "yes" or "no" answers, which tell the instructor nothing. If he wants to probe the depth of the employees' comprehension, he has to ask questions in a way that requires a response. For example:

"What would you do if this happened?"

"Why do we do this first?"

"What would happen if we didn't do this first?"

"When does this step come into the operation?"

"Who would you call if that happened?"

"How would you define 'management'?"

"What are some of the reasons managers don't delegate?"

"What is a 'performance standard'?"

"What is the difference between 'motivation' and 'manipulation'?"

Or, to change the pace, simple statements are just as successful in evoking trainee response:

"Define 'counseling' for me."

"Compare this new method with the one we've been using."

"Describe the steps of an effective orientation program."

"Outline the actions you would take if a subordinate filed a grievance."

"Explain the difference between Theory X and Y."

"Give me an example of the self-fulfilling prophecy."

"Tell me what you can about the Managerial Grid."

These are indirect, low-structure questions and statements that request a reply of some sort. None can be answered with a simple "yes" or "no," and the feedback tells the instructor whether he's conveyed his message and to what depth the trainee comprehends.

Another way to encourage trainee questions is for the instructor to make this type of remark:

"What have I said that may have confused you?"

"What words or terms might I have used that threw you off track?"

"How could I say it differently to get the point across?"

"To what extent are you still uncertain about the procedure?"

"When did I begin to lose you?"

"What other questions can I answer?"

These are designed to maintain a climate of freedom in which the trainee knows that questions are wanted and will not result in recriminations or loss of face. Note the phraseology used: most of the examples put the blame on the instructor if trainee confusion or uncertainty exists. They say, in effect, that *I* am the one who confused you, threw you off track, lost you, said it poorly.

When the instructor accepts the blame, it is easier for the trainee to speak up and ask questions to clear the air. It's already been acknowledged that failure to grasp a point wasn't his fault, so there's no risk in admitting his own lack of understanding. And, once again, there is no loss of face.

PROVIDE REINFORCEMENT

To bring "reward," "punishment," and "reinforcement" back into the picture momentarily, reinforcement theory plays an important role in the training process. Some measure of reward or punishment should be bestowed, but in a manner that encourages the trainee to continue the things he has been doing well and discard those that are producing negative results.

To illustrate: the trainee has been doing something well or responding correctly to questions. The instructor provides positive reinforcement (also called confirmation or reward):

"Keep coming. You're on the right track."

"Good summary. You said it well."

"You did a good job on that."

"Come on—you've almost got it."

"That was well done. Keep it up."

"I like the way you analyzed that."

"You ought to be pleased with the progress you're making."

On the other hand, negative reinforcement, or "punishment," is no more than:

"You seemed to have a little trouble there."

"It didn't work out well, did it?"

"No, you're not quite on course."

"How satisfied are you with these results?"

"What other way could you do it for better results?"

"Easy now. Think it through. What comes next?"

"What weak spots do you see in your argument?"

To the maximum extent possible, keep the trainee informed on how he's doing. Don't leave him in the dark, wondering whether he's succeeding or failing. He needs to know at all times where he stands, and he appreciates both positive and tactfully applied negative reinforcement.

For those familiar with programmed instruction, this type of feedback is one of its major benefits to instructor and trainee alike. The trainee gets almost instant reinforcement regarding the correctness or incorrectness of his response. When programmed presentations aren't practical in an overseas training facility, it becomes the instructor's responsibility to provide the reinforcement through gestures, motions, and the types of questions and statements illustrated above.

Basically, the whole concept boils down to this:

Stimulus + Response + Reinforcement = Desired behavior

The *stimulus* is what moves the trainee to study, to learn, to master. The *response* is what he does, says, or answers to periodic questions and tests. *Reinforcement* is learning whether his responses were right or wrong. And *desired behavior* is his ultimate ability to perform according to predetermined behavior objectives.

A Suggested Training Program for the Local Manager

In this book, the focus is on the training and development of local national managers, not the training of laborers, clerks, or other non-management personnel. Many of the same principles apply regardless of job level, but there's a difference between training a welder to weld and a manager to manage. The first is a mechanical task; the second is primarily a methodology and, in many ways, is more difficult to impart.

Workers, be they nationals or third-country employees, usually can be trained to a reasonable level of performance. Some of their equipment and tools may not be up to U.S. standards, and replacement parts may be hard to obtain. Further, until they are thoroughly knowledgeable, the workers may misuse the equipment or create unnecessary costs through carelessness, waste, or spoilage. However, once they have mastered every aspect of the job, they'll generally be guilty of these "sins" only if the way they are supervised motivates such anti-company behavior.

That's where the training of the local manager becomes so important. He can make or break his subordinates, regardless of their position in the hierarchy. There are many areas in which he will almost certainly need guidance if he is to function effectively. The most important of these include:

- What the U.S. manager expects of him in terms of duties, responsibilities, and standards of performance (the Job Performance Guide).
- What authority has been delegated to him (the Job Delegation Guide).
- Company and departmental procedures, policies, systems, methods, and rules.
- Production or service standards.
- Management principles and practices, such as how to plan, organize, staff, control, set objectives, delegate, communicate, handle grievances, solve problems, and evaluate performance.
- Leadership styles and skills that create a self-motivating organization climate.
- Interdepartmental relations and responsibilities.
- The organization structure, reporting channels, and who to see for what.
- Procedures for completing necessary records, reports, and files.
- Technical knowledge of the work for which he is responsible, if appropriate.

If the local manager has been hired from the outside, he'll require training in most or all of the areas listed. The employee promoted from within won't need as much instruction in organization structure, policies, or production standards, but in the other areas he'll undoubtedly have to be trained.

What might comprise such a training program? Let's assume that the local employee has the technical know-how but has had little or no training in management. A further assumption: the employee is a first-line supervisor responsible for a group of subordinates and is new to the company.

Every situation is different, but the following areas of instruction are usually applicable:

The job of supervising
    The new role of the supervisor
    Responsibilities of the first-line supervisor
    "Management" defined
    The functions of management
    New knowledge and skills required
    "Managing" versus "doing"

The integration of resources: people, machines, materials, money, time

What the company expects from its supervisors

The company—its business and its purpose

What is "business"?

The essential elements of a successful business

Types of businesses

The company's purpose and goals

Organizing for results

The company's organization structure

Some key organization concepts—channels, span of control, line/staff, and so on

Understanding human behavior on the job

Human behavior—basic drives

Basic human needs

The importance of self-esteem

The power of the group in determining production levels

The principle of reward

Frustration—symptoms and causes

Supervising national and third-country employees

The challenge of motivation

What do you want from your job?

What is "motivation"?[2]

Basic needs and motivation

What counts in a job?

What *you* can do to improve human relations

Attitudes and values of supervisors with regard to workers

Reward and punishment in motivation

Leadership styles

Your role as a leader

Styles of leadership

Becoming a democratic leader

Directing—as part of leadership styles

Why people follow leaders—some principles

Planning

"Planning" defined

The nature of planning

Objectives—the first step

Participative planning

Types of planning

Operating planning—to prevent problems

The steps in operating planning

[2] The average local supervisor/manager needs the *fundamentals* of motivation at this stage of his development. He normally isn't ready for the more sophisticated theories of people like McClellan, Likert, and Herzberg, or for the concept of job enrichment.

Personal planning
Planning to solve problems
Getting the new employee started right
"Orientation" defined
The feelings of the new employee
The seven-step orientation program
Training the work staff
The supervisor as a trainer
Why training often fails
Why and how adults learn
Tips on making instruction easier
The four-step method of instructing (JIT)
1. Prepare the trainee
2. Demonstrate the operation
3. Try out performance
4. Follow up
The job breakdown
Correcting the trainee
The job-qualification record
Personnel benefits and policies [3]
Wage and salary administration
What the salary administration department does
Job descriptions
Establishing salary grades and ranges—how it is done
Merit increases
Getting a job reevaluated
Personnel rules, regulations, and policies
Vacations
Time off
Holidays
Sick leaves and other types of leaves
Travel and travel allowances
Local transportation provisions for employees
Company automobiles
Insurance and retirement plans
Housing allowances
Clubs, employee organizations, recreation facilities
Payroll deductions
Delegating—to get things done
What is "delegation"?
Why managers don't delegate
The meaning of "responsibility"
Some principles of delegation

---

[3] These subjects are best discussed by a personnel or industrial relations representative, if one is on the job site.

How standards are established
Quality standards
Standards and work simplification
Enforcing established standards
Cost control and budgets
The supervisor: the key to cost control
Types of costs
The budget: its purpose and how prepared
The responsibility to live within the approved budget
Finding ways to do things better, more rapidly, more easily, or more cheaply

These are some of the critical areas in which the newly hired local manager needs training. The U.S. manager, however, has to be careful in what he presents and how he presents it. It's easy to become too sophisticated and to lose the trainee in the process. It's easy to talk too rapidly or to use words and terms the local person doesn't understand. And it's easy to argue when the employee says, "That may be fine in the United States, but it won't work here."

Perhaps above all, the manager has to have patience. He has to take it easy. Trying to do too much too rapidly will probably doom the training effort. Training is not filling a pitcher; it's lighting a lamp.

The program outlined above could be completed in a week if it were highly concentrated, but there's a question of how much good it would do and what would be retained. At the other extreme, and a more likely suggestion, teaching one subject a week would produce better results. Admittedly that's 17 weeks or 17 separate sessions, but this is not a devastating sacrifice if the objective is to have a well-trained, confident local manager on the job. The benefits will far outweigh the costs.

Preparing to Train

Whether in the classroom or on the job, effective training demands preparation and organization. Keeping in mind the points previously discussed in this chapter on training adults, consider these preparatory steps.

STEP 1. SET OBJECTIVES

Objectives describe what the trainee will be able *to do* when the training is completed. Unless the terminal behavior has been identified, the training is likely to be disjointed and good parts of it irrelevant, with a fair sprinkling of the nice-but-not-necessary-to-know. Furthermore, without objectives, the U.S. manager will never know whether he's reached his destination. He can't, because no destination was identified. It's the old saying: "If you don't know where you're going, any road will take you there."

Here are a few examples of objectives. When written up, each would be preceded by: "On completion of the training, the trainees will be able . . .

- o To read and interpret at least 80 percent of an engineering drawing without supervisory assistance.
- o To introduce the company's management-by-objectives system within their work units by July 1, 19—.
- o To complete all purchasing and material-requisitioning forms with 100 percent accuracy and in accordance with company policy.
- o To demonstrate the techniques of developing nonengineered performance standards for their subordinates.
- o To identify the five Managerial Grid behavior styles and explain the characteristics of each.
- o To demonstrate techniques for new-employee interviewing and for conducting effective performance appraisals.

Each objective indicates what the trainee will be able to read, interpret, introduce, complete, demonstrate, or identify once the training is over. He may not always be fully proficient in actual practice back on the job, but that's where coaching enters the picture. He has the basics; he's met the required standards in the training setting; he's proved his ability in accordance with the terminal behavior objective. Next will come on-the-job development to sharpen his skills and round off whatever rough edges remain (see Chapter 14).

STEP 2. DETERMINE WHAT IS TO BE TAUGHT

With the objective or objectives set, the manager has a target. Now he has to decide what subjects or materials must be taught in order to hit the target. In instructional jargon, this is the act of "discriminating"—of sifting out the nonessential, or nice-to-know, from the essential, or need-to-know.

For example: The manager is teaching a local supervisor how to fill out the company's performance appraisal form and how to conduct the appraisal interview. In discussing the form, he feels the supervisor ought to have an understanding of the other types of rating systems that exist, so he goes into a dissertation on the graphic rating scale, forced choice, the essay type, assessment centers, the critical incident, and so on.

Meanwhile, the supervisor obtains a lot of "nice" information that won't help him a bit in working with *his* company's system. The trouble is, he may not recognize it as nice-but-not-necessary—unless the manager has made the distinction very clear. He may logically conclude that if it's being taught, it must be important. So his notebook and his mind are filled with inconsequential miscellany. *Someday* the information might be useful, but not now.

It's the instructor's job—not the trainee's—to discriminate, to separate the essential from the nonessential. Unless he does so, the training is likely to fall short of its target.

STEP 3. DEVELOP THE TRAINING OUTLINE

After the key material has been isolated comes the task of organizing it broadly in a logical, sequential flow. Again, start with the known and lead to the unknown; teach the simple first, then the complicated.

Next, the instructor's outline, or "lesson plan," is developed. One mistake inexperienced instructors often make is to put too much in the outline. There are too many details, too many long sentences. Almost everything the instructor plans to say is on paper in front of him. He then tends to rely on the outline and read through the lesson instead of making an informal, off-the-cuff presentation. The outline becomes a crutch on which the whole training program depends.

The outline should literally be just that. It's nothing more than a reminder to the instructor of the points he must cover and in what sequence. Just a few brief words are all that's necessary—*if* the instructor knows what he's going to cover and knows his material. As an example: The manager wants to teach the local supervisors some aspects of motivation. His outline might look like this:

I. *Introduction*
   A. Objectives of today's meeting
   B. Why motivation is important to you
   C. Review of agenda
II. *Periods and characteristics of management practices*
   A. Scientific
   B. Human relations
   C. Participative
III. *Motivation defined*
IV. *Current research and its implications in your society*
   A. Theories X and Y

Why say more—if you know your subject and are prepared?

STEP 4. DEVELOP PERTINENT HANDOUT MATERIALS

Any subject that is taught needs to be supported by written materials. The trainee's desire to record important things the instructor says is fine, but it really isn't fair to put the full burden of note-taking on him. Not only that, but when he's buried in his work manual, his attention is distracted from the here and now. There's no way he can write as rapidly as the instructor speaks, so he's always behind, with the risk that something of importance is missed. Then, as the instructor is moving along at his own pace, come the questions about material that was covered while the trainee was engrossed in trying to make sense out of what was said 10 minutes before.

This problem is further accentuated when the trainee's English language ability is a little on the low side. Trying to capture the information in English, he occasionally finds it difficult, so he seeks an adequate translation in his own tongue. The more this is necessary, the further behind he falls and the more lost he is when he emerges from his notebook.

Providing each trainee with a written text or summary of the subject being discussed minimizes the need for excessive note-taking. The text, however, should reflect what is covered in the training session and not be just a series of photocopied articles from various books or magazines. It should be a specially prepared handout that summarizes what the instructor intends to teach. As such, it is an excellent instrument for trainee use during the course itself and for post-course review.

By the same token, all forms, charts, diagrams, and the like should be reproduced and distributed as handouts at the proper time. Don't hold up a personnel form and tell the trainee how to fill it out unless he has one in front of him. That doesn't happen? Sorry, it does.

Preparing texts and handouts takes time. The benefits to the trainee, however, far outweigh the effort expended. The training will go faster, comprehension will be more complete, and the terminal behavior objectives more likely to be achieved.

STEP 5. PREPARE THE VISUAL AIDS

The old adage that "One picture is worth . . ." applies particularly in the training of nationals. Even if a literal picture is not used, words, ideas, or schematics that are projected visually can both clarify and synthesize what is being said orally. At the same time, they help overcome whatever language barrier may exist.

The major issue for the U.S. manager is not whether to use visuals but how to select those that are most practical in terms of (1) the physical facilities in the training or meeting room, (2) the intended audience, and (3) the reproduction and equipment-repair services that are available in the local community. Regarding the last, it's not like at home where A/V suppliers are in every major city and repairs or temporary replacements can be obtained by just a brief phone call. For example, looking for a cassette recorder that would also pulse a tape for automatic slide advance proved to be a hopeless search in Kuwait City. As an employee of one of the leading A/V retail outlets commented, "We're just not that modern here."

So what is best, considering the country and its state of development? The following may help.

Flip Charts

Flip-chart pages that summarize in a few main headings the points being discussed are easy to develop, are brief and to the point, and contribute to the strength of the presentation. Charts made by a professional are usually more dramatic and eye-catching than those produced by a non-artist. However, even the amateur can get his message across if he exercises a little care, uses ruled paper, and gets a supply of watercolor felt markers (these don't bleed through the paper).

For recording notes or illustrating points during the presentation, a second flip-chart easel with blank paper is more effective than a blackboard. First of all, in many locations, the blackboards, greenboards, or slate boards are of poor quality. Sometimes even these aren't available, and the only substitute at hand is a piece of plywood painted black. The other advantage of the flip chart is that whatever has been written is still there if the instructor wants to turn back to it later in the session. The blackboard, in contrast, has to be erased frequently. This removes forever something that may be needed for subsequent reference.

Sturdy, lightweight easels aren't easy to come by in the developing countries, nor are the pads of paper. In fact, good-quality paper and easels are difficult to find outside the United States. The suggestion, then, is to order both from a reliable A/V supplier, such as the Oravisual Company in St. Petersburg, Florida, and have them shipped over. The time saved and the frustration avoided are well worth the expense.

There's another aspect to this: quality visual-aid equipment makes an impression on the trainees. It contributes to their realization that this is a first-class organization, interested in providing the best possible training with the best possible supporting tools. Relying on flimsy, jerry-built equipment that breaks down or for which the instructor is continually apologizing is not the way to create positive trainee attitudes. The local expects us to be professional in everything we do, so professional we should try to be.

Flannel, Magnetic, or Hook 'n' Loop Boards

Each of these serves the same purpose, which is to display prepared "slaps" to tell a story. In this role, they are helpful adjuncts to the flip chart.

While almost impossible to find overseas, a flannel board can be made locally without much effort. All it takes is a piece of fairly coarse flannel, obtainable in most dry-goods stores, that is then tacked or glued to a piece of plywood. The slaps are pieces of cardboard or posterboard, cut to the size desired, on which brief messages (a word or two) are printed. The only other material needed is the self-adhesive backing that is put on the rear of the slaps and holds them on the flannel. The backing almost certainly has to be purchased in the United States.

This type of aid has one advantage over the flip chart: it allows the instructor to put up one slap at a time, discuss it, and then add another—progressive disclosure. That technique isn't possible with the previously prepared flip chart because all the headings are revealed at the same time. This may be all right, but while the instructor is elaborating on the first point or heading, the trainee tends to read the entire page and misses what the instructor is saying. Progressive disclosure prevents that.

Slides

Slides are a common aid with many merits and few disadvantages. The major drawback is that they require a darkened room for sharpness and clarity. If the instructor uses them intermittently during the session, turning the projector on, turning the lights off, and then reversing the process may be disruptive to a smooth presentation flow. On the plus side, 2″ × 2″ slides can be made locally and can almost always be processed locally.

Transparencies and Overhead Projectors

Like slides, transparencies are effective training aids that are inexpensive and easy to produce. They offer an ideal way to display wiring diagrams, schematics, forms, organization charts, systems, and the like.

An advantage of transparencies over slides is that the room need not be darkened. With a bright overhead projector, the transparency can easily be seen under normal lighting.

Films

Again, this is an aid with pluses and minuses. A well-made technical or management film both supports and reinforces the instructor and, if used properly, generates considerable trainee discussion.

The minuses, for foreign use, include the language problem. With actors speaking at their normal pace, a considerable portion of the dialogue is often lost if the audience isn't proficient in English. Also, occasional slang or jargon may not be understood and a key point missed.

Another factor in using films is the electric current and the power-cycle range. Some American projectors have 110- and 220-volt switches, but if they do not, and the current is 220, a transformer is necessary. That's not usually a major problem, but the availability of a transformer shouldn't be overlooked.

A third factor to consider is the potential problem of importing films. Many countries insist on screening every film before it can clear customs. The screening poses two possible dangers. First, if the censoring official finds anything socially, politically, morally, or culturally offensive in the film, it won't be admitted—even though it's strictly a technical or management training aid. Second, those who do the censoring may or may not treat the film with even reasonable care. One that had been taken into Saudi Arabia was screened by a government official. It was subsequently torn in three places, tattooed with sprocket-wheel marks, and patched up with cellophane tape. Needless to say, it was beyond repair, so $350 went down the drain—and with no recourse.

If the company has established good relations with the customs inspectors, many of these importing problems can probably be avoided. Once the officials know that the company doesn't import banned or borderline articles, they are usually more than cooperative. But the risk of importation is still something to consider. Good films run in the $350–450 price range and aren't items to be treated carelessly.

Even so, if films are to be part of any training program, they should be purchased, not rented. Some American producers won't rent at all if the film is to be shown outside the United States (Canada and Mexico generally excepted). Others will rent but charge for the time the film is gone, which, including shipping time, could be four weeks or more.

Furthermore, the renter is fully responsible for any damage incurred, whether it's his fault or not. And then keep in mind that both the foreign country and U.S. customs will probably screen the film before admitting it. It's thus subject to two inspections before it gets back to the producer.

With these problems, it's easier, cheaper, and more practical to buy. The cost isn't that much more, and the film is always on hand whenever it is needed.

Other Aids

Don't overlook drawings, sketches, blueprints, and enlarged photographs. Mockups and simulators have their place, but they can run into a fair amount of money. Models and physical samples are helpful for hands-on experience. Tape recorders, pulsed tape/slide presentations, and filmstrips are other aids that materially support a training program.

And then there is videotape, with its camera and television playback system. This is an ideal tool to help the trainee see himself while performing manual tasks, practicing a sales presentation, learning how to conduct an interview, or developing customer-relations skills. However, the use of VTR (videotape recording) in most developing countries is questionable because of maintenance problems. This is a sophisticated system that may be beyond the electronic skills of local technicians. When one can't even locate a tape pulser in a city as modern as Kuwait, it's unlikely that a VTR expert would be on the scene. Just trying to get a TV set repaired and back in normal working condition can be a challenge.

In conclusion, which aids the U.S. manager chooses will depend on his personal preferences and on the practicality of the aids in the local environment. If selected wisely, properly prepared, and keyed to the message to be delivered, they are invaluable—frequently essential—tools in the training process. Visual images often "say" more than words. They create a deeper impression that is retained long after the echo of sound has died away.

STEP 6. ARRANGE THE FACILITY

Wherever the training is to be conducted, be it office or classroom, a few provisions need to be taken.

○ The training area should be quiet and protected from interruptions. If it's a classroom, there should be no telephones or pictures on the wall to distract attention. Windows should be curtained or blocked with venetian blinds. Even remove or relocate a clock so the trainees can't see it easily. In other words, eliminate every possible item that could draw the trainees' attention away from the reason for their being there.

○ Ensure maximum possible comfort in terms of chairs, heating and cooling, ventilation, lighting, visibility from all parts of the room, and an adequate working area for each trainee.

○ Be certain that the proper electrical equipment (extension cords, outlets, transformers, plug adapters) is on hand for projectors or tape recorders and that room-darkening facilities have been provided.

○ Set up the room in advance of the training session. This means arranging the tables; having name cards, if they're necessary, in place; distributing text materials, notebooks, and pencils; and getting the entire room organized and ready for the class. All of this should be completed the day before the class convenes, at the latest, so that there is no confusion or last-minute scurrying around when the trainees are already in the room. They won't be impressed by lack of preparation.

○ If a film is to be shown, have it threaded, focused, and the sound level tested well in advance. When the projector is turned on, the very beginning of the film itself should appear immediately on the screen and not the lead-in. At the end of the film, turn the projector off immediately. Worry about rewinding it later.

These may sound like simplistic admonitions, but it's surprising how many instructors, even those who consider themselves professionals, overlook the details of careful preparation. One of the best compliments an instructor can receive is when a trainee says, "You sure had this course organized." The local employee especially appreciates it because he sees it as another example of American efficiency.

How the room is physically arranged is largely the manager's choice. If it's a one-person class in the manager's office, that's one thing. When several trainees are to attend, however, the U-shape placing of tables shown in Figure 10 is one of the better configurations.

This arrangement has the advantage of allowing everyone to see everyone else with a minimum of head-turning. At the same time, the instructor can make eye contact with each participant and, if he chooses, has walking room in the inside of the U. The arrangement lends itself to easy informality among the entire group, which is what the instructor should be seeking.

STEP 7. SCHEDULE THE TRAINING

Those who are to attend the training should be so advised at least a week in advance. Two weeks is even better. Also, give them copies of the course agenda, and emphasize particularly the starting time. You'll have a lot of late arrivals if you don't.

Be sure to plan the training so that it won't conflict with holidays, religious observances, or peak work periods. These should be obvious

FIGURE 10.   U-shaped arrangement for training sessions.

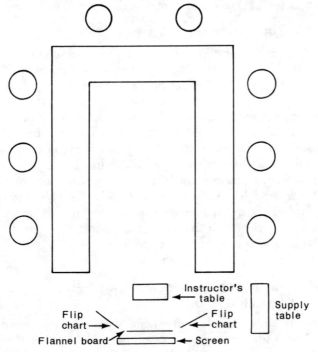

considerations, but U.S. managers often forget about or are not familiar with national and religious holidays.

Preparing to train is about 90 percent of an effective training course. It takes time—maybe 10–15 hours for each hour of instruction—but it all pays off in better employee performance and productivity.

The U.S. manager may feel that he can't take the time. He has a shop to run, an operation to oversee. He's right, but if he doesn't train his people now, they'll learn by osmosis or trial and error. Meanwhile the mistakes pile up, the manager gets busier than ever, and the people become more and more useless. Training is an investment in the future. It costs today and pays off tomorrow. Overseas it's an absolute essential, and is one of the primary reasons the manager is there in the first place.

Conducting the Course

The specific techniques of training are beyond the scope of this book. However, a few suggestions and observations are in order.

START ON TIME AND END ON TIME

As we've discussed before, time is relatively meaningless in the developing countries, so a training class is an ideal opportunity to stress and restress the fact that 8:00 *means* 8:00. By the same token, if you expect the trainees to be ready to go at 8:00, extend to them the same courtesy of stopping when you said you would stop. What with car pools and family obligations, if 4:30 is adjournment time, honor it. Turnabout is fair play, and you will only be inconveniencing others if the class drags on for another 15 or 30 minutes.

Keep enforcing the concept of promptness when returning from coffee breaks and lunch. A 15-minute coffee break is just that. If you're rigid but tactful in your demands for on-time performance, the trainees will quickly learn that you mean business. You'll still have a few who are habitually late, but the majority will begin to conform—in the classroom and on the job.

DON'T SCHEDULE CLASSROOM ACTIVITIES AFTER
NORMAL WORKING HOURS

Even with advance notice, after-hours work can cause family hardships. Homework, reading, or a case study is all right if the assignment isn't too lengthy. But the local manager has his family responsibilities that take precedence over any office obligations. Shopping, care of the children, and helping them with their own homework may limit his time during the evenings. He'll probably do the best he can with an assignment, but it's likely to be a superficial piece of work if it is lengthy or complex.

For the same reasons, formal evening sessions usually won't work. If enforced, they'll be greeted with rebellion, or at least strong vocal discontent. The only really successful way to include after-hours tasks in a training session is to set up shop in a distant out-of-town or out-of-country hotel. Geographically separated from their families, the trainees will then do anything you ask of them. This is an expensive alternative, however, and the benefits may not be worth the cost.

BE SURE THE TRAINEES ARE ACTIVE AFTER LUNCH

The main meal, for most local nationals, is at noon. Having typically had a light breakfast, they're hungry come lunchtime—a fact to which their full plates visibly attest. They're unlikely to go the soup-and-sandwich route.

Since postlunch lethargy is a certainty, schedule something that will require group activity—a tough problem, a case study, subgroup tasks, role-playing situations, anything that will get the people moving and involved. A lengthy lecture will almost certainly fall on somnolent ears.

KEEP ASKING FOR FEEDBACK

Throughout the session, test the waters. Ask questions about how *you* are coming across by using some of the questions suggested earlier in this chapter. If you've established the right climate of friendliness and informality, the trainee will give you the feedback you want so that you can determine what he has learned and evaluate your own performance as a manager/instructor at the same time.

NEVER MAKE FUN OF OR SCOLD A TRAINEE PUBLICLY

The manager's patience may get a little frayed at times, and his irritation may show through. If it does, in the form of sarcasm or public reprimand, the results can prove very serious. The local employees will respond with silence, for fear of exposing themselves to the same inconsideration, and they'll do a lot of talking after class among themselves and to others in the organization. That will just about ruin the manager's reputation as an instructor and possibly even as a manager.

ENCOURAGE ON EVERY POSSIBLE OCCASION

Just as you need feedback on your own performance, so does the trainee. Whenever you can, give positive reinforcement. As you do, you'll be shaping the trainee's behavior along the path you want. Even when the group returns on time from a coffee break, make some comment of recognition. "Hey, a good on-time performance! Keep it up" will encourage a repeat of the behavior that brought a word of praise.

BE *VERY* CAREFUL ABOUT DISCUSSING POLITICAL, RELIGIOUS, OR CULTURAL MATTERS

The best advice is not to discuss them at all. Not only do you risk offending the local employees, but word has a way of getting around—perhaps to your detriment. Something to keep in mind in this regard: there is no way of knowing whether or how often an employee has been asked by his government to report on what's happening within the company or in a training program. One case will illustrate this point. A series of management seminars was conducted in the Middle East for a company's middle managers. Following the fifth or sixth session, one of the trainees, who was in the upper-middle ranks, observed privately to the instructor that the course had been very worthwhile. Then he added, "And the government thinks so too." The instructor's somewhat startled question, in return, was, "The government? What do they know about it?" The trainee's answer: "Oh, they know—and they know all about you, your family, your religion, where you live, everything."

This was a bit of a shocker but yet understandable. The governments of the developing countries, in some instances, aren't as secure as they would like. There's a suspicion of foreigners. If some American is to be closeted with 1, 10, or 25 of their citizens, the people in power want to know what they are being told. Once the government finds that everything is above board, that's all there is to it. But they want to know. They consider in their right, and, more times than perhaps the expatriate realizes, they do know what's going on.

The moral, then, is never to say anything about political, religious, or cultural subjects that could remotely be interpreted as derogatory. This includes the local way of life and living conditions. There's too much to lose and nothing—nothing at all—to gain if you do.

These are a few of the things to think about during the actual training program. If the U.S. manager has done any training in the

States, he shouldn't expect to find it as easy or convenient abroad. He'll run into obstacles that, if not anticipated, can expand into mountains. When aware of the problems, however, he's in a better position to work around them to achieve his objectives. It's not all *that* difficult, but it's not the same as running a program for Americans in a modern, fully-equipped conference room in the home office.

The Importance of Followup

Training is meaningless unless it carries back to the job and unless the manager monitors the trainee's performance to be sure it is in conformance with the terminal behavior objectives. Followup is the only way to determine whether the manager taught and the subordinate learned.

Thus continuing evaluation, up to a point, is necessary. Coupled with it should be positive reinforcement for things done well and discussions of less-than-desired performance. Ongoing concern for the subordinate's progress is one of the more meaningful motivators.

The Manager as a Trainer

After all of this, you may say, "Nuts. I'm a manager, not a trainer." To support that conclusion, it has often been claimed that a manager can be a good manager and not be a good trainer. To which the response has to be: that's impossible. Consider some of the things a manager does in a normal working day, such as correcting a subordinate; introducing a new procedure, system, or regulation; evaluating and upgrading performance; or answering questions. A manager spends considerable time trying to convey ideas and get the proper subordinate responses. This may not be "training" in the literal sense, but it is shaping the subordinate's behavior so that he will do something better, the same way, more accurately, more promptly, or differently. That's training, by any definition. If the manager can't do it well, it's hard to see how he could be very effective in his job.

Once the formal training of the subordinate is over and he is meeting the manager's terminal behavior objectives, the manager moves into another role. He now becomes more of a coach, or developer, of the subordinate. "Trainer," "coach," "developer," or "change agent"—the nomenclature isn't that important. What is important is the manager's recognition of the role he plays in contributing to the growth of those who report to him. If he has hired or promoted wisely, oriented thoroughly, and trained effectively, he is well down the road to molding a local manager who will be able to function independently. The local subordinate still needs help, though, before that goal is reached. That's where development enters the scene and becomes the next responsibility of the U.S. manager.

14

Coaching and Development Opportunities

The training is over. Presumably the local manager has met the terminal behavior objectives. Presumably he has the knowledge to carry out his responsibilities at an acceptable entry-level standard. It's unlikely, however, that his job knowledge is very deep or his skills highly developed at this stage. A foundation has been laid, but the completion of training, thorough though it may have been, only signals the beginning of development.

At the outset, it should be recognized that development is really self-development. The U.S. manager can open doors to growth opportunities, but what happens from there on is up to the local employee. The majority will take advantage of everything that is offered, if they sense a sincerity of purpose on the U.S. manager's part. Through every daily contact with their manager, they can be inspired or disinspired. Which of the two prevails is largely determined by the manager and his genuine concern for the local employees' future. He can't force, but he can expose; he can't command learning, but he can encourage it; he can't order growth, but he can inspire it.

Coaching: What Is It?

Coaching is the manager's ongoing effort to develop the talents, skills, and potential of his people. It's not something that is done periodically or formally. Instead, it's one of many factors in a healthy boss-subordinate relationship. It's not separate from development; it's part of it. As such, coaching includes teaching, guiding, providing direction, appraising performance, encouraging, criticizing, and helping the subordinate learn to think, analyze, judge, and decide.

A manager coaches to expand the subordinate's abilities, to ensure that he develops in his present job, or to help prepare the subordinate for future responsibilities. Coaching, along with whatever technical or management training the subordinate needs, is a critical element of the overall umbrella called "development."

HOW DOES THE EFFECTIVE COACH FUNCTION?

○ *He operates from the sidelines.* He is aware that he can't be everywhere at once. His job is to observe what his subordinates are doing and provide whatever advice, guidance, or instructions are necessary. He can do this well only if he's not personally involved in the details of the operation.

○ *He encourages learning by doing.* Once his people are trained, the effective coach wants them to try out, experiment, practice. He loosens the reins so his subordinates have some freedom to succeed on their own, to learn—yes, even occasionally to fail. We still learn best by doing and best of all doing under helpful supervision.

○ *He adheres to known standards of performance.* This is where the Job Performance Guide comes in. If the JPG has been developed and then discussed with the subordinates, they know what is expected of them in each phase of the job. That is their right. At the same time, the coach never waters down the standards or accepts a less desirable level of performance.

○ *He earns respect through his personal competence.* Unless he is respected by his subordinates, it is most unlikely that the manager/coach can be effective. He may not be able to do every job he supervises better than the people in them, but he must be able to earn their respect through his fairness, his interest in them, his broader experience, his broader knowledge.

○ *He creates a climate of confidence.* To develop, the subordinate has to believe that his supervisor has confidence in him and in his capacity to develop. The effective coach creates this atmosphere and maintains it—even if the subordinate has failed in a given assignment.

○ *He allows for individual differences.* No two people are alike; each is unique in ability and personality. The coach is consciously aware of this and thus tries to develop his subordinates as individuals according to their personal strengths, deficiencies, personalities, and potentials.

○ *He uses questions to encourage thinking.* "Telling" a subordinate what he should have done, other than in a pure training situation, does not increase thinking ability, judgment, or analytical skills. The coach asks questions to force the subordinate to exercise his mind and to decide for himself what he should have done in a certain situation, or what he will do in the future.

○ *He takes time and has patience.* Developing people takes time and demands patience. People don't develop suddenly, but gradually. They advance, fall back, level off, and then move forward again. The coach must realize this and provide the ongoing stimuli to encourage learning even when the subordinate may seem to have reached his ultimate plateau.

○ *He works on one thing at a time.* Everyone has many areas that need improvement. The coach, however, concentrates on one need at a time. That prevents confusion for the subordinate and wasted effort by the manager.

○ *He repeats coaching.* The coach is trying to develop habits, ways of thinking, ways of behaving. A concentrated, one-shot coaching effort accomplishes little. A number of efforts over a period of time are more likely to produce the desired results.

Development Opportunities

To say that one literally teaches or develops is simply not true. Learning and development are internally motivated: "I will or I won't, depending on what I feel and what benefits I see accruing to me as the result of my efforts." This is where day-to-day boss-subordinate relationships become so vital. If they are healthy and supportive, the odds of creating an "I will" motivation are excellent. The reverse is just as likely when a master-slave, lord-serf relationship prevails.

Development, then, begins with that intangible state called "climate." Once the climate for growth is right, the manager can open the doors, with the likelihood that the local subordinate will walk through and take advantage of what is on the other side. As with training, development is not filling a pitcher—it's lighting a lamp.

Assuming now that the right climate exists, what doors can the manager open to encourage subordinate development? Basically, four major opportunities are available: in-company, informal; in-company, formal; out-of-company, formal; and tours and visits.

IN-COMPANY, INFORMAL

This is probably the most obvious and natural method because the local supervisor reports directly to the U.S. manager. The latter, if he's doing his job properly, not only provides continuous coaching, but consciously exposes the subordinate to development opportunities through a variety of situations, assignments, and tasks. For example:

Involvement in problem-solving or decision-making matters. If the local supervisor has the responsibility to decide a certain issue but isn't sure how to proceed, he and his manager talk it over. The manager then leads him to think through the problem, analyze the alternatives, and arrive at his own conclusion regarding the best path of action to pursue. The manager plays a helpful role in the process by causing the subordinate to think, weigh, and evaluate. He doesn't merely tell him what to do and let it go at that. Admittedly, telling is the simple and faster way, but it's not development.

Stepping up a level: when the manager has a problem to solve or a decision to make, and if it isn't a matter of emergency or confidentiality, this is the opportunity to bring the local subordinate into the picture. The manager can then discuss the situation and the solution-finding process he's using to arrive at the most logical answer. The local learns through observation and direct exposure, and is thus better equipped to cope with future eventualities that may be his responsibility to resolve.

Involvement in objective-setting. In this instance, the manager brings the local supervisor into the scene when he (the manager) is establishing his own objectives, plans, and target dates. Not only does he teach the local the techniques of objective-setting, but he solicits the latter's input and suggestions as well. As a result of the exposure, the subordinate is better prepared to go out and do the same for himself and with those who report to him.

Gradually increased responsibility and authority. As the subordinate develops, and as a means to help him develop, the manager delegates—slowly but surely—more and more authority to him by periodically revising the Job Delegation Guide. When development is complete, the individual should have all the authority anyone in his position could rightfully command.

When the point is reached where the local supervisor is performing his own job according to the performance standards, the manager should delegate short- or long-term tasks as further instruments for growth. For instance, could he pass on, temporarily or permanently, tasks that take up his time and involve:

Routine decisions?
Recurring decisions?
Regular time-consuming activities?
Jobs the manager feels least qualified to handle?

Details he doesn't like?
Jobs the local subordinate could do just as well?
Tasks that would provide variety for the local subordinate?
Tasks that would stimulate and provide a challenge?
Tasks that would develop the local subordinate's skills?

Instead of continuing to involve himself in jobs, duties, or tasks like these, which only limit his own vision and ability to *manage*, the manager ought to delegate some of them to his subordinate. An analysis of his daily activities would probably uncover a number of things he is doing that the local person could handle just as well. If so, he should get rid of them.

The manager should remember, however, that effective delegation is the gradual release of responsibilities to another while accountability for what the subordinate does is still retained. It is a *gradual* release. Otherwise, there is the distinct danger of overloading the subordinate to the point where nothing is done well. Delegation is not "dumping," nor is it abdication.

Consider the following case:

For almost three months, Pedro Sanchez had been in his new job as one of several department supervisors. His predecessor, a very capable and experienced man, had been promoted to a managerial position in another division.

On Pedro's first day at work, his manager had reinforced the fact that Pedro was on a 90-day probation. The manager then outlined the duties and the performance standards he was expected to meet. The manager further indicated that additional responsibilities would be delegated as Pedro became more familiar with the job.

The next several weeks were basically a learning period, but Pedro had little difficulty learning what had to be learned and doing what had to be done. As he seemed to have the job well in hand, the manager began assigning more and more responsibilities, confident that Pedro could handle them effectively.

By the end of the second month, Pedro was the first person in the office in the morning and the last to leave at night. His desk was covered with papers, he was continually busy, and he was having trouble meeting deadlines.

The manager began watching him closely during the third month. Signs were unmistakable that production in Pedro's group was slipping, absenteeism was increasing, and people were complaining about the lack of guidance and direction they were receiving. The manager concluded that Pedro simply couldn't handle the job. Three days before his probationary period expired, he called Pedro to his office and told him he was being demoted.

A simple case, but some questions:

1. What common-sense rules of delegation were violated?
2. To what extent was Pedro responsible for his own failure?
3. What should both Pedro and the manager have done before the situation reached the crisis point?

When responsibilities and assignments are carelessly dispensed, when the boss merely watches the subordinate flounder and fails to do anything about it, when punishment for inferior performance is the inevitable result, it's little wonder that local national employees are reluctant to accept delegation. And you can't really blame the Pedros. They don't want to admit their inability to do what the American manager has asked because that would be admitting incompetence, with loss of face a probable fallout. No, the fault here rests solely with the manager. He dumped, then abdicated, and finally punished. It's unlikely that this manager will have much luck when he tries to delegate again.

Delegation to the local subordinate will work when misjudgments are handled wisely and mistakes discussed objectively. If something is not done well and recriminations or scoldings follow, the subordinate won't act independently again. He'll run to the boss for decisions he should make but is afraid to make. In the long run, the manager will realize that he hasn't delegated at all. That's when he says, "It's easier to do it myself." If delegation is to succeed, the local person must know he has the right to be wrong—at least occasionally.

Regular consultation on operating matters. In this area, the U.S. manager makes it a point to keep the local subordinate informed of what's going on—the problems, the successes, the failures, production rates, budgets, budget variances, assignments he has been given by his superiors, and whatever else is pertinent to the operation. In other words, the subordinate knows what's happening, and his vision of the operation is expanded. He is told all that can be told without violation of confidentiality.

Participation in higher-level staff meetings. When convenient to do so, the manager invites the local subordinate to sit in on staff meetings which he (the manager) attends. Because of his position in the organization, the local wouldn't normally be involved, but the manager periodically includes him for the purpose of broadening his exposure to people and events in the company.

Assignment to committees, project groups, or task forces. These temporary, usually short-term assignments test the local employee's ability to work productively with others and to achieve the objectives of the project. They also offer variety, usually provide challenge, and certainly result in a broader job perspective.

Ongoing and periodic performance reviews. Ongoing, quarterly, and annual reviews keep the local subordinate continually informed of his progress. There's no waiting until the end of the year for him to discover what he did or didn't do well. He knows *now* where he succeeded and where he needs to improve. Done properly, the performance review is as much a coaching opportunity as it is an evaluation.

Observation and critique of how the local supervisor is running his own function. His personal effectiveness is one thing. He may be doing everything the manager asks and doing it well. He lives up to his promises, he keeps his boss informed, his reports are in on time, he's energetic and dependable, his attitude and behavior are all the boss could want. But—what's happening below him, in his own shop, among his own people? If all is quiet and routine, fine. If there's trouble of any nature, what is it and why?

How the local's subordinates are performing reveals much about his managerial skill. Perhaps he has established ideal relations with his boss but may be a dictatorial martinet in the supervision of his people. If the U.S. manager is on the ball, he'll keep a close eye on all aspects of the local supervisor's unit and will discuss both failures and successes with him on a regular basis.

Note that it is not proposed that each of the above alternatives be used in every case. They are offered only as examples of avenues open to the manager for informal, on-the-job development. If any do apply in every case, they would be:

1. Ongoing and periodic performance reviews.
2. Observation and critique of how the local manager is running his own function.
3. Regular consultation on operating matters.
4. Gradually increased responsibility and authority.

Within the framework of these four, the other alternatives—involvement in problem-solving and decision-making, involvement in objective-setting, participation in higher-level staff meetings, assignment to committees or other groups—can be employed at the proper time and place. The four, however, are fundamental if the U.S. manager is truly concerned with his subordinate's growth.

One other alternative in this general area, which is occasionally used, is to establish the local national as an understudy. In this role, he is appointed to an "assistant" or "assistant to" position under the U.S. manager. The purpose is to have the subordinate observe his manager—what he does and how he does it—and perhaps carry out relatively routine duties that are assigned.

A variation of this approach is to rotate the local through several jobs and work situations, again as an understudy. The expectation is that he will gain a sense of the breadth and scope of the operation that is not otherwise likely to be obtained.

The basic drawback to the understudy role is that the local never assumes any real responsibility because he's considered to be "in training." He may learn a lot, but his managerial skills remain untested.

IN-COMPANY, FORMAL

Whether a training department is available to the U.S. manager depends on his company. Those with larger, more permanent installations often have a foreign-based technical and management training unit. Others call in training specialists from the home office on an as-needed basis. Still others rely on outside consultants, partially or exclusively, to conduct whatever courses are necessary.

Regardless of who does it, formal in-house training should provide an excellent tool for further development. When the need exists, it is often beneficial to remove the local employee from his day-to-day responsibilities and give him the opportunity for further education. Carefully selected courses can fill in soft spots and develop new job skills. In general terms, formal in-company programs fall into three categories:

○ *Technical* programs, which offer more in-depth exposure to functional responsibilities. Examples are salesmanship, marketing, purchasing, public relations, budgeting, work simplification, electronics, maintenance, production control, and similar technological disciplines.

○ Programs dealing with *managerial principles and skills,* such as courses in management by objectives, human relations, leadership styles, time management, communication, organization development, counseling, and performance appraisal.

○ Programs that teach *growth skills*—skills that are presumably helpful but not absolutely essential to the local person in his current management position. Examples: public speaking, letter- and report-writing, conference leadership techniques, languages, transactional analysis, face-to-face communications, and the like.

If the company has its own internal training department, it can usually be assumed that the courses are well-prepared and structured to meet the known needs of the organization. Overseas, however, it's frequently more practical to hire a consultant to develop, prepare, and conduct one or more programs.

A word of caution if this should be the decision: there are many fine non-U.S. training consultants—and then there are others. The "others" are often several years behind in both knowledge and practice. Therefore, the techniques taught and results produced are likely to be in conflict with the way a modern-thinking, modern-acting U.S. firm conducts its business. A local or area consultant should be thoroughly investigated before a contract is signed. He may offer the advantage of being able to communicate in the local employees' language, but that might be the only advantage.

However offered, in-company courses should be viewed as significant development assignments for the local national. The U.S. manager should not consider them a burden just because he'll be without a subordinate for a week or two. If his unit is well-organized, it will survive the brief absence of the local supervisor. The value derived is likely to outweigh by far that small sacrifice. One example will illustrate this point. In 1972, Saudi Arabian Airlines introduced an intensive, 11-day management training course for its middle managers. Conducted in Beirut to avoid the family distractions that would be inevitable if the course were held in Jeddah, the program ran all day. In the evenings the participants, divided into four teams, worked on problems or case studies. According to recent reports, 80 percent of those who had attended the program between 1972 and 1976 had advanced one or more levels in the organization.

To claim that the course alone was responsible for the advancements would be false. Not only did the airline expand rapidly during that period, but many of the participants were talented in their own right and probably would have moved ahead regardless. On the other hand, to pigeonhole the course and say that it was irrelevant to their progress could be equally erroneous. The part it played can't be quantified, but there is every reason to believe that it contributed its share to the growth of the airline's managers.

OUT-OF-COMPANY, FORMAL

Another source of development is the out-of-company program, often presented by a university, association, or private organization. Such programs are offered in the major cities of Europe, Mexico, Japan, and, of course, the United States. These are the well-advertised seminars ranging from a day or two up to three months or longer.

Examples of nondegree courses are the Harvard Business School's 13-week Advanced Management Program; the American Management Associations' 4-week Management Course; and the AMA's 3- to 5-day seminars. The latter offer a wide spectrum of programs in areas such as general management, sales and marketing, finance, manufacturing, information systems, packaging, and specific courses for those in the international field; the 5-day Managerial Grid Seminar presented by Scientific Methods, Inc., of Austin, Texas; and the Kepner-Tregoe 5-day course on problem-solving.

Degree courses, undergraduate or postgraduate, would not normally be utilized for the average local national. However, they should be considered for the high-potential manager, with the company granting a leave of absence and funding his further education.

Assuring that a staff of educated managers is on hand is one of the best investments a U.S. firm with long-term commitments abroad can make. It is also a significant contribution to the development of the country, and politically can be one more strand that strengthens the country's ties to the United States.

TOURS AND VISITS

A worthwhile development vehicle is to provide time for the local employee to visit the home office. He may never have been to the United States or even very far from his own country. Just visiting the States offers a broadening opportunity that will help him relate more effectively to what the manager is doing and trying to accomplish.

Without physical exposure to the U.S. firm's management and production processes, he's forced to function in a comparative vacuum. Having been reared and living thousands of miles away in perhaps relatively backward surroundings, there's no way he can have a meaningful understanding of the company or what it stands for. If the local person is being asked to function as a modern-day manager, he has the right to know what modern-day management and modern-day technology are. Reading and being told about them aren't enough. That's like trying to describe how chocolate ice cream tastes when the other party has never even seen chocolate ice cream.

Spending some time at headquarters, if the visit is thoroughly planned and coordinated with people back home, can't help but widen the local manager's perspective. Names that were once merely names become people; units or functions that were only boxes on the organization chart become visible entities; procedures, systems, and regulations that may have seemed to be without reason become more reasonable—or at least more understandable.

The other plus is exposure to Western work habits and production techniques. Observation of the typical office efficiency of a U.S. firm gives glimpses of what may lie ahead for the local's own society. Becoming acquainted with what automation can do, the significance of management information systems, or the science of industrialized production can add important building blocks to the local person's development foundation.

When Should Local Employees Be Selected for Courses and Tours?

Despite all the above-cited advantages of seminars, tours, and visits, there are only two situations in which expenditures for these purposes should be made. The first is when the company intends to maintain its overseas installation on a permanent basis, or a least for the fore-seeable future. The second situation is when the company has been retained, on a terminal-clause contract, to manage a locally owned firm and develop its managers so that they can eventually assume responsibility as the U.S. personnel are phased out. When the management contract expires, the intent is to have the firm fully nationalized and managed by its own people.

Further, it is essential that the candidates for tours, visits, and out-of-company courses have the potential to advance. They must be quality people who have demonstrated both ability in their current positions and the capability to assume greater responsibility. The also-ran manager who shows little promise beyond what he's doing today could be enrolled in selected in-house courses, but it's a doubt-ful practice to reward his mediocrity with a company-paid trip to the United States.

So there are strictures. These courses and tours aren't for the zero-potential manager, nor are they apropos if the U.S. firm has a one-shot assignment abroad to build a power plant, a pipeline, or a desalinization plant. That firm is there to *do,* not develop. In all other cases, however, the types of programs and tours suggested warrant consideration in the company's overall development effort.

Above and beyond these strictures, the one element of development that always applies is the first mentioned—the ongoing, day-to-day coaching of the local employee and his continued exposure to the operation. If these efforts need to be augmented by seminars or tours, the base exists for more varied developmental experiences. Whatever the case, the U.S. manager should know what other resources are available that he can tap and that will contribute to his subordinate's growth. He can then plan and budget accordingly.

Encouraging Self-Development and Following Up

If development is primarily self-development, the local person has to be encouraged to take some action on his own. For example, in conjunction with him, set up a reading program of job-related books, articles, magazines, and trade journals. Just reading isn't enough, though. The book or article needs to be discussed with him to determine what he learned and how it applies to his work. Even requiring a brief written report isn't out of line.

Sometimes a formal training program is drawn up for the local person, such as one involving job rotation. But even then, he should be encouraged to visit other departments and operating functions on his own. In one oil company, some of the long-term local managers had never toured the refinery or been out to the pumping areas. Not that such excursions were essential to their own work responsibilities, but this is similar to the salesman who has never seen how the product he sells is manufactured or the airline employee who has never been in an airplane. The better-rounded the person's picture of the business he is in, the better employee he's likely to be.

If a local subordinate attends a technical or management training course, don't just greet him the first morning he returns and tell him to get back to work. Talk with him about the experience. Have him write a synopsis of the course content, what he learned, how it applies to him and the job he holds, what he agreed or disagreed with, what he didn't understand, what benefit the course was to him, and what he intends to do with what he learned. Then see how he applies his new knowledge.

If there's no followup or evidence of interest, the fact that the U.S. manager doesn't really care becomes most apparent. The subordinate may soon view these excursions away from the job as paid vacations, involving no requirement other than to put in an appearance. In extreme cases, the local employee may conclude that sending him off to a course or to visit another department is a convenient ruse to get rid of him for an hour, a day, or a week. Often the local employee is suspicious—until he knows that he can trust his manager. Baseless imaginings may slowly mature unless the manager is careful.

The local subordinate doesn't need or want wet-nursing, but he does expect interest in him and attention to what's happening as he goes through the development process. Followup is essential to maximize the learning experience and keep the employee from feeling that he is being temporarily shunted to the side.

Another important aspect of followup is the way the subordinate's errors are treated. In the early stages, perhaps during the first year or two, he's going to make mistakes. Some will be technical mistakes, some errors of judgment, some behavioral in nature. There will be times when he fails to do as he promised. There will be occasions when he incurs the displeasure of his boss. In these regards, he is like any new manager of any nationality.

Whenever sub-par performance occurs, whatever its nature, it needs to be discussed *now*—not tomorrow, not next week, not during the annual performance review, which may be a year from now. Further, *how* it is discussed will have a significant effect on the local subordinate's subsequent behavior. A harsh reprimand may germinate a sense of inferiority, antagonism, or defeatism. His sensitivity is near the surface, and it doesn't take much to make him bleed. When he does something wrong through ignorance or inexperience, he wants help rather than recrimination. Draw his attention to the problem now, and then coach, guide, or train—whatever is necessary—so that he knows what to do and what should be avoided.

Conversely, don't ignore the things he has done well. None of this: "Unless you hear from me, everything's going along fine." Positive reinforcement, be it in the training class or on the job, rewards the desired performance and encourages its repetition. When rewards are dispensed freely and "punishments" handled tactfully, the local employee quickly senses the manager's genuine interest in him, and he'll respond. He'll learn—if given half a chance.

A Training and Development Plan for a New Local Manager

To tie all the various elements of development together, let's assume that when the U.S. manager arrives on the scene he has to build an organization. It may just be a department or a section, but it's new. Nothing exists. Admittedly, most managers won't find themselves in such a start-from-the-beginning position, but when a company is new in an area, somebody has to get things going.

Let's further assume that the company has a long-term commitment to the area, with the ultimate objective of developing its local national employees to run the operation while phasing out all but perhaps one or two of the very top American executives. And finally, to keep the example relatively simple, let's assume that the purpose of the new organization has been defined and that the necessary structure, policies, regulations, and the like have been established. Now comes the time to fill one or more subordinate management positions.

One useful sequence for a complete training and development plan is the following:

I. Pre-hire preparation
   A. Prepare the job description.
   B. Obtain final approval of the job title, pay grade, and salary range (minimum, midpoint, and maximum).
   C. Develop the Job Performance Guide, listing the expected duties and responsibilities and their corresponding standards of performance.
   D. Prepare a preliminary Job Delegation Guide.
II. Selection of the candidate
III. Orientation of the successful candidate
IV. Training and development [1]
   A. In-company courses
      1. Prepare and conduct technical and/or management courses so the new employee is equipped to meet the basic knowledge and skill requirements of the job, *or:*
      2. Enroll him in a locally conducted, company-sponsored course for the same purpose.
   B. Informal, on-the-job coaching and guidance
   C. Tours/visits during the second year on the job
      1. Schedule the employee for a visit to the headquarters office. Make sure all arrangements are completed in advance, such as his travel itinerary; his arrival date; who is to meet him; hotels; who he is to see, when, and for what purposes; travel funds; passport; visa; and scheduled return date.
      2. Arrange for tours to other company installations, such as plants, warehouses, and factories, that fall within his sphere of interest.

[1] As a rule of thumb, the local employee should spend the equivalent of approximately one month a year in formal training courses (not including the essential basic job training) until he has met all job standards and evidenced his readiness for advancement.

3. Brief him on what to expect in the United States: customs regulations; currency; rate of exchange; local transportation; tipping; how to reach his hotel, if not met; how to reach the office; important telephone numbers; how to reconfirm his return reservation; security of valuables; and so forth.
D. Out-of-company courses
   1. No earlier than in his second year, enroll the manager in short-term (3–5 day) courses to provide training and exposure not available within the company.
   2. Enroll him in university degree courses if:
      a. He is of high potential, *and*
      b. A higher degree would benefit the company and be instrumental in the manager's advancement.
V. *Performance reviews and appraisals*
   A. Provide the local manager with ongoing feedback as to his performance, progress, and development needs.
   B. Conduct without fail the annual appraisal, and provide the manpower planning group with your evaluation of the manager for the purpose of maintaining current information on:
      1. The company's staffing needs.
      2. Promotable local managers.
      3. Potentially promotable managers.
      4. Zero-potential managers.
      5. Replacement requirements—now and in the future.
VI. *"Shadow management"*
VII. *Promotion to the U.S. manager's position* (see discussion below)

"SHADOW MANAGEMENT"—SOME COMMENTS

When the U.S. manager feels the local person is ready to replace him, he often initiates a period of "shadow management": he steps aside from time to time and serves as a consultant to the local. The local employee still retains his old title but assumes some of his boss's responsibilities on a temporary basis, perhaps by replacing the manager when he's on vacation or a business trip. Eventually he might take over on a full-time basis but with certain major responsibilities withheld until he has demonstrated his ability to assume the entire job.

Shadow management provides a testing ground for determining how well the local supervisor can handle the higher-level responsibilities and function under the freedom of greater authority. He's not left alone, however, because the U.S. manager is there to suggest, advise, correct, or insert himself into the scene when necessary. Basically the manager stays on the sidelines or in the shadows as he observes the local person at work in the more advanced position.

With shadow management, the local person actually performs the higher-level tasks, though his boss is close by when needed. In contrast, when the local is serving as an understudy he doesn't become that involved in his superior's work. He primarily sits on the sidelines and observes his boss in action. Both techniques contribute to development, but the greater value, quite apparently, comes from an opportunity to "do" rather than merely be a watcher.

PROMOTION TO THE U.S. MANAGER'S POSITION— SOME COMMENTS

When the local employee has proved his ability to function autonomously in an acting capacity, he is promoted to the higher-level position. The U.S. manager may stay on for a few months as a sort of consultant to the local, but he is the one who is now on the sidelines. The local has the ball.

When the U.S. manager is satisfied that the local national has the job under control, he takes the next and final step. He goes home.

There are many "ifs" and "it depends . . . ," but all other things being equal, a local manager should be ready to move up the ladder within about three years. The variables are his own qualifications and abilities, how well he has been trained and developed, the willingness of the company to put a responsible position in the hands of a local national, unexpected problems that would make it risky to turn the operation over to the person at this time, and so on.

Unfortunately, American managers, in the interests of their own job security, often find a hundred "good" reasons why the local person isn't quite ready yet. "A few more months, maybe a year . . . but not right now." The reluctance to let go is particularly strong when the manager's responsibility for development hasn't been spelled out by the home office, and when he's overseas on an open-end, renewable-every-two-years contract. If he's making good money, his family is happy, and he's not sure what job he'll return to in the States, it is understandable that he would try to hold onto a good thing.

That doesn't help the local subordinate or the other national employees who are ready and eager to move up. The door was opened but then closed—for who knows how long. A commitment is a commitment. Unless conditions make it impossible to do so, it should be honored. If it's not, local employee frustration and anti-American bitterness are highly predictable results.

In looking back over the nuts and bolts of the development program just outlined, it's easy to imagine an American saying, "But that's a full-time job! I have a shop to run. I can't be spending eight hours a day on this sort of stuff."

Right. You can't, and you won't have to. The steps that were outlined—the elements that make up a sound training and development program—are actions taken over a two-, three-, or maybe four-year period. Also, not every step may be necessary in every case. If you're starting with nothing, you naturally have to hire, orient, and train local nationals. Plus you have to provide on-the-job coaching and guidance and evaluate each local person's performance.

Any manager who is worth being called a manager performs those responsibilities. So all that is being added are the in-company or out-of-company courses and the tours, none of which take up your time except for arranging schedules and coordinating the plans. If you're inheriting a going organization, your task will be even smaller. You may only need to do coaching, provide exposure to outside training programs, and set up visits. How much you have to do will depend on how well your predecessor fulfilled his development responsibilities.

The program outlined assumes that the local subordinate is being groomed for vertical advancement. In some circumstances, however, the company might want to expose a high-potential subordinate to a variety of jobs, departments, and functions before assigning him permanently to a specific position. If so, an organized job-rotation plan has to be established in which the subordinate spends four to six months in a department before moving on to the next. Note that this should be a *working* assignment. He should not merely sit around, observe, and takes notes.

The programmed job-rotation plan is usually reserved for supervisors or managers who are earmarked for higher staff or executive positions. It provides an effective corporate overview for the bright college graduate or MBA who clearly has potential. For the specialist, however—such as an engineer, chemist, or computer programmer—the value is considerably less or nonexistent.

A Sample "Training and Develpment Plan" Form

Organizing a logical development plan for the local subordinate isn't as difficult as it might appear. Figure 11 indicates how a three-year plan "to train and develop Phillipe Perez so that he will be qualified

FIGURE 11. Training and development plan.

For_____Phillipe Perez_____ Supervisor____Robert M. Kearns_____

Title____Supervisor, Dept. 931____ Title_____Manager, Dept. 931_____

Date____January 12, 1980_____

Objective: To develope Phillipe Perez so that he will be qualified to assume position of Manager, Department 931, by January 1, 1981.

Plans	Target Dates	Progress Checks
1980 1. Discussion with Mr. Perez of this Development Plan.	1/15	
2. Have him establish specific development plans for his key subordinates no later than:	3/15	
3. Attend Advanced Technical Course #110.	4/23-4/27	
4. Assist manager in developing department objectives, plans, and budgets for 1981.	5/1-8/1	
5. Attend company's 4-day Delegation of Authority Seminar.	7/10-7/13	
6. Visit Department 947 and 981 to increase understanding of their operations and how we affect them.	9/17-9/21	
7. Assist in 1981 budget preparation.	9/24-9/27	
1981 8. Attend Managerial Grid Seminar (USA).	2/15-2/19	
9. Office tour and plant visit (USA).	2/21-2/28	
10. Attend AMA Seminar #2525 (USA).	3/1-3/5	
11. Coordinate departmental MBO objectives for 1982.	7/1-8/1	
12. Assist in 1982 budget preparation.	8/1-9/1	
13. Attend company's Middle Manager Seminar.	10/20-10/24	
14. Objective achieved.	12/31	

Clarifications/Assumptions:

1. Plans are based on known or anticipated training needs. Will be altered accordingly if unexpected strengths or weaknesses appear.

2. Plans assume Mr. Perez's continued ability to grow and develop.

Estimated Costs:

8.	Tuition	$ 500.00
10.	Tuition	500.00
8.-10.	Travel	800.00
8.-10.	Air fare	1,750.00
	Total	$3,550.00

to assume the position of Manager, Department 931, by June 1, 1981" can be condensed to one page.

The assumptions behind the plan:

o Perez is currently a lower-middle supervisor with a staff of first-line supervisors reporting to him.
o He has been in his present position for one year.
o During the first year, he was informally coached and guided by his manager and attended the necessary in-house technical and basic management courses.
o He has just been given his annual performance appraisal in which his strengths, areas requiring improvement, and future career path were discussed.
o He is being developed for vertical advancement.

Note that some of the steps of the plan, as #4, #11, and #12, are to be carried out during the periods indicated in Figure 11 in conjunction with Perez's normal responsibilities. They are not full-time assignments which would divorce him completely from his regular job.

A key word in the written objective is "qualified." Especially in the developing countries, the U.S. manager has to be very careful not to create false expectations. His choice of words must not mislead. Because of language, wishful hearing, or whatever, something like "If you work hard enough, you might be a manager in a couple of years" becomes "I've been promised a manager's job in two years." When the local doesn't get it, the trouble begins.

In the case of Phillipe Perez, he's only becoming *qualified* to move up. Even then, he might not get the job because another local national who is better prepared could appear on the scene.

Those who have worked with this development concept abroad have learned that any hint of a promise may be taken as a promise. They've learned to explain slowly and thoroughly what the development plan is, what conditions the local employee must meet, and the fact that he must be the *best* candidate before bigger things can be expected. They've learned to stress over and over that the plan is a *plan*, nothing more. It is not a contract. And they've learned to point out that even if the objective and no promotion results, the local supervisor is better off and more advanced than if there had been no plan at all.

So, on this point, caution is the word. Don't take it for granted that "qualify" means to the local what it means to you. If there is misunderstanding and the promotion doesn't materialize, expect repercussions. They are guaranteed to occur.

Conclusion

Besides having a basic knowledge of what development really is, the American abroad must be emotionally and mentally prepared to devote time to the growth of the local manager. He can't expect to function as he does at home, because he's dealing with subordinates who may not be as well educated, may not be familiar with business organization and practices, and almost certainly won't be familiar with American ways of doing things. These gaps, coupled with the cultural differences, place a burden on the expatriate. He'll have to make sacrifices if he expects to fulfill his role as an operator/developer.

As has already been said, the heart of development is not the formal courses or the annual performance reviews. It's the day-to-day boss-subordinate relationships. The local supervisor is continually observing the American's behavior—how he does things, his reactions to failures and successes, his emotional stability, his self-control. Whether the American likes it or not, realizes it or not, the local employee is watching, listening, and absorbing. What he sees during each working day is likely to have more influence on his beliefs and behavior than any management seminar, training program, or trip to the home office.

Not that this is radically different from any American boss/American subordinate relationship. But the local national is likely to be more impressionable because of his relative newness to business and industry. It's logical, then, for him to accept what he sees as being right, whether that is the case or not. He's not yet sufficiently knowledgeable to discriminate.

In a healthy relationship, the U.S. manager neither encourages unreasonably nor discourages unnecessarily. False hopes for the future are just as destructive as no hopes at all. The local has to see his strengths and deficiencies as through a sharply focused lens. Otherwise, he will nourish futile expectations or defeating self-doubts. Complete honesty and sincerity, topped with a thick layer of patience, are the necessary ingredients if the local employee is to see himself clearly.

Conversely, if the American forgets his purpose abroad and becomes arrogant, superior, or disrespectful, the local subordinate will surely respond in his own way. Almost certain fruits of a negative climate are personal bitterness and anti-company attitudes. These inevitably translate themselves into acts of overt or covert insurrection. And so the U.S. manager is stuck with a bad apple he probably can't terminate, but it's an apple that he himself spoiled.

Unfortunately, the fruits of poor American supervision have been seen many times wherever American businessmen have ventured. Certainly the developing world wants our technology and expertise. But in the process of exchange, no great love for us has emerged. One would like to think that we, who are presumably there to help a developing country develop, would learn to behave in ways that earn the respect and appreciation of both the people and the government. Many Americans have done just that. But there are those who haven't, and the breaches they have created are difficult to repair. Mistrust, once learned, is not easily erased.

Leaving politics and -isms aside, the Russians have the reputation of arrogance and heavyhandedness whenever they go in the developing world. The same is not true of Americans in general, but identical accusations are often leveled at individual managers. This results in a reputation that is just as harmful to the manager, the company he represents, and the local people's opinions of Americans.

No matter what the U.S. manager thinks, his local subordinates are going to make him look good or look bad. He hires them; he shapes their behavior and attitudes; he is accountable for their performance. Their response is of his making, but their very response puts him in their hands. They now have the power to produce or not, to meet standards or not, to help him succeed or not.

In a very real sense, the U.S. manager is both creator and reaper of the organization climate. If it's a healthy climate, the fruits will be rewarding in every way. If not, he's going to pay the price. How and when is not very important.

For only personal reasons, if nothing else, isn't it worth doing things right?

Returning to an Earlier Case . . .

Now, if you're still interested, go back to Chapter 1 and see if you still agree with the ratings on the scale of 1 to 10 that you gave the four overseas candidates—Larry Nugent, Arthur Braxton, Dan Matthews, and Eric Bennett. The ratings, you recall, reflected your opinion of the probable success of each man in a developing country. If you want to change your mind, do it now and then compare your conclusions with the following.

LARRY NUGENT

Nugent has many factors in his favor. He's single, has no family obligations, is interested in history and archaeology, may know something about the country he'd be going to, and has a strong people orientation. In addition to those attributes, he's technically qualified.

His chances for success, however, are limited. He's *too* people-oriented, if that makes sense after all that's been said. He would undoubtedly get along well with the local employees, but he lacks the leadership power to be a respected authority figure. Because of his leniency and apparent desire to be popular rather than productive, the local nationals would take advantage of him. They would like him, would find him warm and human, and might even invite him to their homes as a friend—which is one of the highest compliments a local can pay a foreigner. But they wouldn't produce for him, and that would eventually be Nugent's downfall.

His chance of success: 3.

ARTHUR BRAXTON

Braxton has what Nugent lacks, and vice versa. His education is probably a plus and his technical qualifications are obviously points in his favor. The fact that he's married, with children 10 and 7 years old, might be a drawback, depending on the country of assignment. On the other hand, it could be a great learning experience for the whole family.

His weakness is, in one sense, his very strength. In his drive to produce, to achieve, he cares little about the people. *He's* the boss, he's the strong authority figure, the *patrone,* the master. What he says goes; what others think is not important. Braxton is a tough, no-nonsense disciplinarian.

The local nationals would work for him under a blanket of fear. The job might get done, but at what cost? "Development" is the last thing on his mind, despite the lip service he might give it during the preselection interview.

Braxton is a good candidate if his role abroad is to be strictly an operator on an in-and-out assignment. As an operator/developer, however, he's a weak candidate.

His chance of success: 2.

DAN MATTHEWS

Matthews is a balance between the Nugent-Braxton extremes—an average, middle-of-the-road compromiser. Familywise, the ages of his children should be no major source of concern, although the 14-year-old might develop some frustrations if he's going into a country where entertainment is minimal and his favorite TV programs haven't even been heard of. Of course, that might do him some good, too.

There may be problems if the family is closely tied to the comfortable, middle-class life of suburbia, with its conveniences; supermarkets, golf club, and social activities.

Jobwise, Matthews seeks a happy balance between concern for production and concern for his people. Which isn't too bad, but it does reflect a pattern, or at least a mentality, of mediocrity. No pusher, this Matthews. No setter of tough yet attainable objectives. His attitude is: go by the book and be satisfied with average production and average morale.

Matthews would probably do an acceptable job. His work would be all right, his people reasonably happy. He'd make modest production improvements and do some developing of his subordinates. They, however, would model themselves after him, and the climate of mediocrity would thus be perpetuated. He's a better bet than Nugent or Braxton for the assignment, even though he possesses neither of their strengths. He's the compromise candidate, and while he'll never be a dynamic success, neither will he be a failure.

His chance of success: 5.

ERIC BENNETT

Bennett has two possible disadvantages. One, his three teenage daughters could find life difficult in a developing country. The 17-year-old might have to remain at home for high school or go to a third country to complete her precollege education. That presents the problem of a family split, which may or may not be something the family wants to endure at this stage in the girl's life. Two, Bennett is a high achiever who wants progress, production, and results. That trait, admirable though it is, is a frequent ulcer-generator in an overseas post, where things just don't get done as rapidly or thoroughly as at home. Unless he tempers his expectations, he could face some disturbing frustrations.

Otherwise, Bennett is a strong candidate. He possesses what the other candidates lack: a high degree of concern for production and an equally high level of concern for people. Further, he uses his people more wisely than Nugent. He's not trying to be loved or to win a popularity contest. He involves the people; he wants their thinking; he delegates; he develops. He knows that he has to have their help and support if the job is to be accomplished, so he does whatever he can to strengthen his personnel and provide a working climate that allows them to satisfy their own needs.

At first he might have difficulty getting the local employees to participate, suggest, or criticize. However, as they come to know and trust him, they'll give freely of themselves. Accustomed to authoritarian bosses, they'll be hesitant, even suspicious, when he initially asks them: "What do you think?" But the doubts will fade away if he persists in the climate of participation.

Bennett is a strong candidate for the overseas position—*if* he is properly forewarned about and prepared for the problems that may face him.

His chance of success: 9.

PART III

And Now,
Some Words to the
Local National Manager

15

Mutual Expectations

As a local national manager, you are undoubtedly aware of the mutual benefits to be gained from your associations with American managers. While your society is probably hundreds or thousands of years older than theirs, they have something to offer you—just as you have so much to give them. Theirs is a business-oriented industrial society; yours probably is not. That is the knowledge they can share with you so that you and your country, without violating your ancient traditions, can make the long leap from "developing" to "developed."

If you have read the preceding chapters, you have noted the emphasis on:

○ The U.S. manager's responsibility to help you learn, grow, and develop in your job.
○ His attitudes and actions in your country.
○ His attitudes and behavior toward you and your fellow countrymen.
○ The need for him to understand that changes are taking place in your country and similar countries that are moving into industrialization.
○ His appreciation of your personal wants, needs, and ambitions.

These responsibilities are his part of the bargain; the remaining chapters will deal with your part of it. Your personal success and the success of the enterprise depend on establishment of a healthy relationship with him, one that satisfies mutual expectations.

Your American manager wants to do well in his assignment; you want to learn, develop, and advance. To achieve his goals, he must depend on you; to achieve yours, you must depend on him. It's a two-way street. Neither succeeds without the support of the other.

What, then, are some of his expectations of you? They're not unreasonable. They're only what any good manager would ask of any good subordinate. For example:

Dependability

The American manager expects dependability in word and action: you will always do what you say you will do. Call it reliability, truthfulness, or follow-through—the meaning is the same. Just as you want to be able to depend on your manager, your subordinates, and your children, so he needs to rely on you.

Promptness

The American expects that assignments will be finished on time and deadlines met. The working day begins at 0800; you're there at 0800. A meeting is scheduled for 1030; at 1030 you're in your seat. Your manager understands that time is relatively meaningless in many parts of the world. However, he does expect you to honor the importance of time as long as you're employed by an American-owned or -managed organization.

The American's concern for promptness and dependability is part of his industrial heritage. Mass production and intricate technologies are possible only when schedules are closely followed and parts or people are in the right place at the right time. What applies to the assembly line or the factory floor applies equally to the office. Administrative efficiency is impossible if appointments aren't kept, people are continually late, meetings don't start on time, and so forth.

In the technically advanced societies, time is critical. If Americans seem continually busy or in a hurry, it's because they are trying to make the most of every minute or hour. They don't always do this very well and, in their busyness, they do waste time (which is one reason for the current popularity of seminars on time management).

Regardless of that, promptness and dependability are basic to the American's way of thinking and acting. He realizes their importance to productive efforts. And that's why he has the right to expect the same qualities from you—again, as long as you are a part of an American-owned or -managed organization.

Honesty

Don't say "yes" when you're thinking "no." If you don't understand something, say so. The manager will respect your openness. He won't respect you if you say, "Yes, I understand," and then prove by your actions that you didn't understand at all.

Saving face is important, but it's better to admit uncertainty now or a mistake now than to have the truth revealed at a later time. Your boss has to rely on your word, so don't give him the impression that you are unreliable by failing to be open and honest with him.

A Balancing of Work Requirements and Family Responsibilities

Your family is important to you. It comes first, as well it should. The nature of your society may require you to do most of the shopping, drive your children to school or to the doctor, and take care of family matters outside the home. Your manager probably understands those responsibilities. At the same time, he has a job to do and may have the same responsibilities as far as his own family is concerned. Both he and you have to balance family demands against work requirements. He has the right to expect you to be on the job each day and for the full eight hours, or whatever the schedule is. Taking two hours off to drive a child with a minor head cold to the doctor when this could be done after work is neither right nor fair.

Independent Management of Your Subordinates

If he's the right kind of supervisor, the American doesn't want to have to step around you and manage your function. He expects you to run your operation and your people. Don't be afraid to act. Don't be afraid to be independent and do what *you* think is best. He doesn't want you coming to him for answers to questions that you should be answering for yourself. Nor does he want to solve the problems you should be solving. The American manager expects you to run an effective, productive unit and to assume the authority he has delegated to you. The major problems—the exceptions to the routine—should be taken to him. Otherwise, your unit and your subordinates are yours. Manage them accordingly.

Results Rather Than Busyness

It's easy to be busy; to produce results and be effective is something else. With your people, and with your manager's approval, set some results-oriented objectives that are realistic, measurable, and challenging—objectives that involve solution of existing problems in the unit or discovery of ways to do things more easily, better, or at less cost. If you are meeting the performance standards of your Job Performance Guide and are also attaining five, six, or seven important objectives, you are undoubtedly producing results. That is progress and what your manager is looking for.

Realism in Asking for Promotions or More Money

If you feel that you deserve a promotion or that your pay isn't equitable, discuss it with your manager on the basis of your *performance,* on what you have produced. Seniority or the fact that "José got promoted. Why didn't I?" carries little weight. Just because José was promoted, perhaps with even less seniority than you, doesn't mean a thing. Performance, meeting the job standards, and achieving objectives—those are what count.

The odds are all in your favor that effectiveness on the job will be recognized, through either advancement or salary increases. You won't have to plead; the results of your efforts will do the talking for you.

Appreciation of the Difficulties the U.S. Manager May Be Facing

Try not to forget that your manager may be having adjustment difficulties of his own. He's in a land that's strange to him, a culture that is different from his. Your ways are not his, your customs not his. He is learning to adapt to you just as you are to him. In some respects his is the more difficult task, because he is confronted with a language he probably doesn't understand and life-styles that are different from what he has always known. If his family is with him, his wife and children are also facing adjustment problems.

At work, he is likely to experience many frustrations. Coming from what was probably a highly organized work environment, he may find the phone service too undependable, the copy machines eternally jamming or the reproduction of poor quality, maintenance work below standard, supplies inadequate, and so on. If he occasionally shows irritation, don't condemn him. He's experiencing a degree of culture shock—and, after all, he is human too.

Your Help and Guidance

Yes, the U.S. manager is there to supervise an operation and help you develop, perhaps one day to replace him. But on the other side of the coin, he needs your guidance and help in return. This applies not so much in the work situation but in the matters of your customs, your habits, your culture. Take time to talk with him and give him more insight into what to do and what not to do, what to say and what not to say. Help him avoid words or actions that would violate your cultural traditions or embarrass him.

If your manager is the right sort of person in the first place, he won't want to hurt or insult others. If he does do so, it will probably be unintentional. Other people may not realize that, however, and might conclude that he's no more than an insensitive American.

If you're a loyal subordinate, you'll alert him to the do's and don'ts. You'll tell him politely when he has made a social error. Not only will he appreciate your concern for him, but he'll respect you for your honesty.

Tactful Disagreement

In work-related matters, he may at times make suggestions, offer proposals, or establish procedures that you feel will produce problems. If so, tell him. Don't let him walk into a trap. You may see things of an operational or cultural nature that he hasn't seen or isn't aware of. If you disagree, explain tactfully why you disagree and then recommend an alternative method, a different plan of action.

The American manager has to count on you for support, but he also has to rely on you for feedback and for assistance in managing his function. The more of these qualities you provide, the more you will rise in his esteem.

Loyalty

Loyalty generally means faithful support of someone or something. Both your manager and the company for which you are working will expect support from you. First of all, it's your job to make your boss look as good as you can. This isn't hard to do when you like and respect him, but it's more difficult when you and he don't get along well. Even then, however, the responsibility is still yours. Undermining him—talking negatively or destructively about him behind his back—is sabotage. It's dishonest. It's the mark of a small person. Dislike him if you must, but support him at all times. He's paying your salary, so be loyal to him.

The same applies to the company. If you can't speak well of it, say nothing. In cases where the organization is greatly at odds with the way you think or believe, perhaps you should stop taking a paycheck from it. Otherwise, the company deserves your complete allegiance.

Conclusion

Each manager is an individual. Some will expect things that others don't. However, most U.S. managers have at least the above expectations of their local national subordinates.

And consider how you would feel if you were in the American's place. Wouldn't you have similar hopes of your subordinates? In fact, except for the one or two that relate to culture, don't you have the same expectations of those who report to you right now—even if you all are of the same nationality?

16

Becoming the
Complete Subordinate

Fulfilling the U.S. manager's expectations is a big step forward. But there are some other things that you can do to gain his attention and earn his respect.

LISTEN AND LEARN

In all probability, the company and the job are new to you. Perhaps you are already a professional in your technical field of accounting, sales, computers, engineering, or whatever. Your training, however, may not coincide exactly with the way the company conducts its business. Furthermore, this may be the first time you have been exposed to the American system of management. So there may be a lot to learn.

If you are asked to attend a technical or management course, don't look on the opportunity as an insult to your level of education or experience. At the same time, don't consider it a paid vacation. The training is for your personal benefit, so pay attention, ask questions, and study.

A small minority of local nationals, when attending courses away from home, think that this is a chance to play. They overindulge, arrive late for class, fall asleep, or perhaps don't show up at all. And then they ask for time off to go shopping, go sightseeing, or engage in other vacation-like activities.

It's fine to have fun and enjoy the freedom of being away from home, family, and job, but there's a time and place for it. If you're sent to a training course, consider it just as much a responsibility as the job itself. You're being paid for both. Back at work, ask your manager for reading materials such as trade journals, articles, and books that will broaden your job knowledge. Suggest to him things you could do to increase your understanding of the operation. Mention to him departments you would like to visit, people you would like to meet, functions you would like to observe. Don't put the entire burden of your development on his shoulders. You're the one who will profit, so take command and contribute to your own self-development by recommending courses of action that you feel will help you grow.

DO YOUR BEST ON THE JOB

While that's an obvious responsibility, what can you do to do your best? A few examples:

Put in a Full Day of Work

If the hours are 0800 to 1630, be there on time and don't leave until 1630. Exceptions will naturally arise on occasion, but if you have established a pattern of punctuality, the exceptions will be overlooked and the boss will be more willing to grant time off when you really need it.

In every job, there's a lot to be accomplished. Each new day offers new opportunities and challenges—for those who are looking for them. It's easy to take it easy, to *react* to what happens rather than be *proactive* and make things happen. To avoid slipping into stagnant mediocrity, look at your shop from time to time and ask yourself a few questions:

Am I satisfied with the work my people are doing?
Are the quality, quantity, and costs what they should be?
Am I at least meeting my standards of performance?
Where are the soft spots, the problem areas in my unit?
What could be done better, more rapidly, more easily, at less cost?
What systems or procedures would I like to see changed?
How can I change my management techniques to get better performance from my people?
In what areas of my work do I feel insecure or lacking in knowledge?
What am I doing to correct any deficiencies my boss has told me about?
Who is qualified to replace me if I should be promoted?

If your questions don't produce the answers you'd like, do something about it. No operation is perfectly managed; nothing is being done in this world that can't be done better. If you just look long and deep enough, you'll find plenty to keep you productively active.

Work Accurately

It's not uncommon for local managers to be a little careless at times, because accuracy and attention to detail haven't been all that important in the traditional societies. There's no substitute for both, however, when it comes to things like financial accounting, reports, records, and jobs involving safety and potentially hazardous conditions.

If you are doing something that demands exactness, ask yourself, when you're through: "Would I sign this off and stake my professional reputation on the completeness and accuracy of what I have done?" If the answer is "no," go back to work.

Plan Your Day and Follow Your Plan

Draw up a "to do" list each day and put down the important tasks that have to be accomplished that day. Then arrange them in an order of priority and start in. This is your work plan. Follow it. Complete it if you can, but if something isn't finished, carry it over to the next day.

Successful managers know what each day holds for them. They have a plan—perhaps only in their minds, but more often on paper—which they follow to the best of their ability, even with interruptions and the unexpected. The amateurs come to work in the morning, shuffle through papers, answer a few phone calls, and then begin reacting to events as they occur. They may be busy all day, but whether they accomplished anything of significance is open to question.

Something else to consider: not everything you do may be as important as you think. Just because "We've always done it" doesn't mean it's worth doing in the future. It's amazing how few things the world would miss if they weren't done at all. The ability to leave out the unimportant, to *not* do something, will give you more time to become involved in results-producing activities. You might keep in mind that only about 20 percent of what you do produces 80 percent of the results. Eighty percent of your efforts account for the other 20 percent. It's the "vital few" and the "trivial many." Discover what the vital few are and concentrate on them. They have the big payoff.

Use Your Time Wisely

If you have a daily work plan and are focusing on the important tasks, the day will be full enough. There are, however, the interruptions and the break periods. Some of the interruptions can't be avoided, and an occasional break from the routine is necessary. Nevertheless, both can turn into wasteful time-consumers.

A visitor walks in on you when you're busy. If you really don't want to talk now, stand up to greet him—and remain standing. He'll get the message in a minute or two. If you have to see a subordinate, go to where he is working; don't call him to your office, unless it's a matter that can be discussed only there. Once he's in your office, you are somewhat a captive. If he overstays his visit, you can suggest that he leave, but that's sometimes difficult. It's the same as when a guest in your house stays on and on after dinner and at midnight has made no move to depart. You can tell him the evening is over, but that isn't a very polite thing to do. You're his victim, a captive in your own home.

Other ways to avoid interruptions: close your door; put a "Do not disturb" sign on the outside; move your desk so that your back is to the door; have a clerk or secretary screen visitors; have someone screen your telephone calls, if that's possible. There are many techniques available that will prevent, or at least reduce, the normal distractions that occur in every office. Experiment, try them out, and seek ways that will conserve your time.

This applies to coffee and tea breaks as well. These are welcome changes from the routine, but they should be "the pause that refreshes," not a half-hour of meaningless socializing. Relax occasionally, stand up and stretch, and have coffee brought to the office. You'll get more done in less time. That can be promised.

DON'T BE AFRAID TO SAY "I DON'T UNDERSTAND"

While this was mentioned before, it's worth repeating. The U.S. manager won't reprimand you for admitting that you don't understand something. Rather, he will respect you for your willingness to speak up honestly.

Of course, if he's explained a point frequently and it still isn't clear to you, it's possible he might become irritated. Should that be the case, however, there's something wrong in the communication process.

DON'T ASSUME—ESPECIALLY WHEN COMMUNICATING

Words have many different meanings, and some, as you well know, can't be translated into your language. Perhaps you can make a general translation, enough to get the sense but not the exactness of what is being said. If you have *any* doubts about what is being communicated, take the lead. Ask, "May I say in my own words what I think you want?"

In this book, the U.S. manager has been advised to question you to determine how well you have understood. But don't wait for him to do this. He may proceed on the assumption that you understood when that wasn't the case at all.

So, again, don't rely solely on him. When in doubt, ask. He'll think more of you if you do—and less of you if you don't ask and you then fail to follow his directions.

SPEAK ENGLISH IN HIS PRESENCE

The American manager probably can't speak your language, although hopefully he's trying to learn it. When you and other local nationals are together with him, do him the courtesy of speaking in English. Reverting to your native tongue leaves him out of the picture and could raise suspicions in his mind about what is going on. It also creates a gap in his understanding.

Many expatriates have commented on this point and the uneasiness they feel. The American manager wonders: Is he using his language to explain something to someone else? Is he commenting favorably or unfavorably on what is being discussed? Is he saying something about the subject—or about me—that he wouldn't dare say in English? The manager has no way of knowing.

Be considerate of him. You have the advantage because you are fluent in at least two languages while he may be proficient in only one. Try to remember the great size of the United States—3,000 miles east to west and 1,500–2,000 miles north to south. With that much territory, the need to be bi- or multilingual doesn't exist.

Americans aren't very proud of their language limitations, and in fact are often embarrassed when a foreign business associate can converse in three, four, or even five tongues. The American's inability to go beyond English works to his disadvantage more times than not. So don't make it more difficult for him by communicating with fellow employees in your language when you are in his presence.

DON'T UNDERMINE HIM

This, too, was mentioned in the last chapter as an aspect of loyalty. But it does deserve a few more comments. If you talk unfavorably about your manager behind his back, chances are that he'll eventually hear about it. In reaction, he might do no more than have a meeting with you to discuss your relationship and what is causing your negative feelings toward him. Or he might take actions that are more harmful to your career. Almost certainly, however, your relationship with him won't be quite the same again.

He has to do a job and has to help you. He deserves your support even if you do not particularly like him as a person. Each of us can find fault with other people, be they boss, peers, or subordinates. No one is perfect.

Your manager is going to make mistakes, irritate you at times, do things that won't meet with your approval, and disappoint you on occasions. But if he's a good manager, those occurrences will be the exception rather than the rule. So allow him the privilege of being human and don't look for faults to criticize. You'll find them, just as he could find them in you if he tried.

There's another aspect of this, too: when someone else hears you downgrade your supervisor, he might wonder, "If he talks that way about his boss, would he do the same if he worked for me?" Word gets around, and reputations spread. The way others look at you will suffer if you become known as a back-stabber. You can't win at this game; you can only lose.

DISCUSS PROBLEMS OPENLY WITH HIM

Instead of undermining him, bring things into the open. There will be problems between you; there will be disagreements. When they arise, go to him, at the right time, and discuss them on a man-to-man basis. Conflict should be put on the table, not buried where it's allowed to smolder and later burst into flames. That's when trouble begins.

There's an old saying: "An ounce of prevention is worth a pound of cure." Here the ounce of prevention is a frank discussion of what's bothering you. Don't let anger or worries build until you're so emotionally upset that no cure could resolve the differences. Furthermore, when problems are concealed, the manager has no way of correcting the situation. He can't do anything unless there's communication between you.

It's not unusual for local employees to hide their feelings in boss-subordinate relationships. That goes for you and your supervisor, and it applies equally to your subordinates in their relationships with you. When culture has taught an individual to respect age and authority, he is naturally reluctant to confront authority when he disagrees with it. Not feeling free to come out and say what is on his mind, he makes his problems known to others, who can't do anything but nod their heads in sympathy. Meanwhile the problem, concern, or dissatisfaction remains unresolved.

Don't let this happen to you. Be respectful of your supervisor but open in your relations with him. And while you're doing this, establish the same climate with your subordinates, so that they will bring their concerns to you with an equal feeling of freedom.

ADMIT YOUR MISTAKES

No one wants to be wrong, and no one likes to have his mistakes brought out in public. But we all make mistakes—you will, your subordinates will, your boss will. When you're the guilty party, go to your boss and tell him what you did, why you did it, and what the results were. Mistakes can't be hidden very long. Sooner or later, he'll find out, so why not get it out in the open now? Trying to cover up something that was done wrong will only be a source of worry to you. Admitting it now will save everyone a lot of time and trouble. Plus it enhances your image of honesty and reliability.

DEVELOP YOUR SUBORDINATES

Just as your American manager has the responsibility to contribute actively to your development, so do you have the same responsibility to your people. The more effort you exert along this line, the better the group of subordinates you'll have supporting you. And the more effective they are, the better you will appear in the eyes of higher management.

The smart manager wants strong subordinates. He knows their performance can make or break him. He's not afraid that one of his people will rise up and take his job away. If someone does rise up and move into the manager's chair, it will be because the manager has been promoted out of it. The only exception to this is when the manager is so weak that a more competent member of the workforce, or someone from the outside, has to be moved in to save the operation.

The fear of a rising subordinate, however, is not uncommon in the developing countries. In one way or another, local managers have been heard to say, "Why should I develop my people? They'll only take my job away." That can indeed happen if the manager is insecure or afraid, but not to the strong leader and developer of others. Again, he may be replaced, but that will be because he has moved up, not out.

An incompetent workforce will be your downfall. You can give a hundred excuses and a thousand reasons for its failures, but in the final analysis you will pay the price. When an army is losing a war, no one fires the troops. It's the generals who are replaced.

So, for job security, put away your fears of a rising subordinate, if any such fears existed. Take the opposite route and get the best corps of people around you that you can. They'll make you look better, and you will profit from their strength.

DON'T TAKE ADVANTAGE OF HOLIDAYS, NATIONAL OBSERVANCES, OR NATIONAL CUSTOMS

Every country has its holidays, every religion has its observances. Whatever these may be, honor them according to custom and your own beliefs. The only request that your manager has a right to make is that you not take advantage of them.

In Moslem countries, it's hard to apply yourself effectively during Ramadan. Even though the working hours may be shortened because of the daytime fasting requirements, be at work on time and put in a full day. Get enough sleep at night so that you're alert on the job. A month of fasting and feasting takes its toll, but even the most devout Moslem can fulfill his religious requirements and still be productive, if he exercises some self-discipline.

Once in a while, you might be asked to work on a national holiday. If so, it may be wiser to agree rather than to refuse on the basis that: "Everyone is off, so why penalize me?" There was probably a real need to have you on the job or the manager wouldn't have made the request. Perhaps he had no choice. In one way or another, you will be repaid. To refuse to work may not hurt you, but it surely won't be beneficial to your career.

No one should be a slave to the company, and this is not a plea for such devotion. You have your rights and obligations, and the American manager should respect them. The only request is that you not take advantage of holidays, religious requirements, and the like. If you do so with any regularity, your manager is likely to start wondering about how important the job is to you and how sincere you are about it.

DON'T EXPECT MORE THAN YOU HAVE A RIGHT TO EXPECT

The principal plea here is to be fair to yourself and your boss. As was mentioned briefly in the preceding chapter, when you do your work well, the rewards for excellence will follow. So don't ask for more or expect more than what you rightfully deserve.

Local managers often have two concerns uppermost in their minds: merit increases and promotions. When their performance is obviously subpar, they feel: "I'd work harder if I got a merit increase. That would motivate me to do a better job, and my boss ought to recognize that." In other words, reward my poor performance and then I'll improve.

Things just don't work that way. A merit increase is not the carrot to encourage better performance. It is the reward that comes as a result of job excellence.

Premature requests for promotion are also frequent. There is apparently a belief among many local nationals that a year or two on the job is enough experience. After that, they feel they should move up a level. "When do I get promoted?" is a commonly heard question. The promotion might come sooner if the employee would expend more energy doing a good job today and less energy worrying about the future.

If you and your boss have worked out objective performance standards, you'll know whether your work is up to par, whether you deserve merit consideration, and approximately what percentage to expect. Similarly, the development plan you and your boss have drawn up will provide a road map for the next step ahead—assuming, of course, that you meet the qualifications and are the best candidate for the job.

Be reasonable in your expectations and demands. This applies to requests for personal time off, extended vacation days, special privileges, a different location of your office if you have one, how your office is furnished, and so on.

For example, just because a peer supervisor has a paneled office and you have bare walls is no cause for demanding that yours be redecorated immediately. What this does is start a chain reaction. Suppose you do persuade someone to panel your office. The other supervisor now demands and gets a wall-to-wall carpet. Because he's one step ahead of you, you ask for a carpet and window drapes. Now you're one ahead, so he orders a new desk—and on and on it goes in this game of one-upmanship.

The game, in which prestige is more important than the job, is a costly one. The appearance of the office doesn't tell who is successful. Only the manager's performance reveals that.

Whether the issue is office furniture or a merit raise, earn what you get and don't ask for what you haven't earned. Your American manager will greatly appreciate your objectivity.

Conclusion

If the U.S. manager is the operator/developer this book suggests he be, your growth and success are of major concern to him. He wants you to do well, and he will help you do well. Your failure is his failure, your success his success.

The coin, however, has two sides. The steps *you* take to become the complete employee are far more significant than anything your manager can do to help you develop and advance. It's like the old saying: "You can lead a horse to water, but you can't make him drink." Your growth and success are up to you. You'll be given the opportunities to learn, but the degree to which you take advantage of them is for you to decide.

Your technical competence will, of course, play an important role in determining your success. Equally critical, however, will be the level to which you develop your managerial and human potential. For a manager on the way up, these are essential talents which become increasingly critical the higher one goes in the organization.

The more you live up to the U.S. manager's expectations and consciously work to become the complete employee, the greater will be the probability of your success. You want a competent boss; he wants a competent subordinate. Together, you can forge an effective team. But each of you must share in the responsibility. It can't be give and take. It has to be give and give. When that sort of a relationship exists, both you and he can benefit. So give and become the complete subordinate. You won't regret it.

17

Welcome to the United States

Perhaps traveling abroad is nothing new to you. On the other hand, it may be a rarely or never-enjoyed experience. Assuming the latter for the moment, let's say that you've been scheduled to attend a training program in the States and visit the home office, or are being sent to the home office for a specific business purpose. What, then, can you expect and how should you conduct yourself?

In many respects, the suggestions in Parts I and II concerning the American's behavior in your country apply equally to you when you're the foreigner abroad. The role is merely reversed. It's your turn now to be tolerant, adaptable, and sensitive to the feelings of Americans. We may have some customs you don't like, but they're our customs and perhaps just as important to us as yours are to you. Empathy goes both ways, and now the burden is on you.

While this is not the place to paint a portrait of America or how foreigners should act here, a few thoughts might be of value if this is your first visit to the country.

PERSONAL BEHAVIOR

By virtue of your upbringing and position in your own society, you may tend to be a little demanding of others whom you have been taught are of a lower class than you. Should that be the case, it's suggested that you control the temptation to order or demand things of others while here. Taxi drivers, waitresses, hotel porters, and hotel maids will respond quickly when *asked* courteously to do something. When they feel they're being commanded like a servant, they'll react with considerable resentment.

By and large, Americans don't consider themselves inferior, even to other Americans. Wealth is the primary element that creates a class structure, not race or nationality. There are no tribes and tribal relationships such as you may have in your society, no religious sects that are considered superior or inferior to others. Over the years in this country, the objective of looking upon all people as equal is gradually being achieved. This obviously doesn't mean equality in intelligence or financial worth but rather in terms of personal dignity and rights of the individual. It means that the coffeehouse waitress deserves the same respect as the corporate president. To look down on her, to treat her as nothing more than a servant, isn't acceptable behavior in our society.

Not that we, ourselves, aren't guilty of such discourtesies. We are, but that doesn't make our behavior right.

Perhaps you have gained the impression from Hollywood films and TV shows that American morals are somewhat on the low side, what with the crime, sex, and violence that are so frequently pictured. It's possible that our national moral standards aren't the same as in your country. But on an individual level they can be just as high, just as strict.

Misreading Americans in this regard has been harmful to some visitors from developing countries. Too many times, they've tried to take advantage of, say, female airline flight attendants. Under the assumption that these women are mere servants, they've been pinched, cursed, and propositioned. They've been treated almost contemptuously. More than once, captains have been summoned to the cabin to inform a local national that his behavior will no longer be tolerated. The visitor should realize that flight attendants are carefully screened, are highly trained, and are on board primarily for the passengers' safety.

This is just one example of an apparent misunderstanding of American moral values. Not that you, as a visitor, would behave that way, but it's worth remembering that what the movies project is not necessarily the way real people are.

CASH AND VALUABLES

Don't flash large sums of money in public. In the first place, it's poor taste. It's showing off. Secondly, there *is* crime here, as there is everywhere. If someone sees you with several hundred dollars in your billfold, you might find your pocket picked and your billfold gone forever.

As for valuables you may be carrying with you, have them placed in the hotel safe, along with any extra cash you have and your passport. Leaving such items in the hotel room can be very dangerous.

TIPPING

Only rarely, if at all, will you find a restaurant that includes tips in the total bill. As a rule, service charges are not "understood" here. How much you tip is up to you. The average, however, is 15–20 percent, with 20 percent more common these days. If you have a couple of heavy suitcases, give the hotel bellman $1.50–2.00. Unlike in many other countries, it's not the habit to leave anything for the hotel maid. But if you've stayed a few weeks and the room has been well cared for, a $5.00–10.00 gratuity might be in order. Just be sure the same person has served you throughout your visit.

Be careful not to overtip. It's easy to do until you learn the value of the currency, particularly the coins. If a taxi fare is $10.00 and you give the driver a $5.00 tip, he'll thank you profusely but may feel he has taken advantage of you. Two dollars for that fare is enough.

AT THE OFFICE

If you have an appointment to meet someone at the office or plant at 9:00, be there at 9:00—or before. You've read it enough, but Americans put great emphasis on time, so don't keep the person waiting.

As you're introduced to people, try to remember their names. It's helpful, if you have the chance, to write down their names in a small notebook. You'll remember them better that way.

Unless you're very familiar with American or English names, you'll probably have as much trouble with them as an American does with those of a German, an Arab, or an Indian. It's difficult to visualize them and thus difficult to remember them.

A little technique that sometimes helps is to get a copy of the company's telephone directory (it almost certainly has one) and study the names that are strange to you. "Brown," "Smith," and "Jones" are easy, but "Ralston," "Stanhope," "Haverhill," "Andreason," "Landrith," and "McClennahan" are less common and harder for a non-American to picture in the mind's eye.

When introducing yourself, say your name slowly. It will probably be strange to the American's ears, with the likelihood that he'll miss it completely unless he can get a mental image of the spelling. "Mohammed Abdul Rahman," said rapidly, simply won't be understood by one unfamiliar with Arabic names.

Ask questions, if you don't understand. This has been discussed in other chapters, and it applies again here. If you're in the United States on a specific business matter, you're bound to miss some things that are said, even though you may be fluent in English. In all likelihood, the Americans will talk at their normal pace, forgetting that a foreigner is in their midst. When you don't understand, ask questions. Get the point clear in your own mind. What was just said might be essential to your mission. Your American hosts won't be critical of you if you speak up. They may be very critical if you don't clarify matters for yourself and then make mistakes later on.

If your trip is a familiarization one, designed to let you see the American office or plant and meet certain key people, ask questions again. Be inquisitive. Learn everything you can; talk to everyone you can. What you're seeing, and the people you're meeting, will be important to you back home. This is the opportunity to change the names on the organization chart to faces, and to change boxes on the chart to living, working departments.

You may have the temptation to relax at night and play a little too much. Caution is advised. Local nationals, in the States for the first time, occasionally overindulge, and then drag themselves to a meeting or appointment the next morning in a bleary-eyed fog. By all means have a good time, but if there's work to be done tomorrow, self-discipline is in order for tonight.

Don't forget that everything you do and say is creating an impression on the home office. Make it the most businesslike impression you can. It's just possible that your future depends on what these people think of you right now.

If any of this sounds obvious, just be aware that some local nationals, if it is their first trip to the States, have not always conducted themselves in a manner that brings them credit. The relative freedom here is sometimes too much for those who have come from a highly disciplined or regulated society. They then take advantage of the opportunities and aren't physically capable of measuring up to their job responsibilities. The value of the trip is lost and their behavior, once it's reported back home, does nothing to contribute to their advancement in the organization.

OUT OF THE OFFICE

Inevitably, you'll find some things here that you'll like better than what you have at home, and vice versa. As the American is advised not to flaunt his way of life in your country, so you should not flaunt yours when you are the foreigner. If, in your opinion, our food isn't as good as yours, don't comment. If you feel that some of our customs aren't in line with your upbringing, remember that they're our customs. If the informality that marks most of our interpersonal relations annoys you, overlook it with courtesy.

You may be asked about your family, your way of life, your political beliefs, what you think of this or that government leader, and your feelings about certain international problems. The American isn't trying to pry into your personal affairs. He asks because he's interested, which is actually a compliment to you. If he didn't like you or respect you, he wouldn't take the time to learn what you think or feel.

You'll find here an easy informality that may not be typical in your country. It's entirely possible that someone from the company will invite you for dinner in his home after having met you only once or twice. In many parts of the world, that simply isn't done on such short acquaintance. Should you go to dinner, you'll probably find the same informality. It'll be a family gathering, perhaps with cocktails first, and then a lot of questions about you and your country. Don't be surprised if business is also a center of discussion. Americans have no hesitancy about bringing up that subject at any time.

Dinner will probably be early, by your standards—1900 or 2000. If the host says, "We'd like you to come to dinner at seven o'clock," be there promptly, or a few minutes before seven. His wife may have a roast in the oven which by 2000 or 2030 will be a tasteless chunk of overdone beef. There's no signal for leaving time, such as after coffee is served. But usually a 2300 hour departure is late enough, especially if tomorrow is a working day. Then send a thank-you note to your hostess. She'll appreciate your thoughtfulness.

Conclusion

This is obviously not a "how to behave in the United States" checklist. But life is different here, and not all visitors from developing countries are prepared for what they'll find. You undoubtedly have assumptions about Americans and attitudes toward us. Some are probably right, others may be wrong. All these few pages have tried to do is offer a half dozen or so suggestions that might help you on your visit to us.

Whenever that visit may be, please read and ask questions before you leave home. We too have had our share of arrogant visitors; we've had those who are late for appointments, inattentive in meetings, careless in their work habits. We've had those who flaunt their wealth, spend lavishly, and try to impress us with their bulging bill-folds. We've had all sorts, and we resent those behaviors no less than you resent them when displayed by a foreigner in your country.

Empathy and sensitivity are the two best allies a stranger in an-other land can have. We want your visit to be a pleasant one, so help us make it pleasant by being the type of guest we ask the American to be when he is with you.

Epilogue

A Western company is in your land. Its reasons for being there may be varied, but probably one or more of these explain why:

- To provide a needed product or service to the community at a reasonable cost.
- To contribute to the growth and advancement of your country.
- To build an organization that will eventually be managed and staffed by you and other local national personnel.
- To provide technical and managerial expertise to a locally owned company.
- To teach local managers to manage the organization according to Western business methods but tempered by your customs, laws, and traditions.

If these, individually or in combination, reflect the goals of the company, you can help them become realities. The Americans who are there can't do it all by themselves. They have to rely on you and the other local employees to contribute fully, wisely, and effectively. They need your knowledge. They need your experience. They need your counsel. Most of all, they need your dedication to the job, to them, and to the organization.

Goal achievement is never a one-man task. It is the result of a team effort—and you, as a local manager, are very much a part of the team. To consider yourself otherwise would be a disservice to the position you hold and to you as an individual.

Whether new or experienced in the job, it is your responsibility to earn your pay and to justify your manager's efforts to prepare you for bigger things. If you do that, and if you support him by both word and deed, you will probably find in him everything that you could want in a manager.

True, it could happen that an individual American would disappoint you. Once in a while, one is sent abroad who is unqualified, either technically or in the practice of management. Should you have the misfortune of reporting to such a manager, don't condemn all Americans because of one incompetent. Furthermore, if he can't do the job, he's not likely to be around long. Meanwhile support him, learn what you can from him, and vow never to manage your unit the way he's managing you. That's negative learning, but there is some benefit in knowing what *not* to do.

The incompetent American abroad is the exception these days. If there ever is a deficiency, it is rarely in technical areas. Rather, it is in managerial practices—which, indeed, is why this book was written. The vast majority of American managers abroad, whatever their human strengths or frailties, want personal success in their own way just as you want it for yourself in your way. In a different culture and facing a way of life that may be difficult for them, they need your support no less than you need theirs.

If you and your U.S. manager can reach a mutual pact to help each other, the benefits will be spread evenly. From your point of view, as you develop and become increasingly professional, your pride in your accomplishments should expand accordingly. Not only will you be growing personally, but you will probably be playing a small but vital role in the strengthening of your country. It's entirely possible that your country doesn't want "industrialization" in the accepted American or Western sense. It doesn't want to modernize at the expense of ancient customs and traditions. The extent to which business and industry are to be a part of the future is up to the nation and its leaders to decide. Almost certainly, however, two goals have to be security and independence. Therein lies the part you can play.

No nation can long survive today unless it has some degree of diversification. Unless there is at least a reasonable balance between natural resources, agriculture, business, and industry, its economic security—and thus its strength—is on an uncertain foundation. In all probability, it's this balance your country is seeking as it moves from "developing" to "developed."

It is important to use the term "developed" in *your* sense and not according to any Western definition. If "developed" means a degree of diversification, some of the benefits of modernization, and retention of most of your religious and cultural traditions, and if the development is such that your country can participate equitably in world trade by giving as well as receiving and is secure in its own right, it would seem that many of your country's goals will have been realized.

Whatever the direction your country is taking as it moves toward a more developed state, you are playing a part in its growth. You are learning and becoming increasingly knowledgeable in the art and science of management. You are contributing to a business or industry that is an element in the nation's economy. Through your contributions you are helping to make life better, easier, or more satisfying for the people in your country. The work you do, then, can assume a significance far beyond the job itself and the pay envelope you receive in recognition of your efforts.

It is a unique opportunity which holds great promise for personal reward and satisfaction. We wish you well.

INDEX

absenteeism, workers' rebellion through, 76, 80

accuracy on the job, local manager's need for, 273

achievement
  and the learning process, 207
  manager's recognition of, 102

adjustment, problems of
  overseas family's, 268
  overseas manager's, 17
  subordinates', 74

administration, manager's responsibility for, 158

Africa, needs hierarchy in, 99

aggression, employee frustration and, 75–76, 79

ambassador, U.S. manager's role as, 37

ambition, as a motivational force, 72

America, *see* Latin America; North America; South America

"American Cultural Patterns: A Cross-Cultural Perspective" (Stewart), 47

American Graduate School of International Management, 46

American Management Associations, 46, 248

American University's Business Council for International Understanding (BCIU), 46

anti-company behavior, reasons for, 131–134

anxiety, learning through, 207

appraisal, performance, *see* performance appraisal

Arabic language, 111, 113

Area Handbook for Saudi Arabia (Nyrop et al), 172

Asia, territoriality in, 121

assumption effect in interviewing process, 187

Augustinian view of work, 31

authoritative management, 104

authority
  assignment of, 168–170, 242
  attitudes toward, 35–36
  defined, 54
  definition of area of, 150, 151, 160
  fear of, 61
  respect for, 74, 104

behavior, employee
  anti-company, 131–134
  basic traits of, 62, 95
  self-centered, 68–69

Belgium, unions in, 176

Benefit Concept, 68–69, 73

body language, communications through, 120–121

bonuses, motivation through, 102

boredom, communications and, 115

budgeting, manager's responsibility for, 158

business tradition
  American, 27–29
  effect of changes in, 28–29

capitalism, U.S. manager's knowledge of, 37, 42–43

caste tradition, locals influenced by, 35